Revolutionary Hope After Nihilism

Revolutionary Hope After Nihilism

Marginalized Voices and Dissent

SALADDIN AHMED

BLOOMSBURY ACADEMIC
LONDON • NEW YORK • OXFORD • NEW DELHI • SYDNEY

BLOOMSBURY ACADEMIC
Bloomsbury Publishing Plc
50 Bedford Square, London, WC1B 3DP, UK
1385 Broadway, New York, NY 10018, USA
29 Earlsfort Terrace, Dublin 2, Ireland

BLOOMSBURY, BLOOMSBURY ACADEMIC and the Diana logo are trademarks of
Bloomsbury Publishing Plc

First published in Great Britain 2022

A catalogue record for this book is available from the British Library.

A catalog record for this book is available from the Library of Congress.

ISBN: HB: 978-1-3502-6928-6
PB: 978-1-3502-6929-3
ePDF: 978-1-3502-6930-9
eBook: 978-1-3502-6931-6

Typeset by Newgen KnowledgeWorks Pvt. Ltd., Chennai, India

To find out more about our authors and books visit www.bloomsbury.com
and sign up for our newsletters.

To the memory of the ever-smiling Nazim, my younger brother.
To the kind of humanity Nazim embodied in his short life.
To those whose voices the world failed to hear.

To a future society in which Nazim's peaceful humanity would feel at home, in a world where there won't be concentration camps, exiles, borders, and painful departures.

CONTENTS

ACKNOWLEDGMENTS

I am extremely grateful to Bloomsbury's editors and teams for working so hard to make sure this book is published in all formats and makes it to its readers across the world. First, Liza Thompson's confidence in the project was key to set off the process. Right from that very beginning, Jade Grogan worked tirelessly throughout the entire process and was always extremely helpful. Suzie Nash kindly helped in securing the final stage of the review process and continued to be of great help throughout the following stages. Ben O'Hagan did an impressive job overseeing the entire production process. As well, I am grateful to Saranya Manohar and Jayashree Aradhyam for their patience and punctuality as they conducted the copyediting.

I sincerely thank the reviewers for their feedback and suggestions, which were very helpful in improving the manuscript.

Also, I am grateful to Vasile-Valentin Latiu for doing the indexing at short notice, and to Rebekah Zwazing and Mona-Lynn Courteau for all their editing work on parts of the manuscript.

I would like to thank my colleagues in upstate New York, especially, Vera Eccarius-Kelly, Laurie Naranch, Zoe Oxley, Lori Marso, Brad Hays, Guillermina Seri, Cigdem Cidam, Tom Lobe, Daniel Mosquera, and William García for their continued support during my time in the area.

I am thankful to all my students in the United States who have not been afraid of joining me to learn via unlearning. I have received some of the most encouraging feedback from them. I am especially proud of my students who have stayed faithful to my motto: a day in which you do not insult a fascist is a wasted day.

Parts of the manuscript have been published as articles and commentaries. I appreciate the publisher's permissions for republication. A close version of Chapter 4 was published in *The World Review of Political Economy*, vol. 11, no. 1 (Spring 2020). Some parts of Chapters 2 and 3 appeared on the Institute for Social Ecology's (ISE) website in 2019 and 2020. The argument regarding my rejection of a prefigurative alternative, mainly presented in Chapter 6, goes back to a paper I presented in 2016 as an invited speaker to the Institute for Social Ecology's Annual Gathering in Plainfield, Vermont— thank you to all the members and the associates of the ISE, as always. In the following year, I presented a related paper at the Left Forum in New York City. Then, I presented a more developed version of the paper under the title of "Negation, Despair, Resistance" at the Northwest Critical Theory Roundtable, which was organized by Joan Braune at Gonzaga University in February 2018. A version of that paper finally made it to *Science & Society*, Vol. 86, No. 3, July 2022, 409–38. That article is primarily focused on providing a Marxist grounding for my negativity argument. More specifically, there, I use primary Marxist sources to show that Marx's communism is inherently a negative thesis, that is, it does not commit the fallacy of basing its rejection of capitalism on an imagined positive alternative.

Other passages, ideas, and arguments throughout different parts of the manuscript have appeared previously in my articles and commentaries in the following outlets: OpenDemocracy, *Telos*, Roar, ISE's website, *Contours Journal* (published by the Institute of the Humanities at Simon Frasor University under the direction of Professor Samir Gandesha), and *LINKS International Journal of Socialist Renewal*. I have also presented some of these themes in a number of invited talks over the last several years. Below, I will briefly mention the place, year, and relevant topic: Wesleyan University, 2021, Culturalism and Education; Concordia University, 2021, Culturalism and Human Rights; Simon Fraser University, 2021, Universal University; San Francisco State University, 2019, Totalitarianism and Space; Seattle University, 2019, Rojava Revolution and Universalism; Simon Fraser University, 2018, Hopelessness, Rojava, and Universalism; Williams College, 2018, Aura and Politics of Space.

PART ONE

Crises

CHAPTER ONE

The Philosophy and the Plan of the Present Work

I

In a socially and politically hopeless world, happiness can only be sought in endless and continual entertainment. However, such a lifestyle is in fact nothing but a perpetual grapple with a paralyzing depression. Being socially alienated, as we are under digital capitalism, renders any reasonable possibility of contentedness impossible simply because we are social creatures. All our meaningful activities are socially rooted and formed, so there is no such thing as isolated individual happiness. In the totalized misery, we have ended up taking happiness to be suppression of despair, psychological denialism. As any psychoanalyst would say, suppression only further intensifies and complicates psychological problems. Yet, we continue to rely on the treatments prescribed by the very system that is the source of our misery. The ideal citizen under the existing totalitarian system is the ideal consumer, a person who is constantly seeking another commodity. For that ideal consumer to be created and sustained, social isolation, political disempowerment, and physiological paralyzation are perfect conditions. Today, Netflix, Instagram, Tik Tok, and Facebook represent the largest asylums for helpless and hopeless addicts. The only way out is to take inspiration from those who are still hopeful and resisting outside this monstruous leviathan. They may be without passports, cars, and fancy houses, but laughter, friendship, and above all building another world is part of their everydayness. They make revolution every day and dance to it because they refuse to be captives of the false dichotomy of hopelessness and entertainment. They may be stateless but live their freedom to the fullest possible limits. The world may have denied them a peaceful space, but they create the space for a better world every day. They did not choose or inflect suffering, but they turn the suffering into which they were born into a struggle for a different world.

In revolution, they make freedom from their propertylessness and stateless-
ness. Those of us with properties and states, on the other hand, often contribute to the perpetuation of the collective misery. The historical situation
is extremely complicated, but if there is one thing this book will prove, it is
that the sun is rising from the margins, and we all have the option of turning
to that human horizon, breaking free from the walls of our properties and
states which have become the walls of our own prisons.

The world is living in very dark times, but sooner or later this will
change. The question is not whether we will live to witness the birth of a
more rational world, but whether now, every moment, through our everyday activities, we are supporting the darkness or those who struggle against
it. That is certainly a difficult area to navigate, but as this book will argue,
two fronts are distinguishable: the front of the silenced and their revolutionary allies who believe in equality against the front of those whose
loyalty is to the clan they happen to have been born into even if that clan
is shaped around inflicting suffering on others. The strongest conviction
of this book's author is that the age of darkness and human suffering will
not end until a time comes when the majority of people will most strongly
defend those farthest from their own groups. Until a day comes when internationalism would not need a word to designate it, until we leave behind
these primordial embodiments of fearing the Other, resenting the powerless,
and worshiping the father figure, the darkness will persist. In that darkness,
however, one can always choose to break free from the tribalist and egoistic
prisons. Of course, that is not always a safe and swift undertaking, but it
cannot be more violent than staying within the walled borders of tribalism. This book will argue that we may not live to see a free world, but all
we need to do to reject the unfreedom including our personal unfreedom
is to switch sides and join those in the margins. To join those in the margins, I assure you, there is no need to travel to the other side of the world.
Unfortunately, there is no city that does not have a big number of them. All
one needs to do is to unlearn the habit of not seeing them and their struggles. Of course, that does not mean marginalization inevitably produces
revolutionary projects. To the contrary, more often than not, marginalization only produces more misery especially for the members of the marginalized classes and groups themselves. Nor am I calling for a moral salvation
through compassion for the condemned. Such theological sentimentalism
would be, and has been, part of the problem of depoliticization of systemic
social exploitation, which is key in sustaining capitalism. A revolutionary
solidarity with the marginalized, first and foremost, needs a revolutionary philosophy and a project. This book is an attempt to introduce such
a revolutionary philosophy, which I call postnihilism. Postnihilism builds
on other revolutionary philosophies in ways that make the negation of the
current crises tangible. Thus, postnihilism is not an alternative to other
revolutionary philosophies but rather an addition to and transformation
of some of them.

Comprehending the scope of the present crises is essential for making another world possible, so this book puts the motto of "dare to know" in action. The assumption that there is no alternative is at the heart of today's totalitarianism. Once we grasp the bigger picture of what is happening, creating an alternative becomes not only rationally realistic but also realistically inevitable.

When social conditions for revolution are absent, revolution becomes even more imperative, if for nothing else then for leading a meaningful life in an otherwise meaningless world. Often, passive pessimism is merely a psychological excuse for not daring to know and, in turn, accepting the status quo. Even for those who are not socially and politically conservative, it is very easy to fall into bourgeois nihilism to further legitimize the political indifference of the bourgeois personality and the hollowness of bourgeois everydayness. From professors of international relations to college students, the so-called realist position, which adopts the most pessimistic notion of so-called human nature, is disturbingly common. Humans are by nature violent, we are told, so those who believe in any egalitarian revolution to bring about a peaceful human society are mere utopians. The same elites who regularly accuse anti-capitalist critique and egalitarian platforms of being unrealistic and utopian have no problem (with) believing in an afterlife world. Somehow, religious myths are neither utopic nor unrealistic, but struggling for a world without massive scale exploitation is utopic and unrealistic. This alone should suffice to expose the nature of ideological hegemony in the age of "post-ideology." Thanks to neoliberalism, all that is political is depoliticized and all that is nonpolitical is politicized. It is the age of idealism without any ideals, the age of the unlimited power of capital or capitalist totalitarianism. The current regime wants us to give up all hope but at the same time seek happiness.

II

I was in the process of completing this book when the Covid-19 pandemic struck. The confused and confusing reactions to the pandemic by nation-states and the immediate crises in the entire capitalist regime from the stock market to the movement of commodities only served to reaffirm my main thesis. The contradictions of the capitalist world system and its nation-state-based international order are now more exposed than ever. What would have been considered another wishful Marxist prophecy, as many former leftists would have said, is now too obvious to be denied even by the fanatics of the market dictatorship and orthodox adherents of the mystified "invisible hand." If there is one thing on which all sides would agree, it is that we are witnessing a moment of historical transformation, but that could mean a fall back into a fascist era if the power of initiative is not taken away from reactionary movements and their populist leaders. The pandemic, in short, has further emphasized the historical significance of the present moment, motivating me even more to publish this book.

Before giving a more detailed account of the grounding and structure of the book, I will briefly address the exposed contradictions of the existing global order and the imminent threat of right-wing movements to ultimately put an end to what is left of representative democracy in some of the most vital regions in the world. While I argue that nation-states are outdated devices that need to be abolished, I realize that the era following the abolishment of the nation-state will be exceptionally disastrous if the decisive actors are those on the right. It is a dangerous illusion to assume that an end of the state would necessarily bring about a less oppressive world. To avoid such a fallacy, which is often committed by some self-identified anarchists, it is crucial to emphasize the Marxist premise that the bourgeois society remains to be the most progressive compared to any other society except for the ones that could be realized through its dialectical negation. After all, in multiple decisive moments in history, communists actually defended political liberalism against retrogressive forces such as fascism and religious fanaticism more adamantly than did liberals. In Italy, from the very beginning of the Fascist takeover up until the fall of Fascism, Italian communists and anarchists did most of the fighting. Another turning point was the 1936–9 Civil War in Spain where anarcho-syndicalist and communist revolutionaries desperately tried to defend the republic, but the liberal democracies' utter betrayal of the republic led to tragic consequences whereby the anti-fascists lost the war against the Franco–Mussolini–Hitler alliance in 1939. We all know what followed that fascist triumph.

In Germany, liberals including social democrats were not prepared to defend the Weimar Republic against the Nazis even via democratic means in the Bundestag while the communists were being shot down or imprisoned one by one. Finally, across the Middle East and North Africa (MENA), communists have been the militant defenders of individual freedoms, gender equality, and freedom of belief, and the rest of what are considered the pillars of the liberal moral system, knowing too well the nightmare the right, in all its forms within and without the state, is capable of bringing about. Today, fascism is not merely a threat here and there; rather, it is a global reality we need to have the intellectual courage to admit and the political will to face head-on. Losing the ability to be shocked by fascism—whether due to the denialism normalized by decades of a culture of self-help or by mass-produced false hope—is analogous to a slow yet certain death from carbon monoxide poisoning.

To problematize and reject the culture of violence, including fascism, we need *the heroic ability to live in the historical moment*. Despite the long traditions that celebrate the cult of death, hegemonic ideologies that normalize utter submission, the culture industry that commodifies all that is potentially rebellious, the nihilism at the heart of bourgeois everydayness as well as fascist reactions to that everydayness, and the threat of a paralyzing absurdity that lies beneath the thin skin of everything we are familiar with, despite all that we are capable of wanting and creating something else. We are capable of negating all that takes part in depriving us of life as such in the name of living. Yet, negation is absolute. It cannot leave a little bubble for the purpose of self-deception in the name of, say, spirituality, culture, patriotism, or allegiance to blood relations. To negate is to rebel. The rebel then moves to revolution. But let us not get too far ahead. As a start, let us first have the courage to look into the present political scene, and as we go the elements of what I call postnihilism will become clear.

Whether democratic or despotic, states draw their legitimacy from their claim to the general will of the public. While this legitimacy fluctuates immensely in different circumstances and contexts, any regressive attempt to replace the power of "the sovereign" with the rule of a particular sectarian or racist group could translate into a Hobbesian nightmare of a "war of all against all." Today, Völkisch movements in several countries are gradually eating away all that could be considered the public foundation of the state. The decline of the bourgeois state will be disastrous in such a regressive scenario.

A pattern of deterioration of the state is now visible from the United States and Brazil to India and Turkey, despite the gulf that separates them in terms of political traditions, institutional practices, and constitutional protections of human rights. In each case, the public sphere is continually shrinking under the pressure of a mass movement that shows three incredibly dangerous symptoms: racism, religious fundamentalism, and a populist leader whose popularity among his Völkisch bases often increases the more anti-democratically he behaves. Undoubtedly, the list can be expanded to include other states such as Hungary and the Philippines, but I will limit this introduction to these initial four cases—the leading democracy in the world, the largest country in Latin America, the largest democracy in the world, and the NATO (North Atlantic Treaty Organization) member state with the second-largest army after the United States. We should also keep in mind that the number of failed states—like Libya, Yemen, and Iraq—will only increase as the economic devastation intensifies in the Global South in the coming years.

It is not difficult to anticipate where the world is heading if a new international order is not realized in response to global challenges to which there can be no national solutions. In a world that is already suffering from extremism and multiple wars, this slide into Völkisch rule could mean the final push into a historical abyss. With the drastic increase of unemployment, it is also easy to anticipate that the ensuing increase in poverty will lead to such a sharp upsurge in violence and crime that political instability will be inevitable. Völkisch movements will find, in such a crisis, the perfect climate to make their ultimate reactionary moves—moves that could, in turn, result in knocking down the state as the (in principle) guarantor of equality under the law.

In the United States, Trumpism had already done more than merely embolden the ultraright groups, from white supremacists to Christian fundamentalists. For the first time in American history, the highest authority in the federal government enticed disobedience against state governments. Armed groups of white men paraded across cities with the utmost ease (Witte 2020)—imagine if African Americans did anything of that sort. Donald Trump realized that his power was directly linked to his popularity among reactionaries, ultraconservatives, and Christian fundamentalists, and he did not show much respect for the division of powers. With his self-declared "war president" authority, the ultimate coup attempt was just awaiting the eruption of a serious crisis, which was almost inevitable given the administration's own failure in handling the pandemic, causing endless chaos in the most vital sectors including public health. Every disaster has its own signs, which are real and physical, like the catastrophe that follows them. We witnessed the (more than) signs of the coming disaster every time we tuned into a White House press conference. One could not help but feel sorry for the representatives of scientific authority in the room. Yet, it was Trump's supporters who rallied in protest without any sense of irony.

Let us not be carried away by the fact that Trump did not win the 2020 presidential elections. Far from being pushed aside as a dangerously popular force, the ultraright is merely enjoying a period of regrouping. From Reagan to Trump, as Timothy Luke (2020) had predicted in 1989, "the screens of power" did their work in mainstreaming the far right. The trajectory since Ronald Reagan's administration (1981–9) makes it clear that the Republican Party has been increasingly moving further to the right. This trajectory can be detected even in terms of the personalities of the Republican presidents. Reagan, a mediocre actor with some diplomatic skills, fulfilled a profoundly decisive task for neoconservatism both internationally and nationally. George W. H. Bush was clearly more right-leaning than Reagan, but when George W. Bush became the president, many were dismayed to see him as the head of the largest power in the world. Yet, compared to Trump, George W. Bush seemed extremely well-rounded as a politician and statesman. Thus, from Reagan to Trump there was a transitionary era during which neoconservatism continually became more extreme. However, "more extreme" is always relative and hardly expressive of the magnitude of the crisis in question.

Even political scientists who likened Trumpism to the interwar fascism in Europe missed the point. Trumpism simply represents the peak of extremism, the final phase of the cycle of fanaticism, the point of total transparency where power becomes a cult leading to endless violence. It is thus the form of right-wing extremism that zeroes the entire traditional conservative affection for "principles" replacing everything with utter vulgarity, perpetually exhibiting force. Trumpism does not possess any form of philosophy, worldview, and doctrine whatsoever. The traditional enemy could become the best friend any minute, a national hero could be vilified for no reason, the highest institutions of the "nation" would become a subject of mockery, and the constitution would be parodied to an unprecedented point. Trumpism is in short right-wing nihilism at its peak. Precisely because of its total nihilism, it makes a much more successful case of fascism than both Mussolini's Fascism and Hitler's Nazism.

Reagan was no genius, but nonetheless he was able to act as a respectful politician. Trump, on the end of the prefascist era, was a reality show buffoon, a misogynist macho, and a public embarrassment for half of the Americans who were not his followers. If Reagan were Napoleon Bonaparte, Trump would be Louis Napoleon Bonaparte. Also, precisely as Marx said in his famous *The Eighteenth Brumaire of Louis Bonaparte*, "the first time as tragedy, the second as farce" (2010d: 103). Here comes the crucial part: we might need to add to Marx's statement, "and then as fascism." Trump was the preface of the real fascist era. The ultraright tested the waters and will most likely take things much further especially as anti-fascism remains marginalized in the United States.

It cannot be denied that the Democrats played a passive role in relation to the growth of neoconservatism and neoliberalism. While George Bush and George W. Bush fall under the neoconservative description, in terms of international politics, the Democrats were barely different. Did not both Bill Clinton and Barack Obama continue the policies of neoliberalism, embargos, and bombings, not to mention unconditional arm sells to oppressive regimes? As a matter of fact, we would be justified to assert that both liberal periods in the White House since the Reagan–Bush era served to keep the game more or less intact while giving the Republicans a chance to regroup and come back with more aggressive agenda. Given that pattern, we can only expect that during the Biden era the fascist chapter is being prepared for the coming Republican takeover. Also, given the profound and unique influence of the American politics on international politics and social movements across the globe, the coming era could very well entail an even worse decline of democracy worldwide in the interest of fascist movements.

In Brazil, where democracy stands on much shakier ground given the country's history of military rule, the danger is even more imminent. Jair Bolsonaro has been more vocal than Donald Trump in his exclusionary, racist, and sexist beliefs (Brum 2018). Like Trump, he too resisted taking the necessary steps recommended by the World Health Organization (WHO) to prevent the uncontrolled spread of Covid-19. He even fired his health minister, who had asked people to practice social distancing (BBC News 2020). To make things worse, he made veiled threats to impose military rule (Miranda 2019) and personally joined rallies asking for a military takeover to end the provincial governments' lockdown policies aimed at slowing down the spread of Covid-19 (Aleem 2020). Following the April 19, 2020, right-wing rallies, the Supreme Court investigated a possible violation of the constitution and the National Security Law, both of which prohibit attacks on democracy in the country. However, in the case of a military coup the

Supreme Court itself, like many other state institutions, will become a victim. Bolsonaro's repeated anti-democratic comments are more than mere flirtations with the army, as became ever clearer in 2019 when he reinstated commemoration of the March 1964 coup that lasted for two decades (Human Rights Watch 2019). As he continues to lose his allies in the government and Congress, he could resort to the military sooner than we like to think.

As for India, Narendra Modi has been an example of a nationalist leader, who manages to destroy all that may hold together a country's diverse peoples. His Bharatiya Janata Party (BJP) barely even tries to hide its discriminatory discourse, especially against perceived Indian Muslims. The increase in sectarianism in both the ruling party's discourse and the government's policies, from Assam (Genocide Watch n.d.) to Kashmir (Perrigo 2019a), directly feeds into Islamist fundamentalism in both India and Pakistan, which in turn will make things worse in the cycle of victimization and demonization. In provoking and magnifying the Hindu–Muslim pseudodichotomy, hundreds of other ethnic and religious groups are subjected to even further marginalization across all regions of India. For months, Indians from various backgrounds, including Hindus, protested against Modi's problematic Citizenship Bill amendment (Perrigo 2019b). However, the coronavirus pandemic provided an excellent opportunity for Modi to impose his rule in a totalitarian fashion. The near future seems breathtakingly catastrophic for a society of 1.53 billion people that already suffer from casteism, extreme inequality, systemic discrimination, and the rise of Hindutva.

In the list, Turkey has been the furthest from what can be called a democracy. Under Recep Tayyip Erdogan, racist and sectarian discrimination has skyrocketed in the last seven years. Erdogan has been manipulating the laws systematically to crush any person or party that dares to oppose his rule (Graham 2016). Erdogan started his campaign of undermining state institutions long before his amendment of the constitution to allow him to rule the country as a president after he had ruled it as a prime minister from 2003 to 2014. The Kurdish region, which had already been brutalized throughout the Turkish state's history, has suffered the most under Erdogan's regime, especially since 2014 (Ahmed 2016). Kurds who choose peaceful political activism usually end up in prison (Khalidi 2018). Currently, most prominent Kurdish politicians are in prison (Amnesty International 2020). In fact, even ethnic Turks who merely signed a peace petition to end the war in the Kurdish majority region were prosecuted by Erdogan's courts (Weaver 2016). As a president, Erdogan expedited his march toward sultanism, which has entailed vast regional interventions through Islamist movements in North Africa and the Middle East.

In 1939, when Mussolini, Hitler, Franco, and Stalin were in power, the entire world population was near two billion. At the time of writing these lines, more than two billion people are ruled by today's equivalent of fascism. What makes each of them stand out is the ability to be "great little men," to use Adorno's expression (2001a: 142), for they assume the role of a father figure and savior who speaks the language of the mass individual, thereby making the process of identification possible. The threat of Völkisch movements has always been present in modern history, but in times of crisis, they could gain enough momentum to seize power swiftly. Today, Völkisch leaders are already ruling some of the most influential global and regional states. It is a matter of course that the upcoming economic crisis will unmask the worst of these leaders and their supporters.

There is not enough space here for me to go into the debate surrounding the use of the term "fascism," but it suffices to state that since its emergence in the interwar period in the first half of the twentieth century, there have been endless attempts to contribute a concrete ideological substance to it, but in vain. To this day, most of the scholars who make a living from the search for a fascist-meter insist to repeat the same fallacy according to which Mussolini's Fascism and Hitlerism must be used as the ultimate fascist worldview, even though the two corresponding regimes themselves had countless differences in their respective structures, politics, and policies. If Mussolini's Fascism is the ultimate fascist philosophy, then even Nazism could not be considered "fascist." On the other hand, if we buy into the orthodox definitions of fascism, which typically include totalitarianism as one of its primary features, even Mussolini's Fascism does not meet the criterion for the simple reason that the Mussolini regime was not a one-party regime except for a few years prior to its collapse. Thus, the fallacy rests in the search for "the fascist ideology" simply because such an ideology does not exist. Just as "democracy" is not an ideology, but a potential feature of certain ideologies and political systems, fascism is a characteristic of certain ideologies, movements, and regimes. By the same token, just as we do not measure democracies according to the first historical models of governance that were defined as democratic, it is futile to use Mussolini's Fascism and German Nazism as the ultimate standard of fascism.[1] Therefore, ultimately, I suggest that fascism is an *ideology form*. In the same way sexism is not a particular ideology with a comprehensive worldview but rather a characteristic of countless actual and potential ideologies, fascism in itself cannot make up an ideology. Any modern ideology that is fundamentally anti-egalitarian and adamantly exclusionary could be described as fascist regardless to whether or not it shares the same categories of in-group versus out-group with historically recognized fascist movements or the same means of deception, manipulation, mobilization, mystification, and so on.

The overall image is more disturbing than that of a bunch of populist leaders' threat on democratic values. If democracy continues to lose ground in the United States, Brazil, and India, we are already speaking of a world in which less than 10 percent of its population will be living under some form of a democracy. Despite its external strength, democracy is arguably the most vulnerable system internally simply because it allows for anti-democratic forces to exploit democratic means. Therefore, it is not surprising that in liberal democracies anti-democratic groups, who by definition do not believe in freedom of speech, appeal to the right to free speech more than liberals and leftists do. In fact, fascist movements across the world use the same strategy to climb to power, that is, democratically. Once they are in power, democracy becomes a sham for a while before it is eventually buried, usually as an immediate reaction to a crisis that is often created by the fascists themselves, whether as a conspiracy or as a result of their bad policies. It is in the period of habitual violations of democratic customs and institutions that the (bourgeois) public begins to lose its senses and sensitivities. Fascist absurdities, cynicism, and vulgarity are increasingly absorbed by the public with a mixture of apathy and exhaustion (in the American case, live comedy shows seem to be the third ingredient). The bottom line is that when the public loses the ability to be shocked, one can be sure fascism has already arrived.

The crises ensuing from the pandemic will make things substantially worse, unless new movements across the world emerge forcefully and urgently. Fascist movements will not miss this opportunity to push for full control. The old world is becoming monstrous, both microscopically and ecologically. A new one must be created.

III

We are facing catastrophes caused by capitalism and nation-state politics, and our only hope is to courageously reject the existing violent order in order to create space for better possibilities. The widely encouraged mass behavior is denial, but I argue that comprehending the magnitude of the current historical crisis is absolutely essential for negating it and progressing toward a better future. I build on the experiences of several revolutionary movements and philosophical traditions to construct "postnihilism." This philosophy in its theoretical methodology and practical function depends on what I call the dialectics of hope and hopelessness. Put simply, hope, unlike anything else, is created and empowered in circumstances where it is least present. Those who are marginalized doubly, triply, quadruply, and so on, such as Kurdish, Zapatista, and Black American women invent the most hopeful emancipatory and revolutionary projects. Even historically, the most universalist revolutionary movements emerged at the margins of the peripheries, but of course they never received the attention they deserve precisely because they are underrepresented.

Postnihilism is a philosophy rooted in the experiences of those who have been marginalized on multiple accounts, and it is articulated with an awareness of the politics and privileges of knowledge production. It is a philosophy that resists hegemony on every level, while teaching that a truly free life can only be initiated from the point of despair because such a life would not be founded on social privilege; rather, it would be resilient because of the hopeless circumstances which it had already resisted. The revolutionary projects of those at the margins of the margins, by virtue of the experiences of the revolutionary subject, are sensitive to all forms of oppression and, therefore, are the most universalist. At the margins of the peripheries, capitalism is experienced as droughts, external and internal imperialism, and both physical and symbolic violence in addition to the immediate consequences of global class exploitation. This revolutionary subject, therefore, has an epistemic advantage over everyone else. Her resistance offers what we collectively need. That is why this book is written. That is why it will be read as long as we live in a world in which even imagining an alternative is made impossible.

Postnihilism unapologetically and categorically rejects all forms of false hope, whether rooted in superstitious belief systems, bourgeois pragmatism, the cheap self-help culture industry, patriotic mass sentiments of belonging, or hedonistic consumerism. I show that the first step toward both personal and political freedom is to become aware of one's state of unfreedom. I call this the courage of living in the present historical moment, which requires the ability to be shocked. When we lose the ability to be shocked and continue to believe in false hope, fascism will take over before we know it. We live in a state of fatal denial. Every day, we refuse to see what happens right in front of our eyes. Among such things, we refuse to see, are the lynching of Black men and teenagers committed by people in uniform, the caging of refugee children by powerful states, and the enslavement of girls and women by state-backed fundamentalist forces. We refuse to see how bad things are, and this will only make things worse. The denialism we live in is nothing but sleepwalking toward the abyss of fascism and ecological catastrophe.

I criticize the dominant culture of mass commodification as one of the foundational grounds that led to the rise of exclusionary populist movements, but I also advance a philosophy of auratic existence cultivated through creative negation. My project aims to expose the debilitating effects of the culture industry and introduce the emancipating aspects of what I call a postnihilist philosophy centered around auratic existence. The book first lays out its own negative dialectics both as a framework and as a springboard to initiate a critical theory of revolution.

Like many in the Marxian school, I avoid anything resembling an autobiography simply because the subject that deserves primary attention is the historical collective struggle, which will continue with or without my contribution. My justification for including the autobiographical passage that follows is to clarify what, I believe, qualifies me as a revolutionary philosopher in terms of my standpoint, expertise, and approach to knowledge production. In fact, I have more reasons for *not* including autobiographical information despite the significance of my experiences with movements of resistance in shaping the overall postnihilist perspective I aim to theorize. Unfortunately, there are two common tendencies in the way in which immigrant authors are perceived. The first tendency is to cast doubt on our ability to be "objective," as if a nonimmigrant author's views are not equally subjective or as if our subjectivities stand outside what is historical and political. Therefore, I avoid whatever might feed into the tendency of personalizing my philosophy. My second main reason for avoiding autobiography is in reaction to the somewhat common tendency of exoticizing the Other. The phenomenon of exoticizing immigrants' views has especially become widespread in the age of culturalism, which I reject in my social critique both in this book and in other works. The non-Western Other's research is often perceived or interpreted as a homogeneous part of what is presumed to be their cultural universe. If there is an obvious clash between the research and the perceived cultural identity, the first tendency, to subjectivize the research, becomes even more convenient as an effective prejudice.

Put as briefly as possible, as a member of a persecuted minority who grew up under one of the most fascist regimes in history; as someone who has always been stateless and internationally homeless; as someone who has been forced to escape political persecution multiple times, with the first being at the age of nineteen and the last at the age of forty-four; as someone who has experienced being imprisoned in three extremely oppressive states, escaping death row at the age of nineteen, and other fatally hopeless situations; and finally as someone whose activities have always been shaped around resisting the dominant wherever he happened to be, I came to realize that my philosophy of revolution is worth formulating in a book.

In addition to its obvious political purpose, I have a personal purpose in writing this book. The personal aspect is the same as writing a letter to those who are living in hopeless circumstances, on the border between worlds, belonging to all and none of those worlds at the same time. That is the kind of letter I wish I had received at some point in my life, as I had been desperately searching for sound ways to resist as a means of survival, meaningfully. Even more importantly, writing this book comes as a desperate way to revere the memory of the anonymous one to whom the world was too exclusionary to allow a space. It is simply my way to deal with my sense of shame as a member of a humanity that has been so insensitive toward its gentlest children. The anonymous whose life and death we failed to notice will always be absent, but our failure to make that absence present can only mean an ultimate abyss, philosophically, historically, politically, and personally. It is by means of making that absence continually present that we can guard against the eternal return of a nihilistic abyss. It is precisely that aura that has the potential power to transform utter hopelessness in a world of utter cruelty into a revolutionary will for transforming everything, both historically and spatially. The aura of the nameless stands for what is most definitive of us as a species, our existential loneliness, our ontological state of being lost, the courageous recognition of which as the universal truth (about being human as such) is also our only hope, both individually and as a species. Personally, I think the uncompromising and continual fidelity to the anonymous, to the nameless whose life and death in the margins of the margins of the margins we failed to notice, is my only way to live auratically.

The more hopeless the auralessness of the current totalitarian regime in the world becomes, the more adamantly I abide by the hope that is rooted in the struggles of the most marginalized.

IV

It is precisely the unimaginability of equality within the existing order that makes the revolutionary total negation imperative. Our inability to hope for a world without marginalization is not a reason for accepting capitalism but rather a reason for negating it. The way out of this dark age is not de-marginalization of some margins, which will always be at the expense of other margins, or decolonization of some colonized groups at the expense of others, but rather the ultimate and universal negation of a system that is inherently marginalizing of spaces of life and centralizing of power and privilege. These centers of political hegemony and capitalist power propose solutions to today's pressing crises only to sustain the very system that is the main source of the crises. In the meantime, in the margins of the margins of the margins, the mere act of living can be a lesson in revolutionary imagination, while a revolutionary project can create the kind of auratic space that is impossible to experience under any circumstances of privilege. The centers' morality is a murderous belief system, aesthetics is an obnoxious mode of perception, and truth is an industry of falsehood. In the centers, language is structured around authority and thought around conformity; the privileged are cognitively too paralyzed to realize their own state of unfreedom; truth is reduced to "what is," while "what can be" is removed from the most essential aspect of human creativity, namely, the striving to be what one is not. In the radically marginalized margins, the revolutionary subject knows too well that the actual is dysfunctional and, therefore, new truths must be made as a matter of course.

This book's ultimate message is a revolutionary one inspired by the struggles of the hopeless ones. Dialectically speaking, working toward a universalist and inclusive revolution is the only way out of the depressing world in which another world is not even dreamable. Precisely because we cannot imagine an alternative, because the existing order leaves us with no space for imagination outside its totalitarian manipulation of all aspects of life, the existing limits of the possible must be radically altered. The actual is extremely irrational and unsustainable socially, politically, and ecologically, so any rational course for moving forward necessitates the negation of the actual. Such a course of progressive movement is by definition, I argue, a revolution.

The negation of the actual must be radical so as to alter not only the boundaries of power but also the limits of what is imaginable and what is knowable. Under the dominant modes of knowledge production our modes of perception are paralyzed, and the impossibility of imagining an alternative world is habitually used against revolutionary projects. I argue for the very opposite of that false reasoning. More to the point, not despite but because of the impossibility of imagining an alternative world, a cosmopolitan revolution is imperative. Capital has been totalizing domination across geographies and universalizing sameness across all arenas of life for centuries. "Globalization" denotes the totalitarian system in which all that is human is subjected to exchange value. The infinity of exchangeability is capitalism's ultimate world order whereby inequality is imposed universally. Precisely because of this, the negation of today's totalitarian system necessitates a revolutionary project unlike any other in terms of scope. The revolutionary project must be premised on: (i) the total negation (of the imposed totalitarian negation) and (ii) the universalist emancipation from the domination of capital. That is to say, the universalism I defend in this book, and elsewhere, is negatively defined. The uniqueness of every space can be reconstructed if and only if capitalism's totalized domination and globalized sameness are negated, which necessitates a universalist scope of the emancipatory project. For difference to be made possible in every particular case, negativity must prevail universally. For every spatial aura to be made possible, the universalized regime of oppressive spatial standardization must be negated, which, again, can only be accomplished through a universalist revolutionary project.

Capital has imposed patterns of sameness, mass-produced "identities," and complete flatness of all social spaces. The alienation of all from all is infinite. It is no wonder then that fascist movements continue to multiply in every part of the world endlessly spreading violence, both physically and symbolically. These fascists' fetishized violence against each other is in fact a war of similarities, not differences as we commonly assume. They are similar in their pathological response to alienation and in their falling captive to the same tribal mode of perceiving the world. This war among the mimics whose difference is mass-produced is rooted in fascism's legitimate parent: nationalism. Because nationalism is essentially a fallback into the primordial tribal tendencies of endless xenophobia, the age of nationalism, when it reaches maturity, can be defined by two intertwined features. Namely, the existential antagonism outwardly and the political oppression inwardly; the drive to wall up the local against the Other who must be excluded at any price and the strife to produce oneness inwardly at any price; the unlimited Othering of the excluded and the unlimited suppression of the included. Thus, nationalists inevitably create an ethos sickly shaped by the exercise of power. Precisely because they are similar in their irrational perception of difference, that is, identity, they end up not tolerating any difference both internally and externally. Also, precisely because the bourgeoisie has succeeded in universalizing this particular mode of perception, that is, nationalism, the unlimited hegemony of capitalism has become possible. On the ideological level, the capitalist world order is a world of manufactured mythology, of the fetish, that aims to displace democratic political energy, steamroll difference qua aura, and create endless patterns of sameness. Fascists will continue to fight for a world in which there is one center and infinite margins. This war of mimicry by the mimics provides capitalism with the perfect conditions of total hegemony.

Postnihilism is universalism insofar as it is a negation of a totalized negation. It is also the rational form of anti-fascism because it is aware of fascism as an *ideology form*, and it is capable of rejecting all fascist movements at the same time (a common problem many in the left fall into is that unknowingly they end up supporting certain fascist movements in the name of rejecting a particular fascist front). The universalism I argue for is the rejection of the kind of relativism that has universalized totalitarianism via its active production of endless bubbles of absolutism. Postnihilist universalism, therefore, implies both (i) the rejection of the absolutist ideologies of exclusion everywhere and (ii) the negation of the dominant/globalized ethos of essentialism. The first is the rejection of modern forms of tribalism, including nationalism and religious fundamentalism, whether they advance old-racist or culturalist discourses. The second has to do with the negation of capitalism as a totalitarian world system that is fundamentally built around the objectification of people, fragmentation of space, and totalization of exchangeability. A postnihilist world is auratic by definition. In other words, it is a world where the conditions of oppression are universally negated, allowing for the ultimate condition of the infinity of unique spaces and spatial experiences. That condition, again, can only be defined negatively, that is, in terms of negating the conditions and ideologies of oppression.

V

This book aims to conceptualize revolution in light of our historical moment and from the standpoint of the ongoing emancipatory movements in order to frame a philosophy of revolutionary praxis. Why is such a philosophy necessary? It is necessary in order to make the goals of those revolutionary movements more attainable through gaining more solidarity across classes, societies, and groups. I argue that we need to support movements like Black Lives Matter, the Zapatistas, and Rojava, not merely for the sake of the oppressed who started those movements but for the sake of all of us. To be able to become revolutionaries, we need to negate our conditions of privilege first.

Privilege is both a cause of our intellectual unfreedom and a symptom of our social unfreedom. We have fallen under the spell of the bourgeois superstition believing that private property or accumulation of capital is the key to our individual happiness. In reality, we have become captives within the sieges that surround our private properties and barbed wires that isolate our countries. The walls we have built to keep the threat of the Other out have eventually become the walls of our prisons rendering us lonely, dysfunctional, and miserable as we live under the omnipresent eyes of policing regimes we continue to fund.

As for those of us who do everything and have nothing, there is a stream of ideological opium given to us to submit to our miserable reality. If we were to dispel some of the subliminal messages and put them into words, they would be something along the following lines:

- It is all worthwhile for the patriotic cause. Our insignificance gains meaning when put in the service of our nations. What matters most are the flag and the power of our nation.

- There is a threat on our nation because the Other, the fundamentally different Other, who envies us, hates us, and is on her way to destroy our superior way of life. Never mind every day of our lives is just more banality seasoned with shopping, we are told. What matters is our national security and the survival of our civilization both of which are facing an existential threat as the barbarians come closer on feet and boats and as the left conspires from inside to destroy our values and unity.

- Every day we do experience the unhappiness that eats away our lives, but we are told happiness is a state of mind and joy is in the small things—only if those small things were not so small to be completely imperceptible by a sober mind; only if those who preach about the small things agreed to give us their stupid big mansions in exchange of all our small things that are filled with magical joy waiting to be lived.

- If we are still miserable, it is because we do not how to take deep breaths, and keep inhaling more polluted air, until we find the inner peace. All we need is the yoga mat available on Amazon and the latest self-help book that was written by a Californian who, after realizing she was bored to death with her life, went to India and found the shortest path to the nirvana (and, of course, she found it, as she was being served as a royalty thanks to her class status and the privilege of whiteness).

We are told our misery has to do with not running every morning—so now we have to also stress about getting up even earlier to run in search of the lost paradise that will supposedly pop up in the muscles. Running and sweating will make us happy, so we keep running and sweating to make it to the mysterious happiness the other sweaty runners are supposedly experiencing.

We are told all we need is open hearts and minds for the voice of God who undoubtedly loves us. We keep trying to open the heart and the mind like the mainsail and jib of an exhausted boat, yet we always end up oaring as the yachts of the golfers, pedophiles, and manufacturers of weapons of mass destruction pass by on their way to their private islands. We wonder if

God knows another way of expressing his love to the poor, but having such devilish thoughts will only make us feel even more criminal. For the unlimited divine love seems to be dependent on never questioning domination.

Before leaving the boat analogy behind, it is worthwhile to draw from a dark joke of a group of refugees. First, however, a linguistic clarification and a bit of context might be necessary. There is an expression in several Indo-Iranian and Semitic languages that would be translated as "God is big," but the implied meaning is something along the lines of "ultimately God is all-powerful and as such capable of making miracles to save people in need of rescue." This expression is commonly used by ordinary people when facing calamities or potential approaching danger during times or situations of uncertainty, which is to say most of the time for the poor. In terms of the context, keep in mind, it is typical of boats that smuggle refugees across the Mediterranean to be overloaded, obviously, because the smugglers want to make maximum amount of money for each risky journey of sailing across the sea, and the refugees who take that route are desperate enough to risk their lives for a chance to make it to Europe.

A group of refugees are in the middle of the Mediterranean Sea when water floods into the boat and sinking increasingly seems to be absolutely certain. In the middle of the rising terror and anxiety, one of the refugees says what many in such a situation would say: "Everyone, don't worry. God is big." Another refugee replies, "I know God is big, but the fucken boat is small."

There are countless such jokes that originate in the tragic absurdities of refugee routes from Asia and Africa to Europe. What I appreciate about this particular one is that it carries the signs of both the original invention and the ultimate death of God. That is to say, just as at some point of human history actual circumstances of hopelessness and sheer terror gave birth to the idea of God, hopelessness at some point in human history can also diminish it as a mythical source of false hope. These two moments are also not uncommon on the level of individual human conversion to and from religiosity. It does not take much investigation to realize that a so-called born-again believer is a typical story of someone who experienced emotions of guilt, remorse, and fear and turned to the magical savior, behind whom there are centuries of mystifying cannons and ritualistic practices. The moment of conversion is the moment of sacrificing one's freedom, the sources of all ecstasies and horrors at the same time, one's continuation into the unknown, which entails both death and a renewal of life. In short, as the biblical, and later Quranic, story makes it clear, one must sacrifice one's Isaac.

Let us imagine the story with a different personality of Abraham. According to the biblical story, God asks Abraham to take his only son, Isaac, to the mountain and sacrifice him like an animal. That way Abraham would prove his faith in God. An Abraham with some philosophical intelligence would not simply go ahead to commit the act merely to win God's rewards in return. We could imagine a scenario in which Abraham would deduce something very logical. Namely, the moment he receives the request to kill the innocent Isaac, Abraham would conclude that God is not all-good and all-knowing simply because an all-good entity would not ask him to commit such an unethical act and an all-knowing entity would be able to know Abraham's sincerity without the need to examine him. Abraham would turn around the table to test God, and God would have already failed on all accounts. If God is not all-good and all-knowing, then by definition God is not God. The realization would make Abraham live in uncertainty, but that is the price for freedom, for the very act of life as such. The terrible experience would transform Abraham from a fearful person to a free one. Needless to say, this scenario could not have been the case in any religion, for that would neither be a religion, nor would it be dominant in a world of unjustifiable social inequalities because the perpetuation of imposed inequalities requires the moralization of submission.

In effect, the statement, "I know God is big, but the fucken boat is small," is a disapproval of faith, because it implies that if God existed, we would not end up in this situation in the first place. Hope and its absence can only be based on actual, material, concrete means and conditions, such as the boat and its capacity. Taking it one step further, we could imagine the same character adding a political proclamation along the lines of "it is exactly the belief in a 'big God' that created such a hopeless world from which we were forced to escape so desperately" or "the hopelessness we are facing at this moment is already a consequence of the hopelessness sustained by the belief in a 'big God.'"

The absence of real hope is the reason that false hope is invented. Yet, that is only half of the story, the psychological half. The more important half, the social and political half is the reverse of the same statement: the absence of real hope is the result of false hope. That is to say, false hope is continually manufactured in order to keep the hopeless away from creating real hope, that is, from changing their state of hopelessness by changing the world, from bringing down the social systems that inevitably will keep the majority of human society in utterly miserable conditions of enslavement in order to maintain the hierarchal system of privileges and luxuries. In the pyramid of social classes, castes, genders, geographies, it is impossible to settle on a level where one is neither exploited nor being exploited because such a level does not exist. As Adorno brilliantly said, "Wrong life cannot be lived rightly" (2005: 39). The only rational act is to work toward bringing down the hierarchy altogether as a system so that nobody will have others stepping on them and nobody will have to step on others to survive.

In situations of utter hopelessness, out of sheer desperateness, people tend to believe in supernatural powers. In fact, as I clarify in this book, for Feuerbach, Marx, and Freud that is the bottom-line explanation for why or how humans created God. For Feuerbach the confusion is philosophical, and theology must be relocated to where it belongs, namely anthropology. Marx's materialism, on the other hand, sees religion as a symptom, a product of actual life conditions, and its abolishment takes much more than a philosophical declaration. It takes the abolishment of the brutal dehumanization that is definitive of class society, which means it takes a revolution. Freud's theory explains the human creation of God in terms of primordial fear of the unknown and the guilt that might have resulted from the actual murder of a father figure by the sons. Human tribes created God as a universal replacement of the dead father figure to gain a sense of certainty in the face of the horrors of existing in an unknown universe. Whereas Freud does not offer a political philosophy, his theory is extremely useful to make sense of group psychology and what makes suppressed people follow a demagogue.

Facing hopelessness for what it is without falling into self-deceiving superstitions, whether political or spiritual, is essential for any actual hope for emancipation. If nothing else, the courage to face hopelessness in all its actual absurdity and injustice amounts to an autonomous rejection on behalf of one's own subjective stance in the world. On the other hand, disguising hopeless circumstances, whether through means of entertainment, spirituality, patriotism, or whatever else, translates to a state of denial. Living in the state of denial entails two major problems. First, it will most likely make the person a participant in the process of making the situation worse; so politically, denial is worse than rejection. Second, the person will not enjoy a moment of intellectual, and therefore ethical, autonomy; so denial is subjectively degrading. In short, denial makes the failure of both the political and the subjective inevitable. However, rejection fulfills the first condition of a revolutionary project and subject. Therefore, having the courage to accept the magnitude of our current historical crises is essential for the possibility of creating any real hope for a real, progressive, change. Here, of course, the implied premise is that the rejection of a reality is not possible without first being prepared to perceive it with all its actual horrors. By the same token, refusing to perceive the hopelessness of a reality renders the subjective illusion stronger and the existing reality more durable.

Even if we assume the hopelessness is absolute, that is, changing the world is absolutely impossible, at the end, there is something intrinsically more meaningful in being a failed revolutionary. If nothing else, living one's last years, hours, moments, if one is (un)lucky enough to have time to reflect before death arrives, it is nicer to realize that one did not live as a complete loser, that one lived as a revolutionary despite all the hopelessness. At the end, what one is most responsible for is one's own stance in the world. It may be all meaningless, but one can choose not to contribute to the meaninglessness. In fact, there is nothing too ambitious in saying one is always capable of a degree of negation. Personally, I believe a day I do not offend at least a fascist is a wasted day. On a broader level, I think a human life that is not dedicated to lessening unfreedom, inequality, and violence is a wasted life.

By negating illusionary meanings, false hopes, and artificial presuppositions of belonging, the subject positions herself face to face with the reality of despair and the despair of the reality. Only after such an act of negation will the subject begin to gain the strength needed for the prolonged march toward a different world, regardless of the popularity of the cosmopolitan movement at that specific historical moment. In that very lonely first move, the revolutionary experiences her freedom in the fullest form thus far. The post-despair sense of freedom is the only way to live meaningfully because prior to that one's psychological life is framed by a totalizing state of denial, not to mention that such a predetermined life also contributes to the general unfreedom and misery of the human condition as such. Once a person decolonizes her own consciousness and starts on the path of her meaningful way of living, she is potentially becoming a revolutionary. Actively rejecting her privileges that allow for marginalizing others is the other necessary condition that makes the formation of a revolutionary subject possible.

Contrary to dystopic nihilism, which sees the human condition as fundamentally irredeemable, the hopelessness I revisit as the first dialectical moment is perceived as a historical condition. For the revolutionary subjects who emerge from the midst of the hopeless, the sheer struggle of living confirms the fact that all historical conditions of hopelessness must be transcended. The revolutionary project of the hopeless, therefore, is necessarily a cosmopolitan project of emancipation.

In the time of revolutions, among many other views, two opposing but equally problematic views surface: the optimistic position that believes the revolution will bring about a world free of the injustices of the prerevolution world, and the typical pessimistic position that claims it is going to be the same: some people will take power and we will be back to the beginning of the cycle again.

The optimist voice often comes from revolutionaries who are too involved in the revolution to let negative doubts creep into their revolutionary motive and therefore their immediate will to action. It can also come from the supporters of the revolution who are too detached from the ugly stage of the events: of the publicized violence and the chaotic nature of revolution. The actual motive of a revolution, however, comes from a despair that turns against the reality that led to it. Revolution is rooted in despair as much as it is motivated by some sense of hope. Despair and hope immediately imply each other in a dialectical relationship. After a certain point of injustice, the dominant question no longer will be whether a revolution that fixes the world is possible or not. The question will instead be whether there is anything worth being afraid of losing anymore. Marx and Engels put it profoundly when, at the end of their *Communist Manifesto*, they state, "The proletarians have nothing to lose but their chains. They have a world to win" (Marx and Engels 1978: 500). By the last sentence, "They have a world to win," Marx and Engels do not mean that the proletarians will necessarily win *the* world. Rather, they mean, the proletarians can, in principle, determine the next stage in world's history by winning *a* world: a horizon of possibilities in which they can continually actualize their creative will.

Having nothing to lose is the actual creative force that sparks a revolution. I do not need to know what perfect justice would look like in order to reject and rebel against injustice. Hope unlike anything else is present in its very absence. That is to say, a hopeless reality is precisely what gives birth to hope. If there were no oppressed people who live their day-to-day lives in hopeless and inexcusably cruel realities, we would not need to think or speak of hope in the first place. Besides, no matter how hopeless we feel about changing the world, the moment we become truly aware of the sufferings of others, we have no choice but to change, or perhaps destroy, the existing order. There is a type of revolutionary who starts or joins the revolution not because she believes in the possibility of creating a tolerable world, but because she believes that her reality is not tolerable anymore. Abolishing an unjust world does not have to imply the creation of a just one. Abolishing the existing unjust order is a necessary, but not sufficient, condition for creating a just world. Revolutions are unavoidable until the history of absolutism, exploitation, despotism, and domination is negated. We might never reach that point, but we can always step forward.

Then there is the second voice that says, "it is pointless: the revolution negates its own principles as soon as it becomes victorious." The excuses and arguments for this position are too many to be listed here. What I want to criticize here is the fashionable intellectual-elitist opinion that pretends to see through history. "Why bother if I know the human condition can never be fixed?" "Humans are by nature competitive and power thirsty," and so on and so forth. It is much easier to be hopeless and passive than to be hopeless and revolutionary. Moreover, often those who do not believe in justice represent the very forces that make justice impossible. Hobbesian types of statement about human nature are, like any other form of ideology, a reflection of certain historical and material conditions of life. Of course, they present their "truth" about "human nature" and "history" as metaphysical truths. Like religions, their claims come from certain material conditions but want to speak in the name of an all-knowing God. The task of revolution is not only to invalidate such metaphysical beliefs but also to end the conditions of their production.

The new horizon of possibilities is dependent on the degree of the destruction of what has constituted the perceived reality thus far, including the standards of evaluating reality and truth. Therefore, the opinions and "truths" of bourgeois intelligentsia are not only unnecessary for progressive revolutionaries, but they are exactly what should be trashed by the revolution. What we need to believe in as revolutionaries is that a different reality will create a different set of truths, that we are what we make of ourselves, that we indeed can reshape our "nature" and our history, that "what is" is never the whole truth because "what can be realized" is at the heart of the ontology of truth, and that we can—and should—enlighten the bourgeois intellectuals by introducing them to this new reality in which their truths are no longer true.

In the contemporary debates of the left, especially within the Marxian tradition, there is arguably nothing more divisive than the question of the feasibility of an alternative to capitalism. Fundamentally, that is the question that separates the two main camps of socialists: communists and social democrats. Speaking in general terms, the question of the attainability of an egalitarian alternative and the best possible means to reach such an alternative whereby human emancipation can finally be actualized could not have been more divisive in the history of progressive social movements since Marx's own time. Of course, this issue could easily be traced back to the French Revolution at least insofar as it defines Jacobinism and its reformist critiques within the left, but the issue gains a much deeper philosophical and political dimension right at the historical moment when Marxism started to own socialism in a manner that seemed to be more valid and effective than other socialist ideologies. By the end of the nineteenth century, Marxism had already surpassed other claims to socialism throughout Europe. We would be justified to denote that historical moment as the two decades that followed Marx's death, which took us into the twentieth century. Right from that beginning, Marxist socialism as a social movement was divided around the question of the realizability of a socialist alternative and the realistic means to that end. Ironically, two of the immediate authorities of Marxism, second to none other than Marx and Engels themselves, took a nonrevolutionary approach. Those were Eduard Bernstein and Karl Kautsky (see Kautsky 1946; Bernstein 1893, 1897, 1909), but one could argue that even the main dispute between Marx and Ferdinand Lassalle, the German socialist leader who died in duel in 1864 at the age of thirty-nine, was centered around the same question. To the revolutionary camp, Kautsky and Bernstein became known as the revisionists, a charge that has always implied the betrayal of the Marxist philosophy of revolution. Whether referred to as revisionists, reformists, or, later, social democrats, or even "social fascists," the fundamental issue remained to be one and the same: a revolutionary alternative versus gradual reform, the imperativeness of revolution versus the reformability of the bourgeois democracy, the feasibility of a revolutionary alternative versus the inevitability of the same path of slow and gradual development.

After taking power, the Bolsheviks quickly turned against those who upheld the revolutionary position, which proved to be catastrophic even for most Bolshevik leaders including the founder of the Red Army. In the Soviet Union, and by default most of the rest of the countries where communist parties took power, the line of perpetual international revolution came under a deadly attack,' resulting in the defeats inflicted on revolutionary communism from 1936 to 1940. Those attacks were embodied in the Moscow show trials (1936–8), the Stalinist conspiracy against the anarcho-communists in Catalonia and Aragon (1936–9), and, of course, the endless assassinations including Trotsky's murder by a Stalinist agent in Mexico on August 21, 1940, exactly four years after the first Moscow show trial.

Within the century that separated Marx's first critiques of the liberal Hegelians in 1840–1 and the ultimate triumph of fascism in Europe in 1940–1, a universalist hope was born, lived, and died. Nonetheless, all the problems the hopeful internationalist movement desperately tried to solve remain unsolved today. A version of communism might have become completely outdated, but the communist questions are even more urgent today. As both Badiou and Žižek argue, the communist thesis remains to be valid not only as a negative (revolutionary) thesis but also as anti-dystopian project of realistic politics of hope, as a project of a necessary alternative to be willed and made.

What makes the Marxist thesis far more valid than today's dominant doctrines—such as that of the end of history otherwise known as neoliberalism or culturalism, otherwise known as clash of civilizations—are the simple truths about lives of actual humans in the most concrete sense. Those truths have to do with the basic human needs that have never and will never become less relevant to history. As long as there is hunger, homelessness, and humiliation, the communist thesis will continue to live one way or another. To put it very directly, as we should, the failure of a form of communism does not amount to the end of revolutions. By the same token, the end of a form of communism does not make communism, that is, the striving to end inequality, any less political. To the contrary, only the realization of equality will mean the end of the communist struggle. Communism, like feminism, will continue until a world is actualized in which communism, or feminism, is no longer necessary. Communism is a negative thesis. It is more about what must not be allowed to go on today than it is about what could be actualized tomorrow.

The revolutionary is a subject whose politics is grounded in historical knowledge, as opposed to moral judgments of what is and what ought to be. The historical knowledge itself necessitates the temporality and inevitable disappearance of the existing order. The revolutionary question, therefore, is neither a question of utopianism nor realism; rather it is essentially a question of *making* truth. To make truth is to render the very singularity of and within the imposed circumstances the material for historical subjecthood. The only way we can become the subject of history is to consciously understand the unique circumstances of our unfreedom and negate them.

Denying our circumstances or negating circumstances that are not ours (at the present historical moment) would amount to nihilism, which is extremely common under neoliberalism and its appropriated sects across the world. The postnihilist, on the other hand, has the courage of being more realistic than everyone else. She has the courage to be shocked and the nobility of wanting to keep that ability. The postnihilist does not aim to numb her modes of sensible perception in the actual lived world of everydayness. This is what makes her affirmative existentially and historically. At the same time, she rebels against those very frames of existence through conscious politicization of every social given and problematization of everything that is institutionalized ideologically. Therefore, revolution for the postnihilist is not utopia; rather, it is an everyday lived truth. Every day, the postnihilist subject negates "what is" at the very space and moment she happened to live. By living postnihilistically, she negates the imposed unfreedoms of the reality. This, in turn, amounts to the postnihilist making of truth. Thus, the postnihilist's most damning proof of the revolutionary alterability of the reality is her own daily life. She makes truth by negating the circumstances of her actual social existence, and by doing so she gives shape to the alternative everyday. The postnihilist's critique is praxis in the fullest possible sense, and her daily life is critique/negation in the fullest possible sense.

As Žižek often emphasizes, even up until the 1980s, the question of an alternative world was considered a matter of political orientation and philosophy whereas now it is for the most part absent from the public sphere. Today the Bernsteinian social democrat would seem radical compared to the common center. Indeed, Bernie Sanders, whose "social democracy" did not call for more than the bare minimum, such as public health care and free education, sounded too radical to the Democratic Party. More generally, today's culturalism was the default worldview of the twentieth-century fascists who saw the world as composed of fundamentally different national characters. Of course, the category of race has been replaced with that of culture even though "race" remains to enjoy a considerable weight both cognitively and discursively, thanks to the deeply racist systems of education, which has metaphysicalized race precisely by reducing racism to a moral problem. It is that very post-Second World War system of education that has perpetuated the modes of racist perception. While the old-fashion racists base their belief in race on the natural sciences such as biology, which is precisely why such a belief is refutable, culturalists justify their racism on mystifying bases provided by the established pseudoscience, namely the so-called social sciences. Precisely because those disciplines are failed imitations of the natural and pure sciences, their entrenchment in ideologies of domination is totalitarian, their mystification of the world in the name of positivism is absolute, and their incapacity to accept any invalidation of their metaphysical assumptions is improbable; liberal education's tribalization and essentialization of the world is more effectively ideological than old forms of fascist education. There is no way to use the social sciences in order to prove the mythical nature of any particular assumption or debase any false paradigm such as the paradigm of culture. Given the neoliberal domination in today's world, culturalism as the most effective form of racism continues to expand its hegemony across societies. Every year thousands of people are recruited in PhD programs who knowingly or unknowingly reinforce the paradigm of culture, even if it means self-culturalization. If the universal doctrine of human rights is liberalism's most important philosophical and historical doctrine, liberals themselves have been its oldest violators, first in the name of biological racism, which was used to justify colonialism, slavery, and endless genocides, then in the name of culturalism, which perpetuates the same crimes only more disguised through neoliberalism's creation of special economic zones of slavery and through climate genocides. In the meantime, the most sectarian and imperialist forces outside the West happily endorse the European and American culturalist myth to tell their victims that the cultural autonomy and authenticity require their silent submission to the hierarchies imposed on them. The Iranian or Pakistani victims of their respective regimes are supposed to believe that their fate is determined culturally, and as such their only option is infinite submission.

The implicit alliance between liberal culturalists and religious fundamentalists can best be described as a fascist pact. Thanks to this pact, the victims of multiple forms of global, regional, local, social, political, and economical forms of oppression are left in complete hopelessness. Both sides are in agreement that only whites are subjects of human rights, that every non-white group is subject to something nonuniversal, something sectarian and tribal. This is precisely where the fascist aspect of neoliberalism is located. In the meantime, luckily, some of the victims in the margins of the margins of the margins refuse to accept the fascist reality imposed on them. Naxalite Maoists, Mesopotamian Ocalanists, and the Zapatistas in Chiapas are among today's most oppressed and, at the same time, the true universalist revolutionaries. The ambassadors of Shia Islamism, like Hamid Dabashi, and Sunni Islamism, like Tariq Ramadan, continue to exploit the Eurocentrism that is at the heart of culturalist essentialism prevalent among many post-Marxists and postcolonialists who believe that they denounce European colonialism but unknowingly embrace the European colonialist image of the Other, an Other who can only be defined racially, culturally, and religiously, an Other whose ontological center is defined exclusively in relation to Europe. Fortunately, however, every Middle Eastern leftist would find it laughable to consider any such figures as leftists, progressives, and so on. While the liquid sentimentalists of the culturalist intelligentsia in the West happily ingratiate with fascist forces outside the West, who in turn happily exploit the same culturalist myth, those in the margins of the margins of the margins have created new modes of perception as a part of their revolutionary negation of today's global dark age. While some of today's celebrities of Western left in the academy, such as Judith Butler and Susan Buck-Morss, endorse the fatal enemy of the left and feminism in the Middle East, militant feminist and revolutionary organizations across the Middle East are on the rise because, luckily, those revolutionaries, whether in Kurdistan or Sudan, have better things to read than what the post-Marxist Western left has produced. Therefore, there is indeed hope, and that hope is created by those who come from some of the most marginalized places and voiced by them and their allies.

I must emphasize that the fashionable feel-good advocacy around hope as positivity is exactly what this book is NOT committing. Any talk of hope without the courage to comprehend the scope of the actual crises is a part of the industry of false hope, which inevitably ends up serving the existing oppressive order. *Hope in the Dark: Untold Histories, Wild Possibilities*, authored by Rebecca Solnit (2016), is just one example of that kind of industry of false hope. Despite the intriguing title, Solnit's approach and (lack of) philosophical stance is representative of precisely what I refute, namely the *liquid sentimentalism* of elite liberals who want a revolution without a revolution, who voice their moral opposition to conservatives but are dismissal, or antagonistic, to the revolutionary left. The pseudo-leftism of liberal elites is a fascist enabler because: (i) it plays a major role in constructing false hope among the oppressed groups and (ii) it systematically tries to delegitimize genuine anti-fascist movements. Far from being a serious critique of the existing order, or even a useful political commentary, *Hope in the Dark* could be placed in the self-help section of bookstores. It might make readers feel better but only by misleading them to believe that things are, after all, not that bad under capitalism. In addition to false information about the environmental crisis (implying that it has improved since the 1960s) and countless other false or unsupported claims, the author, without any sense of irony, wants to make the case that the peace movement won despite its failure to stop the invasion of Iraq. The author rhetorically asks, "What could be more democratic than millions of people who, via the grapevine, the Internet, and various assemblies from churches to unions to direct-action affinity groups, can organize themselves?" (Solnit 2016: 26). What she provides as the ultimate proof of a triumph for democracy can easily be seen as the ultimate evidence of civil society's political ineffectiveness under capitalism. Does not the fact that the war took place despite popular opposition tell us just that? How much comfort would the Iraqi victims take from Solnit's celebration of her activism as a peace protester or her declaration that "we were able to oppose a war with compassion for the troops who fought it?" How absurd does Solnit's celebration of victory sound when one recalls that at the time of the publication of her book the Yezidi genocide had already been underway for two years?

Solnit's book is a call for the culturalization of politics (i.e., the depoliticization of everything for the sake of feeling good). What needs to happen is the re-politicization of culture. Her book invites readers to feel joyful, avoid despair, and be satisfied with gradual change because "revolution doesn't necessarily look like revolution" (Solnit 2016: 26). Such hopefulness is precisely the problem, and having the courage to endorse despair is in fact a necessary condition for moving beyond hopelessness and creating any meaningful political hope for an alternative world. Solnit's standpoint is based on a position of privilege and a pseudo-revolutionary politics as it becomes clear from her personal stories or superficial references to non-Western examples of dissent, such as, of course, Gandhi. It is precisely through this kind of commodities of the culture industry, as Solnit's book, that the dominant system manages to "drown out the screams of its victims," to borrow Adorno's expression (1973: 365). It is due to this kind of bourgeois heroism that preaches us about being positive and hopeful that the real hopelessness of the existing world order is largely concealed while many of us continue to perpetuate systems of oppression and benefit from the miseries of others. It is also because of these false-hope makers that the real hope that is created by revolutionary subjects of the margins, such as the Maoists in India, has not enjoyed a chance to guide the world toward new horizons of possibility.

A Summary of the Rationale

Postnihilism is formulated on the basis that the struggles of the most marginalized have the potentiality of creating some of the most emancipatory spaces. The revolutionary projects of those who have been subjected to multiple forms of marginalization are the most promising sources of inspiration for the next international emancipatory revolution capable of creating a way out of the current historical deadlock. Thus, this book recapitulates the crises caused by capitalism and nation-states and simultaneously concretizes a philosophy of revolutionary hope. Hope does not exist metaphysically; its conditions must be created. Also, unlike anything else, hope is most strongly present when it is absent. For the hopeless ones, to continue living and to create hope is one and the same. For them, life is a struggle to negate their hopeless condition; life is bearable through the present struggle for a better future; living itself is the cycle of struggle that continually redefines life both historically and ontologically, thereby making it worth living.

Walter Benjamin stated, "Only for the sake of the hopeless ones have we been given hope" (2004a: 356). While this statement is central to my work, in this project, I reverse it in terms of the subject and the object: it is the revolutionary projects of the hopeless ones that give us hope.

Far from committing a grotesque romanticization of misery, I think it is only reasonable to expect more misery to come out of misery. For instance, violent crime, not poetic works of art, is the likely outcome of poverty. By the same token, the transcending subject who creates a horizon of hope is not the normal outcome of hopeless conditions of life. How, then, could hopelessness be the condition of the subject for whom life is transcendable through her act of living? How could the most militant and powerful feminist movement appear among the population of Kurdish women, who are in every sense among the most oppressed, even within the peripheries as a stateless population, and even within the Kurdish society itself? Obviously, no form of oppression or combination of forms of oppression suffices to create an emancipatory episteme. As we learn from the Iraqi thinker Kenan Makiya, victimhood "is not a quality but a *condition*" (2006: 108, emphasis from original), which is why those who identify as the oppressed in one sense could very well be oppressors in another sense. In fact, there is nothing in being oppressed in terms of x, y, or z that would guarantee not being an oppressor in terms of x, y, or z.

Given that the conditions of extreme unfreedom necessarily produce more unfreedom, and that the privileged are not in a position to produce emancipatory knowledge—as we learn from Freire (1968) and more powerfully from feminist theorists, such as Dorothy Smith (1979) and Sandra Harding (1986)—how is a revolution of the oppressed possible? To answer this crucial question, I construct a philosophy of praxis that has grown out of oppressive conditions and is epistemologically well situated to negate conditions of oppression in their complex multiplicities. Neither oppression nor privilege, both of which are always circumstantial and relative, can make a revolutionary subject. Ultimately, it is a revolutionary worldview, philosophy, ideology that has the potential capacity of transforming a person or a group of people to a revolutionary subject.

Submissiveness has become so dominant in the general intellectual climate that it is not uncommon even for leftist discourses to reflect the belief that capitalism cannot end but with the end of the world in its entirety. While problematizing this intellectual pandemic of passivity is necessary, the revolutionary truth remains the same: only the revolution of the oppressed can put an end to oppressive systems. If anything, the Covid-19 pandemic or the looming ecological catastrophe only renders revolutionary action against capitalism more imperative and urgent. Therefore, I juxtapose the hopeless historical situation and the revolutionary historical truth to extract a philosophy of revolution. Speaking in Marxian–Hegelian terms, this book shows the irrationality of the existing reality in order to move beyond it. Thus, after pausing on the scale of the crisis of the present historical moment, the book explores the realizability of what is rational. My ultimate aim, therefore, is to convince the reader that it is a rational imperative to negate the existing reality, to make revolution. Negating the existing reality, however, is not an act of nihilism or denialism, just as the alternative cannot be an arbitrary process but rather a rationally crystalized horizon for actual hope for human emancipation.

There is an urgent need for a postnihilist philosophy that has the courage to cognize the magnitude of the existing crises, which in turn will necessitate figuring out a new horizon of possibilities. Effectively, the practical aspect of this philosophy, even if not fully theorized, has always been at work among the oppressed of the oppressed, that is, the doubly oppressed, who choose rebellious action over submission. If nothing else, such a rational will has the historical effect of denying the ruling system its totalitarian absolutism, because one rebellious act is sufficient to prove to everyone that the system has failed to impose unlimited hegemony, that nihilism has not been able to annihilate all free will, that the door of possibilities is still open. Philosophies that are not prepared to face the darkness of the historical moment and be inspired by the struggle of the hopeless are doomed to fail and fail us. Only such a postnihilist philosophy can face the magnitude of the current historical crisis without falling back into the rich tradition of false hopes and redemptions or sheer apocalypticism.

Structure

In Chapters 2 and 3, I address the ongoing crises in terms of the Covid-19 pandemic and their deeper political implications. In Chapter 3, I introduce the reader to the ecological crisis by presenting some of the latest scientific research in an accessible language. Then, I explain what is lacking in those scientific reports, namely, by pointing to the fact that what has caused the crisis is the capitalist modes of production. The crisis is not an ethical one, but rather a sociopolitical one that necessitates a revolutionary change in human society as such. I argue against the widespread attempts to moralize the ecological crisis as if with a few adjustments by consumers, corporations, and nation-state policies the crisis could be resolved, as if the crisis were not an inevitable and immediate consequence of capitalism. Thus, after explaining the structural ways in which capitalism is anti-ecological, I conclude the chapter by arguing that there is no alternative to going beyond capitalism if we are to curb the ecological catastrophe that is approaching so fast that those who are twenty years old now might very well live to witness the complete extinction of one-third of today's animal and plant species, according to recent scientific research. The conclusion of the three chapters is that the dual power of capitalism and nation-states must come to an end, rationally speaking.

However, the cosmopolitan revolution I allude to is nowhere to be found on the visible horizon. Then the question is: why is that so? Hence, one of the main undertakings of this book involves critical analysis of the current ideological crisis. Narrowing down my diagnosis of the ideological crisis, in Chapter 5, I argue that culturalism is at the root of the rise of fascist and other exclusionary ideologies across the world. While the paradigm of "culture," unlike "race," does not entail hierarchy, when it is used in this quasi-anthropological sense and to classify identities of the Othered, it is tantamount to "race." Deindividualization and essentialization are inherent to the paradigm of "culture," only less perceptible as a subject of critique than the paradigm of "race" in today's dominant climate of opinion. We assume that there is such a thing as a Chinese culture, an Indian culture, or an Ethiopian culture, and with that assumption we commit precisely the fallacy that multiculturalism was supposed to correct. In other words, in the name of recognizing diversity, the non-white other is homogenized under a mental blanket called culture. The culturalization of people has been effective in depoliticizing their struggles and creating a fragmented world of extreme identitarianism. This ideology started to become dominant around the same time the popular hope in the communist project started to decline and neoliberalism started to rise, namely in the late 1970s and early 1980s. By the end of the twentieth century, "class" had long since fallen out of fashion even for many former leftists, and instead the sectarian worldview of culturalism became the norm, which is something the far right in the

West and elsewhere was quick to capitalize on. Of course, following Slavoj Žižek's lead, I refute culturalism, arguing that even what used to be called economist centrism of Marxism offers a far more inclusive and critical analysis of today's world than the dominant culturalist ideology of neoliberalism. At the end of the first half of the book, I return to the main question. Specifically, why did we lose faith in the possibility of a cosmopolitan horizon of emancipation? Why have we ended up internalizing the Fukuyaman thesis of the end of history and capitalist liberalism as the final stop of our evolution, and the Huntingtonian thesis of culturalism as our normal way of seeing the world, which is something Žižek has noticed and brilliantly expressed in his work?

Only then will the book reach a point where offering an alternative, albeit a negative one, can make sense. Therefore, in the second half of the book, I try to critically diagnose the crises behind this frightening loss of faith in the human will for emancipation, which has led to a fallback into climates of religiosity, tribalism, and apocalypticism. Inspired by Žižek's outstanding observation and commentary on Fredrick Jameson (see Žižek 1994: 1; Jameson 2003: 76), almost in every course I have taught in three American universities, I have asked the participants the following two questions. First, can you imagine the end of all forms of life on the planet as a probable eventuality? Second, can you imagine perpetual peace in human society as a possibility at some point in the future? Every time, I have been shocked by the results. Almost all the participants answer positively to the first question and negatively to the second. Even when I try to push them to change their position with regard to the second question, for instance, by emphasizing that the "future" in this context means infinity and that the issue at hand is whether such a thing is a possibility, not whether it will happen, at best one or two students would reconsider their first responses. This illogical pessimism has ideological roots. Educators, opinion makers, and parents are at least partly to blame for creating such a pervasive outlook.

The problem of ideological internalization of nihilism is so widespread that it has devastating political outcomes as a self-fulfilling prophecy. There is nothing natural about today's dominant nihilism, but its roots and origins are not evident by any means. Such a passive pessimism with regard to the potentialities of the human society—or even a rather modest goal such as perpetual peace, which should not seem unattainable even if one simply considers some of the partial progress we have made since the Second World War—should be viewed as a symptom of a much wider crisis. My research addresses various aspects of the current global crisis, including its ecological and societal ones, and its main approach falls under the interdisciplinary spectrum of critical theory centered around ideology critique. More specifically, I argue that if the 1990s and 2000s were the Fukuyaman era of the "end of history," based on his well-known declaration of liberal democracy (albeit in its capitalist guise) as the culmination of our search for the most just system, we are witnessing the ultimate end of thesis of the "end of history." If anything, we are at the zero point of a new search for cosmopolitan solutions to the endless global and planetary crises with which we are faced. Nation-states have long proved to be inventions of enduring tribalist mentalities. The current fever of nationalism in different parts of the world could be the last historical chapter of this antagonistic, discriminatory, oppressive, and totalitarian ideology. We will either give in to its barbaric impulse represented by the apocalyptic visions of its offspring that is (neo)fascism, or we will be motivated to create another horizon of possibilities before reaching the abyss of the ultimate ecological collapse. This book may not be a guide for a way out. However, I am equally certain that sooner or later we must turn to the reasoning realized by this kind of project. Moreover, all great changes start with a few, usually unnoticeable, steps in the right direction.

Through a method of negative dialectics, I reject psychological positivity, arguing that despair is an essential moment that could dialectically shape revolutionary will. Oppression is both situational and political, so critical theory must be universalist in its negativism in order to be sufficiently sensitive to local progressive struggles. Negating moral sentimentalism, I argue that critical theory becomes devoid of its revolutionary potential when it is reduced to moral criticism, as opposed to the critique of the totality of unfreedom inherent in bourgeois society and its reactionary poles. Chapter 6 will function as the foundation for my overall philosophy of revolution. I argue that the alternative can only be defined negatively. Therefore, prior to even raising the question of alternative, we must be able to comprehend the magnitude of the crisis. For without knowing the seriousness and scope of the crisis, any discussion of alternatives will necessarily amount to searching for a solution to a problem that does not exist. The logical conclusion of the chapter then necessitates a diagnosis of the crises in their broadness and complexities, which is why I dedicate the first half of the book to introducing the scope of the crises facing us under capitalism.

In the first stage, I argue that in order to know what is wrong and reject it we do not need to know what is right. In the second stage, I argue that in order for the conception of an alternative to be possible, we need to free our thought from the existing conditions, which in turn necessitates abolishing them, per historical materialism. The fact that Marx never gave a positive account of what communism would look like supports my position and the position of critical theory more broadly. Critical theory bases its praxis on negating the normalized and internalized relations of domination, instead of claiming any positive solutions. In fact, the critique of solution-driven mentality is itself a subject of critique by critical theorists (Cox 1981). Then, linking my critique to Marx's well-known eleventh thesis on Feuerbach—I argue that the mental–physical division of labor is part of the problem of the impossibility of prefiguring a viable alternative to the existing order. That is to say, alternatives must be realized by the oppressed themselves within the revolutionary activity that is neither abstract thought nor thoughtless work.

Revolution insofar as it overcomes alienation is both the process of changing the world and the model of the changed world. Here it is crucial to recall that alienation, as the French Marxist Henri Lefebvre (2014) defined it, is the combination of separation and abstraction. Accordingly, the philosophy of revolution is inherently anti-philosophy because it must renounce all forms of metaphysics and ethics that have assumed realms beyond and above the history and materiality of actual human beings. It also denounces the bourgeois nihilism and its aesthetic commodities. For such commodities, otherwise known as works of art, are nothing but bourgeois boredom, emptiness, and depression meticulously manufactured, polished, framed, packaged, commercialized, and sold.

In the remaining parts of the book, I argue that there are already revolutionary individuals and movements who have been constructing an alternative world. However, because of Eurocentrism, culturalism, and the internalization of the neoliberal outlook, actual ongoing revolutionary projects have been ignored. Also, in line with the argument in Chapter 7, where I revisit a few extraordinary revolutionary figures, I argue that in our search for the revolutionary subject, in our search for revolutionary hope, we should look at the margins not only in and of the West but also in the margins of the margins, where many more people have been forced into hopeless material conditions of living. The world can be perceived more accurately from the margins and by those who are excluded. If nothing else, this is what the history of serious literature also tells us. Only in the margins of the margins are the capitalist, nationalist, racist, and sexist layers of oppression experienced in the fullest possible way. Moreover, the revolutionary subject that is formed in the margins of the margins invents revolutions out of hopelessness, as opposed to utilitarian calculations or bourgeois pragmatism.

A dialectical-spiral method is followed in constructing the main philosophical theory and its concepts. Ideas, arguments, examples, analogies, critiques, and observations are not dealt with in a leaner way. Rather, they are often revisited at different points of the volution according to which the theory evolves, moving between the multitude of negations. Dominant ideologies are embedded in linguistic structures and normalized modes of research, so even if one's overall position is critical (or even revolutionary), one will inevitably end up reproducing the aspects of the prevalent order in an infinite number of ways. If nothing else, the dominant mode of perception, according to which the text will be interpreted by readers, will ensure the reproduction of the norms. Given this, that is, the near-impossibility of moving beyond the totalitarian grip of signs and signifiers, texts and interpretations, production and reproduction, the only way of making progress within a critical project is to engage in a continual process of dialectical negation aimed at creating new planes of significations that will create rapture after rapture with the normalized regime of hermeneutics. Negation is either absolute or it is only a momentary type of negation that will easily be reprocessed within the positive totality. To accomplish the completion of a negation and enable other movements of conceptual negations in all directions, on each level, the temporal movement must correspond with the spatial one. Thus, my method in this book is itself inseparable from the critical theory the book advances. That said, my reader does not need to grasp the methodological dialectics to be able to make sense of the theory. The only reason I touched upon the method is to emphasize that what might feel like repetition is anything but repetition. Such points in the reading should, in fact, be perceived as signs of arriving at a different stage in terms of the broader dialectical movement. Put differently, some similar propositions are used in multiple locations of the manuscript, but each time each proposition is used as either a premise within a new argument or a conclusion reached via a new path.

My hope is that by the time the reader reaches the last sentence of Chapter 8, she will have not only comprehended the philosophy but also become confident in using its concepts to negate, to resist, to move beyond the nuances of nihilism in whatever way that is possible in her particular set of circumstances.

CHAPTER TWO

The Indispensability of Universal Anti-fascist Solidarity: A Return to Normal Is Neither Possible nor Desirable

Only now, after two decades of stubborn persistence, has the twentieth century come to its ultimate end. The world of the twenty-first century is taking shape by the hour. The old world will not come back despite all the prayers. It is in the nature of perception to lag behind events of this scope. Did not most people believe that what would later be known as the Great War would end before Christmas of 1914 and everything would go back to normal?

If the twentieth century was the age of the nationalist plague and the total capitalist domination of the world, this century, after long uncertainties and turmoil, could be both postnationalist and postcapitalist. However, the two-headed beast of nationalism and capitalism will not wither away with a poetic whimper but with a violent bang.

The emerging world is not predetermined. The process is not one of unfolding, and old recipes—whether leftist, rightist, or divine—are useless. We, human beings currently living, are responsible for this ongoing reshaping of the world. The ruling elites who dream of going back to "normal" desperately want to force a resumption of the capitalist machine. Yet a return to the pre-2020 normal is neither possible nor desirable for the billions who have been forced into labor prostitution, endless wars, and social alienation throughout their lives.

At certain historical turning points, the objective conditions of existence across human society change so drastically that they open up the horizon of possibilities for a universal rearrangement of societal and political relations. Nonetheless, the way in which this rearrangement takes place makes all the difference. Even though the demise of the old world is certain, its burial and the crystalization of its replacement are contingent upon the presence of progressive emancipatory forces to counter and defeat oppressive retrogressive ones.

Reading Crises Critically

The existing state of the world continues to make a dignified life for billions of humans less and less attainable. This crisis is just as ecological as it is political, for ecological crises are fundamentally political, and the domination of the naturalized politics of nation-states has catastrophic ecological consequences. The less obvious dimension of today's ecological crisis lies in the very nature of capitalism, which, as discussed in Chapter 4, is inherently and entirely dependent on the exploitation of labor and the natural environment.

Yet, the nihilist disbelief in universalist struggles for emancipation is by far more prevalent than any other time at least since the First World War, and in Europe, certainly since the 1848 revolutions. The fact that over two billion people live under fascist leaders, who came to power through elections, tells us something about the darkness of our age. The rise of fascism during the last decade cannot be dismissed on the basis of culturalism, so-called economic development, or religious fundamentalism alone. In Chapter 1, I gave four examples of the fascist leadership, the United States, India, Brazil, and Turkey, but certainly we could add others on every single continent. The point of my selection was precisely to show that the phenomenon—having been present in the West, East, North, and South—can no longer be dismissed on some reductionist basis or portrayed as some isolated exceptions in a few corners of the world.

Therefore, we desperately need a critical analysis of the massification of people who are made to act according to the irrational rationality of their systems of oppression. Voicing an urgent question for many Marxists during the first half of the twentieth century, Wilhelm Reich wrote, "What is to be explained is not why the starving individual steals or why the exploited individual strikes, but why the majority of starving individuals do *not* steal and the majority of exploited individuals do *not* strike" (1946: 15).

Like last century, and the centuries before it, with a few exceptions of moments of revolution, the vast majority of people seem to choose to act against their own freedom, which can be a frustrating fact if we do not adopt a more sophisticated historical worldview than liberal individualism and idealism. Why do millions of oppressed people become the very instruments of their own oppression? Why do people who are already marginalized further disempower themselves and often empower a man who would not be fit to run an animal farm let alone govern an entire country? Of course, there are answers to these questions, but the extensive division of knowledge into isolated fields of expertise, along with the capitalist relations of knowledge production, has led to approaches that are for the most part reductionist and more often than not ideologically distorted.

Most of the critical theorists of the Frankfurt School offered their own multidisciplinary theses to tackle the question of the fascist massification of the working class, and these theses still have a lot to offer us today, as this same phenomenon continues in various places in the world. For instance, Adorno's thesis of the culture industry is crucial in exposing the methods that are used effectively for achieving an ideological hegemony that "democratically" renders the oppressed at the heart of the process of domination (Adorno 2001b). Today's culture industry is far more effective than old-style fascist propaganda in creating a moldable fascist mentality characterized by the same traits Adorno attributed to cultural commodities: standardization, predictability, and mechanically reproducible patterns of sameness (Ahmed 2008a). The new modes of ideological production heavily involve the 99 percent, which is exactly why they are more successful in securing the position of the 1 percent. What we are witnessing is a democratically produced and protected type of totalitarianism. The old model of totalitarianism proved to be a failure in achieving the end goals of both total control and durability (Ahmed 2019c).

Both Fromm and Reich used Freudian theory to unpack the phenomenon of fascist individuals' identification with authority, and for both of them the roots of the authoritarian personality go back to the patriarchal family structure, where suppression and obedience to authority begin. Reich relies heavily on his theory of sex economy to explain the behavior of the individual who cannot free herself even if a unique opportunity for freedom presents itself, as happened in the 1905 soldiers' revolt in Russia, according to Reich's interpretation. He writes, "*Sexual inhibition alters the structure of the economically suppressed individual in such a manner that he thinks, feels and acts against his own material interests*" (Reich 1946: 27; emphasis in original).

To Fromm, however, the individual's identification with the authority figure also has to do with his/her entrenched sense of insignificance and inability to stand the prospect of his/her own freedom. As a result, Fromm concludes, the individual's thoughts, wishes, and acts are determined by an outside authority. These subjects desperately need to obey, and even when they express their wishes and opinions, they merely express the wishes and opinions of the authority to which they submit. More or less like programmed automatons, potential fascists march when they are told to march and kill when they are told to kill. This is part of the sad truth we have resisted and continue to resist more than one hundred years after the Armenian genocide by the Young Turks, whose Kamal Mustafa Pasha, later to be known as Ataturk, would become Hitler's "star in the darkness," as Hitler himself put it (Ihring 2014: 116).

The fascist mentality adopts a collective self-image that is both pitifully self-victimizing and mythically self-aggrandizing. Parallel to this, the demonized Other, the imagined enemy, is depicted as both a merciless conspirator and a weak enemy. Indeed, in their remarkable book on fascism in the United States, Leo Löwenthal and Norbert Guterman noted this "fantastic fusion of ruthlessness and helplessness" of the Other in speeches of anti-Semite agitators in the 1940s (2021: 69). Of course, we should also keep in mind that it is precisely the "powerlessness" of the marginalized that "attracts the enemy of powerlessness," as Horkheimer and Adorno brilliantly put it (2002: 138). Ultimately, there is a double bifurcation at work, of both the fascist in-group and its othered Other. This double bifurcation is among the decisive features of the fascist form of ideology, and this method of conceptual problematization will prove to be helpful for critical analyses of fascist ideologies across geographies and histories.

On the level of individual personality of the followers, the fascist narcissism is manifested as an irrational idealization of a father figure and some form of naturalized patriarchal moral criteria. The obsession with the father figure can result in any number of social and political expressions depending on the specific societal norms and political hot topics. Essentially, it is an obsession with the cult of power, which can be embodied, for instance, as the demand/striving for the extensive exercise of power against the Othered, or more directly as the Führer principle, the unconditional loyalty to the in-group leader. Whatever the expressions of the obsession of the cult of power may be, the image of an enemy is absolutely essential. The enemy as an existential threat to "our" nation, culture, community, and so on is needed not only to stimulate the urge for the exercise of power but also to glue the individual members of the in-group together. The automated and alienated individuals are incapable of intimacy as such, so what brings them together is the common revulsion of the same object of hatred, which is essentially a projection of the suppressed self-image.[1] Again, for the fascist, as Löwenthal and Guterman write, "the Jew is not the abstract 'other,' he is the other who dwells in themselves. Into him they can conveniently project everything within themselves to which they deny recognition, everything they must repress" (2021: 89).

The Apocalyptic Vision of Reactionary Ideologies

One of the problems that lead to a dark age being prolonged is the general inability to gage and recognize the age as being dark. However, there is nothing noble in this statement, and indeed such a claim is more often than not made by spiritualists who have even less faith in reason than the average educated person. Conservatives habitually tend to romanticize the past and describe their contemporary times as decadent. To conservatism, the world continually worsens and any movement forward is a movement downward, so all that can be done is to slow down the decline. Foucault insightfully ties this conservative tendency to the myth of the pure origin, wherey history is not seen as progress but rather as a continual fall. Reinforcing Nietzsche's critique of "the belief that things are most precious and essential at the moment of birth," Foucault states, "we tend to think that this is the moment of their greatest perfection, when they emerged dazzling from the hands of a creator or in the shadowless light of a first morning. The origin always precedes the Fall" (1984: 79).

This fear of change is at the heart of reactionary violence manifested in the language and practice of various fascist movements. No wonder the communists in Nazi Germany were among the very first enemies who had to be wiped out ruthlessly. For as much as the image of the German peasant was idealized as everything that embodied the authentic spirit of the *Volk*, the purity of the blood, and the sanctity of the soil, the Marxist revolutionary progress and its rootless, propertyless, urban, and bastard protagonist, the proletariat, is the very equivalent of devil. The Marxist actively works to realize a rapid abolishment of the very nationhood of the nation, including the uniqueness of its identity and its traditional way of life. Marxist communism, therefore, to fascists, is the absolute hell of complete decay where there is no lower level.

It is the same hatred fascists express, sometimes explicitly and sometimes subliminally, against the city. The city is not only the birthplace of the bastards of the world who are now trying to unite under the banner of Marxist communism to destroy organic hierarchy and sublime value systems but also where all castes and races inevitably share the same space. The city, in this perception, completely strips the individual of everything that has depth. The fascist experience of the city is one of ultimate departure from the security of the primordial tribe, the line of nobility, the sacred warmth of the home (the womb), and nature as such. Even within the city, every change is another painful burring of the traces of the past and familiarity. Eventually, the faceless and nameless city dweller will eat away everything the way worms eat away the heart of a nobleman. The fascist, therefore, is on a sacred mission as the tragic hero of her diminishing world to join the brothers and sisters who are united in their struggle against the decay, which reached a catastrophic level in the first half of the twentieth century.

Being at the edge of complete extinction, obviously, the peasant could not put up any fight at this point. The fascists, therefore, turn to the city to recruit their fighters among the worthless bastards themselves, whose sacrifice for the sacred mission is the best and only role they could play. The role of the mob is instrumental. Even a few hundred of them marching on the streets suffices to attract other potential fascists to join the movement, so the growth of the fascist movement can be rapid. Moreover, under certain crisis-ridden circumstances, a few hundred armed fanatics could control the population of few hundreds of thousands of ordinary citizens. In all cases, a fascist movement needs the spectacle of the military-style marches of recruits in order to perpetuate growth of its physical power until it reaches a point where it can swiftly impose its totalitarian rule of terror. One of the most recurring scenarios of the rise of fascism is that of the demise of the revolutionary left, which is most profoundly expressed in Žižek's formulation of a Benjaminian insight: "behind every fascism there is a failed revolution" (Žižek 2008a: 386).

In her *Origins of Totalitarianism*, Arendt explains that one of the crucial aspects of the fascist enterprise is the massification of classes, especially the working class. That is to say, the first fascist political task is to find ways to allure workers to the degree of making them fight against their own class. At first glance, massification might seem contrary to the atomization of individuals, which is also attributed to fascism. However, this atomization is, if anything, extremely helpful in making the fascist fraternity ever more appealing to the individual whose need for dissolving into a collective identity is tied to escaping the unbearable sense of isolation and loneliness, which is also asserted in Fromm's notion of "escape from freedom" (Fromm 1965). The authoritarian individual's attraction to the vulgar spectacle of masculinity and the violent exercise of power against the marginalized is an immediate attempt to deny a shameful sense of weakness and insignificance, as we learn from Adorno (2001a).[2]

Spirituality for the Sake of Perpetual Submission

The social and political forces dedicated to perpetuating the old structures or reimposing new social hierarchies are numerous. Of course, there are all kinds of conflicts, alliances, and enmities among those retrogressive forces. However, so far, it has been forces on the right that have almost exclusively dictated the battlefield, as they are not confronted by a universal, emancipatory, and egalitarian movement. The fatal mistake is to assume that the liberal pseudo-opposition and their bureaucratic establishment will keep the extreme right at bay.

The belief that the end is inevitable and the best one can do is to passively submit to the mythical doomsday and focus on finding so-called inner peace is a form of apocalypticism that has deep roots in mysticism. Also, it must be noted that, especially in times of crises, ruling groups encourage the masses to turn to spirituality, to seek individual inner peace, lest they reflect on their perpetual enslavement and seize the opportunity to break those chains. This is precisely why during the Covid-19 pandemic, houses of worship were declared "essential" in theocracies and liberal democracies alike. The psychic chains imprisoning and tormenting the body have always been manufactured in spaces of spirituality. In houses of worship the miserable are taught to postpone their lives until the promised afterlife. It is there that they surrender their senses and crucify reason in mass frenzies. The violence materialized in existing social hierarchies and the death cult that saturates spirituality reproduce each other. Thanks to the mystifying powers of spirituality—whether in the Indian subcontinent, the Middle East and North Africa, or the Americas—the poor are made to love their own individual miseries, hate each other collectively, and defend the very system that exploits them both nationally and globally.

It is always easy to give in to indifferent passivism, whether in the name of realism, spirituality, existentialism, or some other excuse. It is also easy to live as if some other authorities, whether actual or fictional, hold things together despite all the objective signs to the contrary. One of the reasons fascism rises during times of crises is that the disempowered, alienated, and isolated individual tends to seek an escape from the general anxiety by submitting to the authority of father figures. Freud (1949) used the same theory to explain the secret behind the collective enthusiastic submission to a fascist leader without using the term "fascist." Freud saw an immediate relation between the longing for the missing father figure and the invention of God as a universal authority to resolve the problem of the horrific fear that accompanies the realization of one's freedom in the world.[3] Predating French existentialists such as Jean-Paul Sartre and Albert Camus, he discovered that God had been invented precisely to trade in freedom for a sense of security and metaphysically managed universal order (Freud 1961: 17–19, 24; 1962: 19; 2001: 172–3).

No wonder, to this day, religiosity in its most extreme forms directly correlates to conditions of social insecurity, such as poverty. Ultimately, believing in a metaphysical form of justice is less demanding and more comforting than accepting the fact that the only way out of endless injustices is our own, innovative, step-by-step march toward the construction of a different world. Above all, the fascist strife for total control, with the omnipresent father figure at the top, is a strategic imitation of monotheistic theology. What has changed in the age of fascism mainly has to do with the technologies of power. In 1944, Horkheimer and Adorno were already well aware of this when they wrote, "The *Führer*'s metaphysical charisma, invented by the sociology of religion, turned out finally to be merely the omnipresence of his radio addresses, which demonically parodies that of the divine spirit" (2002: 129).

Faith in father figures promises immediate relief, which is the real reward that the weak cannot resist. It is not that believers cannot give up the promised (after-life) heaven; rather, they cannot give up what such a belief provides them here and now. This is precisely why believers often insist that in order for you to see the effect, you must have faith. Despite the discernable circular logical fallacy in such a statement, there is a psychological truth in it. One is promised salvation under the fundamental condition of believing in the savior, and all one needs to do to test the truth of the claim is to test it out empirically. Of course, what is being tested is not the metaphysical truth claim but the psychological claim. The confidence with which people are invited to assess the efficiency of religion is far beyond the confidence of any salesperson selling any commodity. The trick is accomplished subjectively, with the subject and object of the experiment being one and the same. The immediate outcome of belief is by definition an unmistakable feeling of certainty, which simultaneously dissolves the subject's ontological anxieties. Marx's (1970) well-known statement that likens religion to opium remains one of the most insightful observations about the subject. Opium's irresistibility to those who "just try it once" is similar to a religious experience. Opium empirically proves its power. Like religion, the power of opium remains a fiction, or at best something to be imagined, to those who refuse to try it. The bottom line is that changing one's perception is incomparably easier than changing what is perceived.

The entire culture industry is devoted to creating a thought-numbing sphere in which the consumer continues to perceive with all five senses, except that everything the consumer perceives is thoughtless, and therefore entertaining. Thanks to mass culture, changing one's perception is not a demanding task at all. In fact, all one needs to do is to stay connected to the stream for as long as possible during one's waking hours. Even while doing something as mundane as walking, driving, cleaning, or exercising, to ensure one is shielded from negativity, uncertainty, and angst, one needs to be "connected." Wi-Fi is a lifeline so essential, it often makes drinking, eating, and sleeping secondary needs, resulting in all kinds of disorders. Not to be connected is to be exposed to the fatality of thinking about the world right there and then.

Perception is our most essential medium of all knowledge, so feeding the senses what is manufactured for the purpose of constant enjoyment can only lead to a more deserted reality. A reality that is not perceived is, at least politically, no longer a reality, but of course, it continues to exist materially with such an absoluteness that death is the only escape from it. A subject, no matter how delusional, remains a constituent part of this material reality. The subject's passivity, too, plays a direct role in what today's reality will become a day, week, year, and century from now. Passivity is itself an activity, only with effect of objectifying the subject. The more people choose passivity, the more powerful and influential the ruling elites become. For every withdrawn subject, a sociopolitical space is given away to the dominant. By the same token, with every single case of withdrawal into passivity, the public as a whole becomes less free.

The Train of Fascism Is Speeding Up

If we allow the absolutism of capital and the tribalism of the nation-state to determine another century, we will be no less irresponsible than those who looked the other way as Nazi trains traveled to and from the concentration camps. They too preferred to focus on their daily "small pleasures" and remain positive. They too wrote stupid poetry and exchanged gifts to reaffirm their fragile humanism. They too turned to spirituality and cultural entertainment when they felt reality needed a mystical surgery to make it less unbearable.

This death train is operated by fascists; calling fascism something else will not make the damage to lives and life systems less violent or less painful for the victims. By the same token, then as now, those of us who believed that barbarism could be avoided were silenced by liberal governments and elites. Even then, the petite bourgeoisie and scholastic priests of the dominant class were more annoyed by the leftist use of the word "fascism" than the actual rise of fascism. Today, the same faithful minds of the absolute authority of textbooks act as a paramilitary force, censoring and interrogating leftists to reinforce the ban on real anti-capitalist and anti-fascist criticism.

The moment the victims make it to the other side of the barriers that keep them silenced and invisible, the elites react in terror drawing public attention to alleged danger to "our" civilization, culture, norms, liberties, and ways of life. Just as the protests that followed the murder of George Floyd began to gain popular support, an aggressive campaign of criminalization of the movement was launched. Words like "looting," "vandalizing," and "violence" became part of the news reports and commentaries. The oppressed is perceived not only as a threat but also inherently barbaric and uncivil. Just as police violence is portrayed as exceptional cases caused by "bad apples," no matter how peaceful a protest movement, the immediate depiction of it by the elites is criminalization and demonization of the movement in order to reinforce the ordinary silence on the marginalized. While the right-wing media outlets openly demonize such protest movements, the liberal leaning outlets and elites use the language of neutrality and moderation to do the same thing, only more effectively. In news reports that cover protests, the overwhelming images that are aired endlessly are those of broken bank machines and store fronts rather than broken heads, arms, and legs, of the protesters. Any act of breaking into a store could be aired endlessly precisely to criminalize the act of protest whereas the public is never given a glimpse into what takes place inside police cars and stations. In short, the liberal impartiality essentially comes down to the use of extreme partialities for purposes that are particularly illiberal. It, liberal impartiality, is rooted in the strong bourgeois tendency to preserve the privilege of the ruling groups.

A case in point is an open letter published by *Harper's* Magazine on July 7, 2020, in which about 150 academics, authors, and journalists recognize "powerful protests for racial and social justice are leading to overdue demands for police reform, along with wider calls for greater equality and inclusion across our society, not least in higher education, journalism, philanthropy, and the arts." "But" they add, "this needed reckoning has also intensified a new set of moral attitudes and political commitments that tend to weaken our norms of open debate and toleration of differences in favor of ideological conformity" (*Harper's* 2020). While on the surface the letter is supposedly a call to defend "free speech," it is the left that is implicitly accused to have created an intimidating climate. By accusing "all sides," the authors of the letter put Black Lives Matter and anti-fascists into the same cage of suspicion as the alt-right and KKK, which practically amounts to charging the protest movements and discharging the criminal organizations. Without any sense of irony, the signers of the *Harper's* letter, in the name of defending the right to freedom of expression, reacted against the protests that were inherently both an embodiment of free expression and a protest against suppression. The intellectual superficiality of the letter is especially appalling when it insists to claim the voice of reason and "open debate."

Somehow the free speech argument has become a source of an incredible amount of dispute at the expense of the actual content of speech and its political implications. Somehow the mention of "free speech" is supposed to make the speaker the ultimate representative of the right to free speech and freedom as such. Do religious fundamentalists not speak in the name of justice? How irrational would it be if we assume that only because of their mention of "justice," any opposition against them would be an opposition to justice? The irrationality of allowing fascism to go on unchallenged in the name of "free speech" is just as irrational. Anti-fascism is inherently a movement of freedom, including free speech, and, by the same token, criminalizing anti-fascism is diametrically against the right to free speech, and freedom at large. It simply does not matter that fascists use the free speech argument. The use of the free speech argument has nothing to do with the political orientation in relation to free speech as a universal right.

Why does the debate around the right to free speech become a main topic of dispute every time anti-fascist movements make progress? I think the answer to this question is the same as the answer to the question of why protest movements of the marginalized are immediately associated with violence, crime, and civil chaos. The victim is never allowed to be even a victim. Imagine a Nazi regime that would let its victims to express their suffering. Would not that be a symbolic gain for the victims and, therefore, empowering the victims at the expense of the domination of the Nazis? Misrepresenting protests and distorting their purposes is just another strategy of silencing the disadvantaged whether it is done in the name of order, free speech, or security. In one of his brilliant insights, Adorno writes, "If thought is not measured by the extremity that eludes the concept, it is from the outset in the nature of the musical accompaniment with which the SS liked to drown out the screams of its victims" (Adorno 1973: 365). While in all patriarchal societies the cult of power entails an unconscious repulsion against the powerless, the inability to tolerate the voice of the victim is an unmistakable symptom of fascism. Also, the hegemony of a fascist ideological form can be recognized by the normalized repulsion against the powerless, which in turn is rooted in the suppression of the image of the weak self, the self that is desperate for the omnipresent father figure.

Fascism goes a step further in its repulsive urge to suppress the weak Other constantly as a way of escaping and denying the weakness that defines the self-image. If the military attracts those who are addicted to the sadistic exercise of power, fascism is a movement of militarization of the entire society. Here another crucial aspect of fascism is formed: the constant need for an enemy. Corresponding to the narcissistic collective self-image, as both mythically heroic and tragically fragile, the imagined enemy must have a dual character. It must be both existentially threatening and extremely powerless, defenseless. Thus, the image of the enemy is divided between an outside enemy and an inside conspirator. The outside enemy represents the existential threat while the inside enemy is the pollution that has prevented "us" to reach "our" ultimate glory of indivisibility intrinsic to our identity, say, as a nation. According to the fascist modes of perception, "our" indivisibility, of course, depends on our collective ability to preserve our purity, and as long as we tolerate any form of human pollution, we carry the seed of our destruction. The inside enemy is what Agamben called "the banned," the excluded who is included by virtue of being excluded (1998: 28–9, 105, 110). The banned is the ultimate object of the fascist hatred, which holds the in-group together.

Universalist egalitarian voices are suppressed mainly by the same forces that passively empowered fascism in the early twentieth century. As the extreme right gradually takes over, the self-assured, always positive, fundamentally apologist liberal discourse is more concerned about losing their own privileges than anything else. Describing the liberal elites' hypocrisy in terms of maintaining both an ethical appearance and, in practice, indifference toward the rise of fascism in the interwar period, Arendt dwells on several cultural events, starting with the reception of the performance of Brecht's famous play *Dreigroschenoper* in Germany in 1928, which "presented gangsters as respectable businessmen and respectable businessmen as gangsters" (Arendt 1979: 335). Arendt continues, "the bourgeoisie could no longer be shocked; it welcomed the exposure of its hidden philosophy, whose popularity proved they had been right all along, so that the only political result of Brecht's 'revolution' was to encourage everyone to discard the uncomfortable mask of hypocrisy and to accept openly the standards of the mob" (1979: 335).

The moment the eternalized and moralized violence of capitalism comes under threat, liberal enablers of fascism break with their bourgeois manners of performative politeness and nonviolence, maliciously exposing their fundamentalist spite against egalitarianism. They ingratiate themselves with forces that commit femicide and pedophilia, yet they lose every celebrated principle of their proudly claimed liberalism once they are faced with an even loosely defined communist discourse. Today, we are all riding a train operated by fascists and would-be fascists and heavily guarded by a hypocritical liberal establishment.

The current anti-racist protests in the United States could be viewed as the "American Spring," and unfortunately it might have the same fate as the

Arab Spring. In the absence of a universalist, revolutionary leftist movement, the Arab Spring was doomed to be exploited by the right (Ahmed 2011). Nearly a decade after the beginning of the Arab Spring, this is precisely what we are witnessing with the imperialist rise of Islamist fundamentalism (Ahmed 2019c). The American Spring too could very well be exploited by white fascism and Christian fundamentalism. Even before the murder of George Floyd, armed white militias had started to make their vulgar presence felt in multiple cities (Ahmed 2020)—with the explicit approval of Donald Trump (Sollenberger 2020; Krieg 2017).

Liberalism is not a revolutionary ideology with a doctrine of social justice, nor are liberals revolutionary agents who could or would prevent the rise of fascism. While they may show sentimental support for anti-racism and anti-authoritarianism, their class position situates them against egalitarian anti-fascist movements. Therefore, even if passively, their pressure on egalitarian movements will continue until the rising fascist movement no longer needs them.

The Fascist Reality

One of the senses in which liberals functioned as fascist enablers was their habitual insistence on underestimating the threat of fascism, even when fascist groups vulgarly made their presence known, from the streets to some of the highest loci of state administration. Sometimes, the lack of wide anti-fascist resistance in the interwar period is blamed on the lack of historical precedent. In other words, people generally were either caught by surprise or could not imagine what fascist movements had in store for Europe. While now we should know all too well what the danger of the extreme right can translate to, there is a general tendency among oppressed people who do not identify with the right to buy into the false hope provided by liberal elites. The assuring liberal discourse simply resonates with a lot of people's desperate need to believe that things are fine or will be fine soon.

There is an academic orthodoxy that continues to portray fascism as something historical, and even those who perceive the present danger articulate their warnings in terms of a potential *return* of fascism. Unsurprisingly, such warnings are met with rebuffs that point out the obvious differences between, say, Trump and Hitler or Modi and Mussolini. At best, the warnings by some liberal academics and journalists seem to be taken as an exaggerated analogy between present populists and past fascists. On the other hand, there is a tendency to use the term merely as a swear word, as a moral/political accusation. The effect is the fictionalization of fascism. It is similar to the use of terms such as savage, barbarian, bloodthirsty, and so on, which are metaphorical and contain an intended degree of exaggeration. In short, the pejorative use of the term "fascist" also ends up undermining the actual threat.[4]

While some have been warning of the return of fascism, the overall debate remains predominantly marginalized. The scholarship has constrained its analytic potentiality by relying on Mussolini's Fascism and Hitler's Nazism as the main, if not only, standards of what should or should not be considered "fascist." Of course, there is a debate about generic versus historical definitions among the scholars of the field,[5] and for the most part, the framework has started to move away from the orthodoxy that holds the features of Italian Fascism and German Nazism as the original and therefore definitive standards.

I think those early examples should be considered as the least developed or as simply two specific models of fascism among many other actual and possible variations. Again, if we measured democracy by the earliest historical models in ancient Greece, we would not be able to justifiably designate any contemporary system of governance as a democracy. In fact, "representative democracy" would be a contradiction in terms, which is one of the anarchist arguments, but such voices are quite marginalized.

The main problem with the liberal accounts of fascism is their dismissal of fascism's capitalist character. By reducing it to a mere moral-political crisis, the liberal accounts almost entirely leave out class analysis.[6] Directly attacking the liberal tendency to deny the capitalist dimensions of fascism, in 1939 Horkheimer wrote, "whoever is not willing to talk about capitalism should also keep quiet about fascism" (2005: 226).[7] In the age of neoliberalism—especially with the extreme concentration of power in the hands of the bourgeoisie, tribalization of the oppressed, and the culturalization of grand political and social conflicts—the totalitarian structures of capitalism and fascism have become more indistinguishable. As David Harvey argues, to maintain its global rule, neoliberalism explicitly uses "authoritarian, hierarchical, and even militaristic means" (2007: 195). More recently, in a book on fascism in the United States, Shane Burley asserts, "fascism is an attempt to answer the unfinished equation of capitalism, and, instead of challenging the inequalities manifested through this economic system, it hardens them" (2017: 38–9). Burley also realizes that it is too misleading to reduce the problem of fascism in the United States to Trump's administration. As he puts it, "if Trump had not existed, fascists would have invented him" (2017: 35). He explains that movements such as the Alt-Right had been growing for a long time, and it was time for them to mandate someone to "rebrand genocidal racialism as red-blooded Americana" (2017: 35).

Liberalism is officially dead, thanks to its anti-universalist turn at the hands of culturalist ideologues and identitarian tribalists. Everything that was once progressive in liberalism has been buried by the liberal bourgeoisie. The universal values of the Enlightenment are being defended in the margins of the global South, while, at the same time, liberals enjoy their prolonged honeymoon with reactionaries of all kinds. Today, from Indonesia and India to Bolivia and Guatemala, the progressive universalist values are defended by those who continue the struggle of the twentieth century's murdered revolutionaries. As women fighters struggle against the two empires of jihadism led by Ankara and Tehran respectively, as the Sudanese and Darfurians struggle to save the only place where the Arab Spring has not been defeated by fundamentalism, and as Peruvians and Brazilian progressives resist the ultimate demise of hope, American and European liberal elites fight to keep the status quo through an endless reproduction of false hope. Barack Obama arguably has been the most vivid embodiment of the liberalist mass production of false hope. Suddenly, as it were, the otherwise revolutionary goal of changing the world became attainable without any revolution whatsoever. Suddenly, millions of African Americans were supposed to believe that the age of racism had just ended, and the sun of equality had finally risen from the capital city of the republic. What an ideal way to beat out every prospect of mass protest and turn potential dissent into extra reinforcement of the establishment against the possibility of real change.

The liberal elites have an ideological sense, or a class instinct, which immediately alarms them of the threat of universalist egalitarians. As a result, at the historical crossroads between fascism and universalism, they swiftly yield to fascism but remain intolerant of egalitarianism. When fascism takes over, they either become its loyal social engineers or return to the infamous line of "I am not interested in politics." In the end, their stock shares and properties require full and unconditional submission to the ruling political system.

The liberal affair with fascist forces does not necessarily imply a resemblance between the liberal and fascist moral positions. Liberalism, even in its prime in the mid-nineteenth century, reduced nearly all social and political questions to merely matters of moral values. This should not be surprising, given its early submission to capitalism, and therefore, its careful normative curbing of all that could possibly point to the material bases of social and political problems. The liberal elites, therefore, are religiously against any changes in the fundamental social foundations of capitalism. To them, a few superficial plastic surgeries here and there are sufficient to keep the status quo and make it as good as new. This is precisely why today's crises are expressed in a neutral language in which both the crimes and criminals are disguised. For instance, extreme class exploitation is depicted in terms of pseudocritical terminologies such as food deserts, food insecurity, development, economic initiatives, humanitarian aid, and so on; racism–antiracism in terms of diversity, inclusivity, and interculturalism; and ecological destruction in terms of climate change, global warming, and environmental sustainability. The discursive distortions are inseparable from the ideological strategies that aim to further the totalitarian hegemony of capitalism in and across societies. At the end of the day, we are made to believe that all these crises can be solved with a few lifestyle adjustments from the side of the ruled and a few reforms of management methods from the side of the rulers. While the crises and their endless consequences intensify, the oppressive language of liquid sentimentalism and the pacifying language of managerialism leave the door wide open for fascist forces to exploit popular frustration while revolutionary potentialities, including prospects of anti-fascist resistance, are policed in every possible way, morally, pedagogically, politically, and militarily. Those who sit at the very top of the market dictatorship are celebrated as the world's philanthropists. The same governments who, in a reasonable world, would easily be designated as eco-terrorists of the worst kind shamelessly hold climate conferences as if they are part of the solution.

As far as today's ruling elites are concerned, the totalitarian system of capitalism must persist eternally, and this is exactly where their anti-egalitarianism is rooted (not in their moral value system). In times of crises, when fascist alliances are prepared to seize the opportunity to push for ultimate control over the state and society, liberals' false hope does little more than guard the fascist train. The systematic suppression of the left not only guarantees a swift fascist triumph but also adds a democratic touch of legitimacy to this triumph, thanks to the biparty theatrical disputes in farcical parliamentary settings. In Arendt's words, "Double morality as practiced by the bourgeoisie … is always pompous and never sincere" (1979: 335).

The faithful guards of the train that is speeding toward the abyss of fascism will, of course, disappear in the face of fascist terror. Once again, only a vibrant left will remain to single-handedly defend the principles of political liberalism and establish a peaceful and genuine democratic order. When these gloomy days, and the gloomier days to follow, are over, the lesson that must not be forgotten is that the opportunism of bourgeois elites is just as fatal to the prospect of a democratic and egalitarian society as flag-waving fascists.

Whenever the principles of liberalism in a Western country have come under fascist threats, liberal elites have not only failed to put up resistance but have also censored and persecuted leftists involved in anti-fascist mobilization. Whenever a society was about to achieve emancipation anywhere in the world, liberal governments did not hesitate to support fascist forces against socialists and communists. This is exactly how fundamentalists and/ or nationalists became the main players in most regions of the world by the 1990s.

Notwithstanding the historical distortions of Cold War propaganda that systematically demonized communism by equating it with Stalinism, most murdered communists were, in fact, victims of Stalinist regimes. How many Americans know that some of the earliest modern communist projects were actually attempted in the United States before Karl Marx became a communist? Or that Marx was an adamant defender of liberal ideals, such as freedom of speech, and that he worked for a major American daily newspaper, the *New York Daily Tribune*, for almost ten years? (Hosfeld 2013: 93; Marx and Engels n.d.). Thanks to the dogmatism disseminated by the advocates of social hierarchy, not many know that communists and anarchists started their desperate struggle against both fascism and Stalinism right from the beginning, in the 1920s. They bitterly intensified their struggle in Spain in the three years leading up to 1939, while liberal governments imposed an embargo on the struggling republic and all those who were fighting on its behalf against the Franco–Mussolini–Hitler alliance. The historian, Enzo Traverso wrote,

> To get an idea of the prevailing atmosphere in Spain during the conflict, we need only recall the words with which Captain Gonzalo de Aguilera, Franco's press attaché, defined the objectives of his army to the American journalist John Whitaker: "Kill, kill and kill" (matar, matar y matar) all the "Reds," in order to liberate Spain from the "virus of Bolshevism." The number of victims testifies to the ferocity of this war. Historians give the following tally: 100,000 dead in combat, 10,000 dead from bombings, and 50,000 dead from disease and malnutrition caused by the conflict. The political repression, for its part, claimed 200,000 victims, at least three-quarters of these being objects of Francoist violence. (2016a: 115–16)

Of course, there is always the typical objection that insists on associating communism with Stalinist crimes, simply because most Stalinist regimes claimed they were communist. Yet those who refuse to distinguish between Stalinism and communism on the grounds of association should also be prepared to apply the same logic to other comparable phenomena as well. For instance, should they not associate liberalism with war, given the numerous wars declared by liberal democracies? Should not the same logic compel them to define liberalism in terms of the use of nuclear weapons, given that the world's leading liberal democracy alone has used them? If Christianity and Islam were to be defined by the barbarianism committed in their names, should not their institutions be banned? Clearly, the logical fallacy that moves from alleged association to historical equation is used selectively and deceivingly by liberals and conservatives in order to mislead the masses.

The internalized ideology that equates communism with Stalinism is false through and through. There is nothing intrinsic in communism that entails gulags, just as there is nothing intrinsic in liberalism that necessitates using weapons of mass destruction. Let us recall that insofar as Marxist philosophy is concerned, a "communist state" is a contradiction in terms. Even in the case of the Soviet state, from the outset, anti-Bolshevik leftists denounced it on the basis of being a case of "state capitalism." In the years and decades that followed, arguably most of the men and women who perished under Stalin's totalitarian regime were self-identified communists. Stalinists were the bloodiest enemies of communism, and they managed to destroy the movement quite effectively. Nonetheless, the conditions that gave rise to communism as an international socialist movement have only intensified.

Somewhat similar to the Stalinist blow against communism, today, bourgeois elites act as the fatal enemies of liberal principles. To such liberals, everything is relative, except their private interests, so their romance with fascism is more than merely an affair; in fact, it is almost always fascists who break up with liberals. Fascists are bloody criminals, but fascist groups do have certain moral codes, however unethical they may be. Pragmatically, fascists find it risky to cement a partnership with moral relativists and egoists. This distrust is almost intuitive, insofar as fascists know that those who permitted fascism to flourish cannot have fidelity to anything, unless they have been fascists all along. Therefore, once the liberal contribution to fascist political economy becomes dispensable, on a nice sunny day, fascists will announce the end of the affair. By that point, previously self-identified liberals will swiftly blend into or actively join the new norm, if they have not done so already.

But the breakup does not constitute an end to this symbiotic relationship. In fact, the moment fascism triumphs by taking over the state is when liberal elites' social allegiance becomes fully apparent. The process is one of continuity rather than transformation. The same unconditional submission, the dissolvement of every trace of rational autonomy, has been the essence of the liberal personality. We only need to recall the long history of the liberal affair with representatives of foreign fascism, such as Islamism, Hindutva, and various nationalist fascist regimes outside the West. Conversely, from the point of view of liberal Islamists, such as the Muslim Brotherhood, Khomeinists, or factions among the Sangh Parivar, the foreign partner in the love affair is European fascists. In other words, it is not only white liberal elites who have been on good terms with non-white fascism for a long time, but non-white liberal elites also usually have warm relations with white fascism. Thus, the social fascist that exists inside some liberals does not surface only when political fascism takes over the state; rather, despite the fluctuations in its visibility, which is dependent on time and place, he is always there. All of us have seen Western liberal leaders who happily and voluntarily abide by the rules of their fascist hosts, say, in Iran, while knowing very well that such submission cannot be considered, for example, feminist, by Iranian feminists (contrary to the cultural-relativist assumption prevalent in the West).

Conclusion

Of course, most liberal bases are victims of their leaders' bad faith, and those bases can be won over if a new, forceful, and unapologetic universalist movement emerges. Short of such an effort, we should be prepared for the velocity of the fascist train to increase as it draws nearer to the abyss. Now is the time for a decisive anti-fascist struggle and a democratic, egalitarian, universalist mobilization of people. We should unapologetically denounce the *liquid sentimentalism* of bourgeois liberals and aim for nothing less than universal emancipation. If the ecological crisis is not deemed urgent enough to motivate such a movement, the approaching fascist abyss should be more than enough. Those of us who have means for democratic action should use that freedom, protect it, and advance it while it is still possible.

It is misleading to speak of the threat of fascism when fascism (in its various forms) has become the norm in the neoliberal global order, including its anti-American and allegedly anti-imperialist terrains, such as Erdogan's Turkey. Despite the gloominess of the overall picture, there are truly infinite ways to approach a new world. Let us begin with the fundamental premises. No matter how many more decades or centuries pass and how many more egalitarian revolutions miserably fail, the truth is, the most essential needs of all humans have been, and will always be, food, clothes, and shelter. Prioritizing those needs and universal health care and education is not any more utopic than abolishing the slave trade was in the early 1800s. Those who tell us universal equality and freedom are unrealistic wrongly assume that the existing reality, which is based on hierarchy and exploitation on every level, is functional. Even for typical conservatives, things are different during these times of uncertainty. The point is: what kind of social force will be able to seize this historical moment to determine the direction of change.

The Covid-19 pandemic has destabilized the existing order immensely. The question is whether we can construct a broad social movement quickly and forcefully enough to prevent the continuation of the exploitative hierarchy within and among societies. In the United States alone, by the end of May 2020, more than forty million people became unemployed, and this was within the first ten weeks of the ongoing crisis (Cohen 2020). Mobilizing only 10 percent of the unemployed population would be more than double the number of all the members of both ruling parties in the United States. In India, the desperately marginalized make up a population larger than all the armies of all nation-states combined. No state machinery would be able to defeat a democratic grassroots movement of such a scale. If you, the reader, initiate this conversation with at least one other person, the movement has already begun crystalizing—another multiplying cell of emancipation. Like fish whose smallness in size and largeness in numbers render fishing nets useless, a social movement could overwhelm any police state with astonishing speed.

CHAPTER THREE

The Two-Headed Beast of Capitalism and Nation-Statism

The Covid-19 Test of Nation-States

If there is one political reality the Covid-19 crisis revealed, it is the disastrous inadequacy of nation-states. State officials habitually analogized the coronavirus pandemic to a war. In addition to the typical deficiency of imagination of policy makers, the analogy exposes something characteristic of nation-states, namely, their antagonistic origin and aggressive nature. The irony is that precisely because it was not a war but the very opposite of a war, governments across the world were dumbfounded. Had it been a war, nation-states would have known exactly what to do. Historically, they have excelled in the destruction of the conditions of life and lives. The Covid-19 pandemic put the nation-state—in all its governmental variations—into a unique historical test, a test of the state's capacity to preserve lives on a relatively large scale.

It is important to detect the language of biology, biomedicine, and immunology in politics, as some contemporary thinkers such as Donna Haraway (2013), following Michel Foucault, Gilles Deleuze, Giorgio Agamben, Slavoj Žižek, and Roberto Esposito have done. Of course, the othered Other has constantly been linked to a virus, insect, or a disease against which the genetic superiority, blood purity, and health flawlessness of the in-group must be defended at all costs. What is missing in Haraway's critical account of biopolitics and discourses of biopower is the fact that nationalism has reversed the direction of the analogy. More specifically, instead of the usual likening of the Other to viruses, viruses are likened to the Other; instead of analogizing the Other to a source of disease, diseases are analogized to the Other. That is exactly the logic behind labeling Covid-19 the "China Virus" or "Wuhan Virus" by not only Trump's circle, but also some renowned American scholars. The deeper logic behind this reversal of the analogical construction should be obvious. Namely, average Americans already perceive the Other as the ultimate source of existential threat, so it only makes sense to tie the fatality caused by the virus to the Other. By doing so the ideologues of populist neoconservatism in fact further alarm the American public about the alleged threat supposedly caused by the Chinese and other far Asians. Not surprisingly, just like every other time a part of the world's population has been demonized, racist attacks against perceived Asians in the United States increased immediately. To reiterate, the new logic of bio-fascism is not that the Other symbolizes disease, but rather disease symbolizes the Other; the nationalist does not need to be told about the fatality of the Other but the Otherness of fatality. Thus, in this sense at least, the darkness of our age exceeds the darkness of the age of old fascism.

Today, even the health sector within the establishment of biopower does not have a language other than that of war. Even protecting the public health is repeatedly portrayed as a war against the virus, as opposed to maintaining the lives of human beings. There is no shortage of militarized spaces whether on or inside so-called national borders, yet there is shortage of medical schools, hospitals, hospital beds, ventilators, bottled oxygen, and so on. The mere mention of defunding the police, let alone defunding the armed forces as such, renders one a radical socialist in the United States despite the ongoing police violence against African Americans. At the same time, demanding health care and education for all is resisted just as rigorously. Does this irony not make the death-driven core of nationhood, nationality, nationalism, and the nation-state abundantly clear? When the military budget is a semi-taboo to argue against while at the same time a functional public health care is associated with the intolerable enemy (communism), how difficult is it to comprehend the nation-state's stance in terms of life and death even in the most basic sense?

No nation-state has a shortage of soldiers, who are at best completely useless, and at worst licensed killers, yet the world suffers from a deadly shortage of health workers including physicians and nurses (International Council of Nurses 2021). Soldiers who are trained to kill constitute the typical image of the national hero across nation-states, yet nurses who die on daily bases trying to ward off the imminent threat of death are nowhere to be treated as martyrs. It is crucial to note the gender division between the two sectors, the war industry versus the health care sector. Traditionally, the military is a male-dominated sector with most ranks from generals to ordinary soldiers, whereas most nurses are women. Beyond this obvious disparity in the division of symbolic and material value between the male-dominated sector and the women-majority occupation, this sexist division of significance is indicative of the fundamental link between a nation-state and the violent nature of patriarchal domination, as explained later in this chapter.

When the Other is situated within the sovereign, spatial segregation, demographic apartheid, and complete annihilation have been among the most common policies practiced by nation-states, including the United States, Turkey, the Third Reich, South Africa, Myanmar, Pakistan, Sudan, and Brazil to name a few. At southern borders of Europe and the United States, refugees are treated as nothing but intruders who are vigorously kept out using not only the police apparatuses but the very war machine that is the army and its sophisticated war technology. As if that is not enough to keep the most disempowered out of the body of the sovereign, armed militias are deployed in the case of the United States. In the case of the European Union, the very regimes and movements that create refugees, such as the Erdogan regime and Islamists in Libya, are paid to make sure drowning in the sea is the only option left for the refugees who risk entering Europe. All that because once the refugee makes into the territory of the sovereign, the protection system in place cannot deploy killing means against the intruders. In the world of biology that would be the immune system's limited options for attacking an intruder without causing self-fatality. In liberalism's world, Western governments do everything they can to make sure the refugee will not reach the spatial threshold beyond which she may enjoy the rights to which she is entitled by virtue of being a human according to liberalism's own most celebrated document and its alleged universal principles. The liberalist system wants to preserve its claim to the Universal Declaration of Human Rights but, without any sense of irony, only within its nationalist borders which are increasingly militarized and racialized. Put simply, liberal governments' endorsement of the doctrine of human rights comes down to the prevention of the human from becoming the right holder. This is exactly the problem with idealism, to put it very plainly: the ideal's sanctity is affirmed only in order to commit a total denial of its subject. Notice how in the name of a religious community's sacred values the supposed members of that very community are the first to be humiliated, in the name of realizing the glory of a nation the members of that very nation are symbolically and otherwise stripped of their basic dignity by the very rulers who set out to make the nation "great again." Similarly, liberalism's endorsement of liberties and rights is idealist as opposed to materialist. This is also why, in today's (multi)culturalist ethos, it is the perceived "culture" of the Other that is respected, not the Other's person. In fact, precisely through culturalizing her, she is denied personhood. This is how idealism inevitably falls into nihilism. It produces totalitarianism not despite but because of its fetishism of its own proclaimed moral principles. The idealists' detachment from the actual life conditions is so drastic that often even to the last minute of their demise they fail to realize the utter destruction and suffering they cause. All one needs to do to see the parallelism is to consider the last days of fascist leaders from Mussolini and Hitler to Mohammed Raza Pahlavi and Saddam Hussein.

The nationalist and racist depiction of the Other as a virus has become a familiar story. In fact, treating the othered Other as an unwanted strange body to be assimilated at best, and deported or wiped out at worst, is part of the very birth of nation-states. As the historians of the twentieth century repeatedly mention, suddenly millions of people became the target of mass assimilation, deportation, and/or elimination at the same time as nation-states began to pop-up from Anatolia to central Europe and far beyond, including the European colonies across continents. This is the reason why Hobsbawm maintains that a "world of nations" is not possible because such a world is inevitably nothing but a world of dominant groups ruling over others whose nationhood is denied within each state, while the state begins the process of creating and imposing its alleged origin, that is, the nation (2012: 12). Because the idea of nationality is entirely fictional and fictionizes the past to reestablish a false present, education has become the most central machine for falsification in the age of nation-states. Whether public or private, the educational system in every nation-state is the central apparatus for actualizing total hegemony.[1] The sheer repetition of the mentions of the (political) nation, the (administrative) state, the (geographic) country, often interchangeably, as a naturally existing entity and as a normal unit of study in all fields of inquiry is sufficient to normalize the myth within a couple of generations. Even when and where such nationalist politics lead to resistance from the side of the disadvantaged and racialized Other, the resisting group borrows and reproduces the same language of nationalism by claiming the right to nationhood, sovereignty, and such, especially in the absence of a universalist popular movement. Thus, in the absence of such an emancipatory movement, nationalism simply multiplies, and reactions become increasingly nastier leading to various forms of fanaticism, tribalism, and fascism. A nation-state's very legitimacy is founded on delegitimating the identity of the other groups who live within the same territory claimed by the national sovereign. While every nation-state borrows its legitimacy on the basis of difference, national uniqueness, the right to self-determination, once established, its survival depends on its capacity to eliminate plurality within its borders, which could involve anything from lingocide to genocide. The othered Other sooner or later will act as an enemy if for nothing else then for being treated as an enemy by the dominant whose identity is totalized on the state in the name of the nation. Once the othered Other reacts as an Other, the dominant will take the reaction as evidence for the objectivity of its xenophobia. The process of self-fulfilling prophecies does not end at any new borders; rather it merely multiplies in scope.

There is a rich field of research around the concept of nationalism, but if one thing is certain, it is the fact that it is never clear what a "world of nations" would look like. A million nations? Three hundred million nations? As Eric Hobsbawm observed, "a world of nations cannot exist, only a world where some potentially national groups, in claiming this status, exclude others from making similar claims, which, as it happens, not many of them do" (2012: 78). The reason for this limitless vagueness of nationhood comes down to one major fact: nationality is a fiction. To quote Hobsbawm again, "Nationalism requires too much belief in what is patently not so" (2012: 12).

Like all other fictions, it must eventually give way to something else, something not irrational. Also like some other fictions, it may create a world of real social relations and spaces, but the fiction at the core of all those material realities will nonetheless have to give way to a different mode of perception. Some of the ancient Mesopotamian, Egyptian, and Greek temples are still standing, but in each case, the central ideological fictions have been given away, and, needless to say, the particular societal functions of those structures have disappeared. Irrationality could have a long life, but its demise is more certain than anything else about it. One does not need to adhere by Hegel's idea of Idea to assert that every irrationality is bound to disappear in the interest of something that is more rational, in the long historical context. In the prevalent anti-Marxist climate, utter historical nihilism and outright idealism have become widely acceptable while considerations of potential historical progress are quickly accused of committing teleology. One does not need to be a Marxist to believe that contradictions are immediate signs of change. A system that reaches a certain contradictory point, its collapse is inevitable. And, yes, the broad philosophy of history adopted in this book is Marxist, but while we are at it, let me also confess that I am a Newtonian as well. On the same note, it might be worth stating two basic propositions. Namely, gravity existed even before Newton theorized it. Similarly, what has become known as historical materialism was merely discovered, not invented, by Marx.

Assessing Marxism on the basis of its false applications may be an effective tactic for propaganda, but ultimately Marxism, like every other theory, should be assessed on the basis of its accurate representation, interpretation, manifestation, and so on. Even if this never happens, the truth to which the theory alludes is not dependent on our ability to recognize the plausibility of the theory. That said, of course, the Marxist awareness itself can become a decisive factor in the revolutionary potential and thus the horizon of possibilities. In the absence of the historical awareness and an awareness of the historical significance of that awareness, people are bound to become objects, not subjects, of history, which almost inevitably amounts to the perpetuation of forms of unfreedom, violence, and suffering.

Somehow, claiming that actual life conditions of actual living human beings are significant factors of shaping value systems, cultures, and so on makes one a radical "ideologist" incapable of free, objective, and realistic thinking or a Marxist incapable of impartial and rational judgment. Yet, in today's supposed post-ideological ethos, some of the most absurd forms of denialism are scarcely subjected to any reasonable judgment, even by positivism's own standards. For instance, the complete denial of materialism is, if anything, considered praiseworthy, which is indicative of anti-Marxist fanaticism. The denial of the 6.5 billion years of the history of the planet is not uncommon among decision makers in the arenas of politics and education in the world hub of both liberal democracy and capitalism. Most of these denialists assume that before ten thousand years nothing existed, which amounts to falsity of a ridiculous magnitude (1:650,000). Superstitions, including the belief in an afterlife world or the absolute wisdom of a couple of poorly written texts and the belief in the eternality of the existing capitalist order and the naturality of nation-statism are supposed to be non-ideological and realistic. In the same time, it is Marxism that is habitually accused of utopianism by anyone from first-year college students to professors of the social sciences and humanities, who, more often than not, have not bothered to read a single text by Marx and Engels, whose combined works include tens of thousands of pages, not to mention the works of other Marxists.

As Žižek, the leading figure in the field of ideology critique, would say, today's self-proclaimed anti-ideological or post-ideological elites are by far the most fanatic of ideological recruits of the neoliberal world regime. Žižek's prolific work has exposed this issue better than what I could hope to do here, but this absurd contradiction is, nonetheless, worth revisiting again and again. Stupidity, in the sense of the will to ignorance, that is, making the choice of not knowing, has always existed, but, arguably, it has never been so proudly, widely, and positively embraced as an intellectual merit. In addition to the clear irony in this bizarre link between stupidity and (the fashionable insistence on a post-ideological) intelligence, there is an even more bizarre irony at work. Namely, every possibility of the awareness of what constitutes facts, namely material *factors*, is denounced from the outset in the name of non-ideologicality, free thinking, critical thinking, and such. The political consequence of this is not only the abolishment of active subjecthood but also actively supporting systems that abolish subjecthood. Thereby, by denouncing Marxism, and by association materialism and every faculty of critical understanding, today's intellectual heroes fanatically oppose the possibilities of progress toward human emancipation. By placing themselves at the forefront of idealist reactionism, they insist on pushing what is potentially fascist toward actual fascism. Not only do they fail to perceive the personhood of the othered Other, but they sacrifice their own personhood in the name of autonomous thinking. No wonder today's fanatic defenders of "free speech" are those on the far right; the defenders of the (European) Enlightenment are among the most tribalists; proud liberals are among the most effective enablers of illiberal, including fascist, movements. The self-proclaimed post-ideological thinker is the kind of unfree who is not aware of the conditions of unfreedom, whereas those in the margins of the margins of the margins are, if nothing else, well aware of their unfreedom, and precisely because of that the revolutionary subject that emerges from those margins, against all odds, has a better chance of producing free spaces and spaces of resistance. The unfree who is aware of her unfreedom is by far less unfree than the unfree who is unaware of her unfreedom. Therefore, if there is any realistic hope for an effective revolutionary movement, it is located outside the zones where capitalist liberalism enjoys a near total hegemony. The new regime of totalitarianism surpasses the classical models precisely because it eliminates every trace of destruction through the systematic destruction of aura, wipes out every spatial corner through imposing total transparency, and eliminates every possibility of auratic experiences through the glassification of all surfaces and illumination of all spaces. If the classical models of totalitarianism try to kill those who dare to dream of a different world, the new model of totalitarianism eliminates the dreamability of another world.

The Viral Test of Totalitarianism

The pandemic has exposed irreconcilable contradictions in not only the entity of the nation-state but also the capitalist world system. In my book, *Totalitarian Space and the Destruction of Aura* (Ahmed 2019b), I argue that capitalist liberalism is a more advanced form of totalitarianism than the textbook models of totalitarianism, which are overtly political and violent. Looking at totalitarianism on the societal level, it becomes clear that extensive use of sheer force increasingly antagonizes people and thus widens the gap of trust between society at large and the ruling elite. Because of its nuanced modes of hegemony, capitalist liberalism is therefore more successful at accomplishing total control than traditional one-party totalitarian regimes. After religion, capitalism has produced the most successful ideological apparatuses in history capable of making millions of people give up their own freedom freely.

Advanced capitalism has enhanced the means of total control in such a way that the use of brute force on large scales against the state's own citizens has decreased significantly, but of course violence remains to be the immediate governmental choice of action as soon as a relatively large group of citizens come together to protest against the state or government. No matter how peaceful a popular demonstration might be, first and foremost, it is the state's policing regime that is deemed appropriate to respond. There is barely a qualitative difference between governments in the way they respond to the same type of protests because overwhelmingly they use violence even if by merely exhibiting lethal means. In effect, the purely democratic act of the *demonstration* of the body in the public space is answered by the state's *demonstration* of disciplinary and lethal force. Surveilling, tear-gassing, handcuffing, beating, shooting, and lynching are all within the range of relatively normalized acts of violence committed against the body who dares to exercise democratic protest in the public space that is supposed to be undisputedly a space for democratic action.

The difference between states' reactions to movements of dissent is quantitative, not qualitative. Moreover, this does not necessarily mean liberal democracies always use less violence. The parameter that determines the amount of violence to be used by the state is the perceived threat of the protest on security, as defined by the ruling groups, which could include anything from national security to private property, thereby sanctifying the entire political and social loci of domination. If the state advances its hegemonic means of control, the elites and those in charge of the police apparatuses may feel less threatened by certain protests resulting in what could appear as a more relaxed political climate. However, the moment a progressive protest increases its popular velocity and spreads across large areas of the country in question, the relative level of state violence immediately increases. This is one of the patterns of behavior that exposes the essence of nation-states and, therefore, similarity most clearly. In 2020, in the United States, it became clear once more that any number of armed forces could be deployed by all the three levels of the government to suppress a civil movement such as Black Lives Matters and Antifa. Thus, whether in the United States or Belarus, as soon as a section of the population re-politicizes its actions in favor of broadening equalities and freedoms, the state's reaction is qualitatively and universally predictable, and the procedures involve various degrees of surveillance, physical violence, and detentions. It goes without saying that there are countless differences between the United States and Belarus, but as nation-sates, they are also strikingly similar. In the liberal democracy, democracy is a recognized right but exercising it may put the right holder in serious danger. In the case of the dictatorship, democracy is a nonrecognized right that may put the right holder in serious danger when it is claimed or exercised. In either case, the state does not entertain the idea of conceding to citizens when it comes to the production of public space and the existing relations of privilege.

We need to take a step away from the immediate reality in order to grasp a truer account of the reality. In this context, we should keep in mind the following general premises when we think of the state in today's world:

> Every state is a nation-state.
>
> Every nation-state is inherently racist, bourgeois, and patriarchal.

Even though we need to conceptually separate racism, capitalism, and patriarchy, they do not take place separately or in isolation of the conditions maintained by nation-states.

What conceptualization enables us to do is precisely generalizations that are necessary in order to conceive the heterogeneity of forms and means of domination *within* the totality of the existing order. By the same token, conceptual distinctions between the state versus the market, or political society versus civil society, are necessary to be made without committing the fallacy of assuming the categories as actually separate realms. The point is to conceptually break down reality in order to comprehend it better in its complexity and totality.

Under capitalist liberalism the boundaries between the state and the society are blurry, thanks to the absolute power of capital.[2] The state itself must submit to the sanctity of capital, which is the aggregate value accumulated through the extraction of raw materials and exploitation of the human force that transforms those materials to commodities. Capital is sheer value removed from all its material and social sources, and its absolutism exceeds the limitation of the physical space and the body as if to enter a metaphysical realm of reality where it becomes the determining power of all values. This immateriality and metaphysicalized influence of capital elevates the social and political status of the capitalist to a realm similar to that of the theological God. In fact, the analogical correlation has already reversed: in order for the theological God to be all-powerful again in the social and psychological realms, it has to operate as pure capital and speak the same sacred language of profit. In 1888, Charles Spurgeon, an English pastor, published a book titled *Faith's Checkbook* (2020), and it is still in print; it has only been made more appealing through putting more linguistic and visual emphasis on the banking analogy.

Ultimately, theology lost so much of its political economy to the capitalist metaphysics that now the roles are reversed; theology is forced to reinvent its social persona and enhance its currency by submitting as faithfully as possible to the rule of capital. Capitalism in turn gains an essential ideological wealth from the triumph that left God with no other option but to declare full allegiance to the new universal regime of absolutism. The religious adoption of the capitalist language entails the universalization of capital. For the same reason, the subliminal ideological hegemony of capitalism becomes effectively immediate. Moreover, this allows for the capitalist revitalization of the idle assets of religion, which includes endless nets of reference and meaning and vast infrastructures of value production. Above all, the capitalist conquest of the former theological semiology allows for furthering the diffusion of the power to reach actual limitlessness of control, which is the fundamental definition of totalitarianism (Curtis 1979; Conquest 2000).

The market as the main realm of arbitration has the advantage of defusing those more overt modes by which power is exercised. When the means of control are not detectable, the ideological predetermination of perception too becomes more naturalized. When the market rules, freedom is framed, perceived, and experienced according to an ideology that renders it profitable. Unlike the state, the market grows directly on societal organs, so the capitalist ideological influence is religious in the sense of absolutism because it does not lend itself to rational examination easily and is psychologically effective because it promises everyone ultimate salvation. That is to say, because of its nuanced modes of hegemony, capitalist liberalism is more successful in accomplishing total control. Those who are aware of their unfreedom create a social space to exercise some freedom, whereas those who are unaware of their unfreedom end up being constantly confined in a space that is always entirely transparent to the gaze of power, or what I call totalitarian space (Ahmed 2019b).

Liberalism assumes the inseparability of free market capitalism and democracy. Western leaders, from Ronald Reagan and Margaret Thatcher to George W. Bush and Tony Blair, took the magic formula of laissez-faire democracy (or capitalist liberalism) to heart, and as a result, they were keen on realizing a "new world order." Their ideological support did not come only from classical liberals but also from the new prophets of capitalist liberalism, such as Milton Friedman and Francis Fukuyama. In 1992, Fukuyama expanded on his 1989 article to announce that the fall of the Eastern Bloc had opened the horizon for the eternal triumph of liberal democracy across the world (Fukuyama 1989, 1992). At the same time, Friedman's Chicago Boys set out to inject the neoliberal vaccine wherever and whenever they saw an opportunity, from Latin America to Eastern Europe. The golden opportunity for implementing extreme privatization of all sectors was determined by applying what Naomi Klein (2007) called "the shock doctrine." This describes the situation where a disaster creates a unique window of time during which society is so shocked that its defense mechanisms are paralyzed. As Klein discovered, the Chicago Boys would seize on such moments of utter confusion and helplessness to implement their neoliberal policies. The neoliberal dosages that were too strong even for the United States during G. W. Bush's term were tried out in post-2003 Iraq. The result was nothing even remotely resembling political liberalism.

Neoliberalism proved the exact reversal of liberalism's fundamental thesis of free market democracy. Namely, it proved that laissez-faire capitalism works even better under illiberal regimes. In fact, laissez-faire capitalism strengthens regimes that are already authoritarian. Putin's Russia and Erdogan's Turkey provide two especially obvious examples. The coronavirus pandemic seems to have shown that, compared with the totalitarianism of state capitalism such as the People's Republic of China, free market capitalism is totalitarianism without benefits. While we all know that the state comes first in China, what is less admitted by liberals and those to their right is that under capitalist liberalism capital has the ultimate priority over human rights. This became clear in the way the coronavirus crisis has been handled in the United States and the UK. In that context, there is an uncomfortable suggestion that many in the West still want to be untrue. Namely, the Chinese state seems to have been more effective in controlling the coronavirus outbreak than liberal democracies have.

Even if the Chinese government's published information about the coronavirus outbreak is proven to be inaccurate, it remains true that in the liberal democracies where most sectors are privatized, most governments failed to handle the crisis efficiently. While the Chinese government has been criticized for concealing information and silencing early warnings about the catastrophic potential of the new virus, the United States and the UK also played down the actual threat until they suddenly were forced to change gear.[3]

It might be too soon to draw definitive conclusions, but we have good reason to deduce several points in terms of what forms of government might have some success in overcoming this challenge, keeping in mind that the long-term consequences of this crisis will be far more profound than anything the nation-state could handle. While the domination of society by both political and economic elites should be rejected, there is something critical to be learned when corporate capitalism is compared to state capitalism. My intention in the comparison, of course, is not to legitimize any form of totalitarianism; rather, on the contrary, it is to delegitimize all forms of totalitarianism, including those that are not recognized as such. More to the point, a serious investigation of the philosophical foundation of liberalism leads us to the conclusion that liberalism is fundamentally illiberal. Its premature genealogical union with capitalism had put it on the path toward totalitarianism, at which it has finally arrived in the form of neoliberalism. If anything, neoliberalism has been quite successful as a totalitarian system, but to reach a distinct view about this issue, we need to step out of the hegemonic framework within which the norms of inquiry are situated.

In that context, the Chinese model of the institutionalization of capitalist politics inherently invalidates the liberalist doctrine. Even for political theorists who insist to stick to the old definitions of totalitarianism and naive attribution of liberality to liberalism and illiberality to everything else, the Chinese model should prove beyond any doubt that capitalism and totalitarianism are two sides of the same coin. The plain manifestation of the compatibility of capitalism and totalitarianism would not be surprising to those who are aware of the capitalist foundation of liberalism, that is, the fact that liberalism is inherently founded on an illiberal societal formula. This illiberal essence of liberalism can be further exposed when the capitalist production of space is uncovered (Ahmed 2019b).

If instrumental rationality is an essential condition for capitalist domination, it is understandable why the Chinese model has surpassed the West in the latter's own invention. The Chinese system is fundamentally based on the execution of instrumental rationality, rendering it superior not only in terms of control but also in terms of hegemony. The uncompromising centrality of instrumental rationality also explains the distinctive efficiency of the Chinese model as a totalitarian political system. One of the most crucial aspects of the Chinese totalitarian model is that the state's authority is above and beyond racial and religious constraints, two frontiers with which Western states are still struggling, given the unfinished project of secularism and the states' long history of racial violence. The Chinese state's approaches toward the Tibetan and Uighur questions do not contradict, but rather manifest, the absolute authority of the state. Obviously, the state policies are oppressive, but they are not based on racial or religious discrimination. To the contrary, they are direct manifestations of the state's rule of not allowing any racial or religious challenges to its authority. Looking at these policies from the racist and religious mindsets in which the West is stuck, they seem as if they are expressions of racially and religiously motivated hatred. Even comparing Myanmar's campaigns against the Rohingya, which are indeed both racist and religious, with China's policies of total assimilation of the Uighur would be extremely misleading. The former is indicative of primordial hatred, whereas the latter is the result of the state's near-complete adoption of instrumental reason.

Post-Racial Totalitarianism

In fact, the Chinese state's faithful positivism has also made it incomparably more efficient than traditional totalitarian regimes with racist or sectarian foundations. Historically, Stalinism was far more efficient in its totalitarian governmentality than German Nazism or Italian Fascism. Fascists are too impulsive and neurotic to be able to let a totalitarian system reach its mechanical perfection in terms of the utilitarian exercise of power. Moreover, the racist divisions they create within the society they govern undermine the very ideological hegemony that is essential for a durable and stable totalitarian system. In short, in fascist totalitarianism, the premodern impulsive elements are more dominant than the pragmatism of instrumental rationality (of course, racism and fundamentalism are both modern phenomena, but only as reactions to modernism, as ideologies that fetishize premodern traditions).

What makes instrumental rationality so essential for totalitarianism is that it prioritizes efficient and unlimited control through the means of technological perfection, that is, the mechanization of governmentality. Looking at fascism from this angle helps us to understand why fascist regimes represent a failed model of totalitarianism. The fascist neurotic desire to inflict suffering merely for the sake of suffering or to spread terror for the sake of terrorism directly undermines the utilitarian function of instrumental rationality and thereby both the function and durability of the fascist totalitarian enterprise.

Policies advanced by racist and sectarian regimes are inevitably colored by neuroses, just as their politics are derived from unconscious, destructive, and primordial xenophobia. Therefore, racist and sectarian regimes actively destabilize the totalitarian order they aspire to establish. This is also what made the Stalinist model of totalitarianism more successful than the fascist model. However, the Chinese model is a hybrid model of totalitarianism that borrows from both Stalinism and neoliberalism. The assimilation policies that have targeted Tibetans and Uighurs is the Chinese equivalent of the Soviet Union's Sovietization policies—and, as such, they are carried out as a function of the state's totalitarian machine of social engineering. Of course, we should also keep in mind that Stalinism was squarely capitalist if nothing else by virtue of its manipulation of the means of production, to use the most essential aspect of Marx's definition of what distinguishes capitalism as a mode of production. The Chinese totalitarian model, unlike Stalinism, also allowed for the hegemony of the "free market" to further the boundaries of submission. In short, what distinguishes the Chinese system is that it rearranged the relationship between the politics and economy in such a utilitarian way that maximizes the efficiency of the technologies of power. Eurocentric false dichotomies that remain dominant in the academy have simply prevented the theoretical comprehension of this form of totalitarianism that is exemplary of capitalism and positivism.

Family and the Normalization of Patriarchal Domination

From Plato's *Republic* to modern European political thinkers, despite the profound alterations that happen to the notion and structure of the state, we cannot miss the direct association made between the state and the patriarchal family or the ruler–ruled and the father–family relations. The resemblance between family and state is more than a semiological analogy made by political thinkers. In fact, to the ancient Greeks and in the Roman Empire, the ruler's wisdom remains to be considered crucial for his gaging of the legitimacy of his authority. Therefore, for the Greeks and Romans, one could argue that the association between the father and the government is more metaphoric than it is during the Christian era when patriarchy as such becomes the source of absolute power. In the sixteenth and seventeenth-centuries' political philosophy texts the state–family association becomes a presupposition, something writers take for granted. There are two texts we should recall here: Augustin's *City of God*, in the beginning of the Christian era, and Robert Filmer's *Patriarcha*, at the end of that era. To the former, the emerging rule of God is celebrated on the basis of God's metaphysical authority. To the latter, the threat of the Enlightenment egalitarianism necessitates a defense of the declining patriarchalism. Below is a passage by Filmer, where the immediacy of patriarchal relationship between power and authority is made clear on both theological and political levels:

> For as Kingly power is by the law of God, so it hath no inferior law to limit it. The Father of a family governs by no other law than by his own will, not by the laws or wills of his sons or servants. There is no nation that allows children any action or remedy for being unjustly governed. And yet for all this every Father is bound by the law of nature to do his best for the preservation of his family. But much more is a King always tied by the same law of nature to keep this general ground, that the safety of his kingdom be his chief law. (1949: 96)

Filmer, then, adds, "A proof unanswerable for the superiority of Princes above laws is this, that there were Kings long before there were any laws.

For a long time the word of the King was the only law" (1949: 96). In fact, it is laws that draw their legitimacy from kings not vice versa. Just as God does not have to abide by the rules he established for people, the King is the only one who is exempted from the obligation to follow the laws. Thus, the division is made very clear: as the judge, the father figure's judgment is not the subject of arbitration or assessment, whereas the natural place of people is never to judge and always be judged based on the degree of their obedience. This is the core of Filmer's argument throughout his book in defense of political patriarchy, which is directly linked to the theological foundations determined by the biblical stories.

Filmer and other conservatives' methods of validation are simple: the old way is the right way, because the further we go back in the past the closer we get to God's way. Royalists were right insofar as the monarch is God's shadow on earth, but the more crucial question is: whose shadow is God? God is, of course, man's shadow in the realm of ideas. God is the creation of the father figure to legitimize and perpetuate his rule. Therefore, the authority of the political ruler is originated in the authority of the father in the patriarchal family, and by the same token the state's normalized domination is rooted in the patriarchal family.

Up until Feuerbach, the Hegelian philosophers merely interrogated aspects of religion but not religion as such. To most Enlightenment philosophers, God remains to be the first mover and absolute origin. Only with Feuerbach does philosophy try to reclaim its territory from theology. In fact, Feuerbach aims at the complete and unapologetic abolishment of theology. The main question of his *Essence of Christianity* is the following: what is theology's basic object of study? Of course, theology is the study of God. Contemporary theologians have modified that to claim theology is the study of "religious beliefs," but obviously God remains to be the object of religious beliefs, and, therefore, theology. In fact, claiming that "religious beliefs" are the fundamental object of study makes Feuerbach's thesis, which I will discuss below, even more easily confirmable.

Feuerbach makes the case that God is a product of the human mind, and as such, theology is essentially anthropology mistakenly separated. To say the object of study is not God but "beliefs" is to admit that the object of study is humans, for obviously only humans hold beliefs. Therefore, replacing God with "religious beliefs" as theology's defining object of study, only proves Feuerbach's point rendering the first part of the materialist argument unnecessary. Then, it follows that theology is fundamentally a human science, which is Feuerbach's ultimate point. Feuerbach's project is revolutionary within the context of history of philosophy, but it is not necessarily a revolutionary philosophy.

It is Marx's work that is revolutionary in the full sense of the word because it not only recognizes the gap between theory and practice but also sets out to overcome it. In his famous eleven *Theses on Feuerbach*, Marx basically argues that of course God is merely a human illusion, but there are two points to keep in mind here. First, the illusion is real, that is, pointing to the fact that religion is based on a confused, and erroneous, account of the world would not be enough to put an end to the influence of religion. Second, there are actual material conditions that prolong God's life as an illusion with actual social and political consequences. The only way to put an end to the illusion is to put an end to the entire social relations that gave rise to it and those that continue to sustain it. In other words, we have to *make our truth* by undermining all that produces and reproduces illusions. To Marx, it is crucial not to repeat the idealist mistake in the name of materialism. The valid form of materialism therefore is historical materialism. That is to say, truth is historically constructed and the only way to intervene in that process is to become a historical agent, that is a subject actively and willfully involved in changing the world, a revolutionary subject. There can be no end to the reign of political oppression without demolishing social relations of domination; there is no end to the state brutality without ending the social unit that continues to normalize patriarchal violence and absolutism.

Slavoj Žižek in his book *Event* makes a crucial point in relation to Robert Filmer's argument asserting that Filmer adopted the language of the Enlightenment philosophers, using notions like "natural history," to make his point with regard to patriarchalism and the state. Žižek argues that Filmer's adoption of the Enlightenment language is already a defeat for the old school because the real victory is to have one's enemy adopt one's language (2014). However, one could also argue along with Horkheimer and Adorno that precisely because the Enlightenment repeated the mythology of the pre-Enlightenment, it failed to achieve its universal emancipatory goals (Horkheimer and Adorno 2002). The church on feudalism gave way to the bourgeoisie, and since then the bourgeoisie has been using the state and family to perpetuate and normalize its domination. The Enlightenment notion of "natural history" quickly became a tool for advancing the interests of the European bourgeoisie.

The family is the first institution of patriarchy where social domination is naturalized. Thus, here the signs of free expression are detected and immediately processed to increase access to the child's psyche. After all, from the perspective of dominant patriarchal values, proper growth requires endless monitoring, disciplining, and molding. The objective is to constitute a policing system in the child's own psyche. Ultimately, the superego is a psychic space reserved for patriarchy to exercise its unlimited control. It is where the immortality of the father figure is placed, coded, and locked. By the time the child is six years old and school takes over to complete the second phase of production, the secret dark psychic underworld has already been carved out, as Freud has taught us.

The family is fundamental for the sustainability of the dominant relations of exploitation. Under feudalism, the distinctions were brutally clear. Serfdom was maintained by brute force, so domination was directly expressed within systems of discipline and punishment. From the cultivation of land to the theological grounding of absolutism, the means of torture were creatively invented and reinvented. The miserable child was doomed to carry a cross that was not her cross and hope for a redemption that had no place in her world. Barbarianism spoke the language of saints, while the victim's very existence was nothing but a sin and source of more sins. Imperialist religions meet at that point, diverging only with regard to what each sect deems the most effective way to beat out all that is autonomous in the human individual.

As Foucault pointed out in his *Les mots et les choses*, in the Middle Ages, the order of the universe was one of resemblance, endless patterns of symmetrical replications within and between the micro and the macro universes (1994). In such a world of dizzying parallelism of cosmoses and microcosmoses, there could be no hope of anything but cherishing the sole author of creation, whose omnipotent narcissism led him to chain everything in circles within circles of guilt and submission. Then, there were the armies of theologian–philosophers and artists devoted to aestheticizing, rationalizing, and moralizing that universe of the impossibility of a distance between the individual and community, on the one hand, and the internalization of the myth of an infinite distance that separates the miserable from ultimate good, beauty, and truth, on the other hand.

At the risk of re-Hegelianizing Marx, one could argue that once the family historically succeeded in securing the metaphysics of masculinity against all that needed to be exploited, the time was ripe for the bourgeois reordering of the modes of both production and perception. Of course, the bourgeois emancipation of the individual loosens both the tyranny of the patriarchal family and the grip of religious institutions, but only to reinvest patriarchy in a system where violence is reinvented more effectively to fit the totalitarian role of each institution from family to the market and state.

By now, the individual was allowed to claim a space in the world. She, or rather, primarily, "he," could even be a right holder. Taboos were, for the most part, lifted. In fact, the expression of desire became all that constitutes desire. Exhibition to the degree of absolute transparency, to a totalitarian degree of submission to the gaze, started to frame this unprecedented emancipation of the individual. The individual has become free to choose her way to exploit or be exploited under the tyranny of the bourgeoisie.

Under the bourgeoisie, the mystification of patriarchal power is relocated from the theological realm to that of state militarism precisely in order to perpetuate and expand absolutism. The act of killing gains sanctity, heroism, and material reward if it is committed by those admitted into the brotherhood and sisterhood of the national armed forces. Normally, the brotherhood in an armed force, such as military or the police, attracts authoritarian individuals whose views of themselves and the world are centered around the exercise of power. By giving up their free will, the soldier or police officer gains the power to deprive others outside the brotherhood of their freedom.

In the meantime, femininity is continually reproduced and redistributed for demarcation, that is, as tags that indicate exploitability. "Nature" has become "mother nature" to legitimize its endless exploitability. From the perspective of the bourgeoisie, the world is composed of resources to be exploited. Therefore, there are two main classes of resources: natural and human. Extraction, monopoly, and management of the two resources become the source of that which is the source of all power: capital. Capital, in turn, is the prime signifier of value, and the value of everything is necessarily determined in terms of the principle of exchange. It is exactly through the universalization of capital's hegemony, and thus the submission of everything to the principle of exchange, that a world of sameness and absolute power is established. If the near total isolation/alienation of the individuals of a society is a prerequisite for totalitarianism in that society, the near total isolation/fragmentation of societies is a prerequisite for world totalitarianism. Nation-states have provided the latter condition for capitalism as a totalitarian world system.

Nationhood as a Patriarchal Problem

The sociopolitical creature called "nation" can best be described as a modern reincarnation of the primordial patriarchal tribe. Despite nationalist ideologues' self-authorization to speak in the name of the public against the old aristocracy and monarchs, the new ideology was destined to reproduce hierarchical relations inwardly and imperialist impositions outwardly. Nationalism's mature form is fascism. The same self-victimization, demonization of the Other, romanticization of a mythic pure (tribal) past, and sense of metaphysical mission gave birth to Kemalism, Fascism, Nazism, Nasserism, and Baathism. Supported by bourgeoisiefied mobs, guided by experts of instrumental rationality, and armed with the most destructive means of killing, nationalism simply crafted what it deems natural, the nation—the pure nation. How else could the glories of the past be revived if the nation, with its pure blood and legendary will, is not revived first? How else could the nation be revived in its original purity if not through a process of cleansing to rid itself of any contamination, to resolve the problem once and for all through a "final solution?"

The mythic purity of the "nation" is the ideological preparation for legitimizing genocide in the same way that the masculinist obsession with female virginity is a subliminal expression of the desire to rape. At the end of the day, everything is standardized, illuminated, exhibited, and commercialized in the duality of attractive advertisement and the desire to consume. The commodity is the final production, the pure object, femininity packaged according to the masculine regulations of health and economy of pleasure. Once that which exists for consumption is consumed, it is treated as nonexistent insofar as the consumer is concerned. In the process of profit accumulation, what is extracted from the "natural resources" is turned into garbage, and nature as a whole into a dumpster. The garbage is thrown back into the lungs, blood, and womb of the "mother nature," who is increasingly ruined beyond recovery. What is perversely called "mother nature" at the end is nothing but a sacrifice in the most death-driven patriarchal temple in history.

If the source of mystified absolutism in medieval and monarchic states was God as the religious absolute myth, "nation" is nationalism's absolute myth and source of mystified legitimacy. The exercise of power in a nation-state fluctuates between its mythic and institutional poles. In times of peace, when the bourgeois hegemony is not challenged, the state operates as the umbrella institution of all legal institutions. However, in times of war, severe economic crises, and popular discontent, the nation prevails, allowing fascist paramilitary and small gangs to share the burden of policing through inflicting sheer terror on the marginalized. Fascist leaders speak in the name of the nation to bypass the legal and procedural obstacles of the state as an institution.[4] In this sense, fascism could be understood as a political mode of capitalism that is reactivated when democracy becomes a threat to liberal capitalism.

Just as God is used to absorb and redirect the anger and frustration of the oppressed, the "nation" is an effective myth with the power of absorbing and redirecting the anger and frustration of the immediate victims of capitalism. The appeal to prehistoric fear of the outside world is a technique of psychic manipulation that has the power to make the desperate human act irrationally and against her own prospects of emancipation. Also, like God, the truth of the "nation" is completely dependent on the hegemony of the dominant, the dominant class's ability to maintain mass belief in nationalist illusions. Like religion, the nationalist illusion promises heaven to those who are prepared to give themselves fully and unconditionally over to an otherwise rationally unjustifiable faith. For capitalism to continue operating as a global system, the sectarian and tribalist identitarianism of various populations across the world is essential. That is exactly why just as the crises of capitalism intensify, there is a rise of fascism in its various nationalist and religious forms.[5]

The state, insofar as it represents the absolute territorial sovereignty, is a creature of the seventeenth-century Europe. The concept was invented in 1648 to put an end to one of the most devastating sectarian wars, the notorious Catholic–Protestant Thirty Years War that wiped out about 15 percent of Central and Western Europe's population. Two hundred years later, Europe was in the midst of revolutions and conflicts, mainly between hopeful progressives who tried to continue the Enlightenment as a universalist, humanist, and emancipatory project, and conservative forces who were not prepared to let an egalitarian world take shape. In France, Prussia, Austria-Hungary, and Russia, there were socialists and anarchists desperately fighting for the realization of a borderless egalitarian world, and, on the other side, the emerging elites who would do everything they could to transform a desperate social class in each dying empire into a nationalist mass with a sense of both victimhood and mythic heroism.

In the mid-1800s the conflict between universalists and reactionaries was not yet determined, despite multiple setbacks to the Enlightenment project. In fact, just as German nationalism was about to crystalize the core of its nation-state, in 1848, two hundred years after Westphalia treaty, a young Hegelian from a Jewish background and the son of a German factory owner in Manchester published the *Communist Manifesto*, which would become one of the most influential documents ever penned. In it, they write:

> All previous historical movements were movements of minorities, or in the interest of minorities. The proletarian movement is the self-conscious, independent movement of the immense majority, in the interest of the immense majority. The proletariat, the lowest stratum of our present society, cannot stir, cannot raise itself up, without the whole superincumbent strata of official society being sprung into the air.
>
> Though not in substance, yet in form, the struggle of the proletariat with the bourgeoisie is at first a national struggle. The proletariat of each country must, of course, first of all settle matters with its own bourgeoisie. (Marx and Engels 1978: 482)

A few pages later, they add, "The working men have no country" (Marx and Engels 1978: 488).

The victory of the nationalists in Europe would mean countless genocides outside Europe before that violence would eventually be brought back to Europe, within the lifetime of one generation. In terms of the history of ideas, the Enlightenment is the moment at which the distinction between universalism and tribalism becomes most clearly pronounced. Yet, it is the Haitian Revolution of 1791–1804 that should be called the first universalist revolution in history, as the Argentinian sociologist Eduardo Grüner strongly argues (2020). In fact, the French republic used excessive force to suppress the antislavery revolution in Haiti. The American republic too openly took the side of the enslavers and the institution of slavery.

Then, in Europe, the Paris Commune of 1871 became the most distinctive historical confrontation between universalists and the forces of the status quo. The two sides would confront each other again in 1917 in Russia, 1936 in Catalonia and Aragon, and 1948 in China. Today, the same opposing historical forces are at war in Andhra Pradesh, Kurdistan, Sudan, and Chiapas.

The newly formed German nationalism of the nineteenth century gave birth to nationhood as a distinct and homogeneous identity with an inherent right to "self-determination." However, the "self" that emerged was one naturalized on the basis of racism and realized through cementing social relations of domination. A "nation" remembers its poor and marginalized in times of war, when the unconditional sacrifice of life is needed. Even then though, it is the affluent men who determine the future of the nation and speak in the name of its glories, which are constructed on the mass graves of the miserable.

Nationalism was arguably the first disastrous deviation from the Enlightenment. It was the first contradiction of the emerging bourgeois vision of the Enlightenment that aimed to both open up the world and fortify the walls of an entity more like a magnified tribal village, that is, larger than a city but extremely less heterogeneous, with the power of an empire but without its diversity. The sovereign state is supposedly the national expression of the political will of the nation. The modern state, in other words, is nothing but the political embodiment of the supposed organic community called the nation. The heavier emphasis in France on the republic as the nation maker, as opposed to the German emphasis on the organic idea of the nation as the origin of the state, rendered French nationalism relatively less exclusionary. Nonetheless, nationalism as such was born as a reactionary ideology in opposition to the universalist essence of the Enlightenment project. Napoleon Bonaparte was the first manifestation of the triumph of the nationalist deviation of the Enlightenment after the French Revolution, and Bismarck was in turn the German Bonaparte.

The irrational longing for a mythic pure, safe, and moral community is the direct outcome of the Oedipus complex, masked by an extra layer of mysticism and polished with romanticism to both preserve the fetish and attract the largest number of sexually suppressed individuals. It was inevitable that the fear of a world in which the individual would be born both as an ontological subject and a political right-holder would give birth to a reactionary ideology such as nationalism. Nationalism is essentially a cry for an impossible reunification with the fetishized mother. Homeland, therefore, in the nationalist mentality, is everything that is unconsciously associated with the mother's womb, outside of which there is nothing but the pain of separation and loneliness. Outside the womb, thrown naked into an unfamiliar world, everything causes unbearable pain for the suppressed individual, and freedom is hell. Freed from the divine hierarchies of the father, historical progress is simply a continual fall from bad to worse, away from the kingdom of heaven. If there is one mission for the nationalist, it is the quest of returning to the lost glory and reviving the greatness of absolute domination. How else could the authoritarian personality make the nation great again?

Nationalism's reaction to progress is ultimately a brotherhood congregation and narcissistic ritual centered on the cult of motherhood; it is a call for liberating and reclaiming the violated mother. This is embedded in the subliminal references associated with the homeland's cry for its sons to come to its rescue. The nationalist hero is both fragile and violent. As he sets out on a quest to return to the protective warmth of the womb, he is at the same time inspired by the mercilessness of the father figure, which is why patriots are also the true destroyers of the homeland. Thus, unlimited exploitation of the homeland becomes the pure expression of patriotism, just as the pure expression of love turns into what amounts to rape, the actual unconscious drive to disguise the weak self. It is no wonder then that fascist movements, which usually call for a revival of alleged past glories and the greatness of their nations, inflict the ultimate destruction on the people and country they claim to love so much.

It took the bloody episode of colonialism, crowned by the Great War, for the nation-state to ultimately come into being in its current (de)formation. The idea of a homogeneous group of people with absolute ties to a geographic territory being transformed into a "nation" is necessarily violence-inducing. The production of the nation-state involves genocide because the puritanical creation of the nation itself amounts to a forced extraction of a single element. Like gold mining, everything other than the desired entity is treated as waste and, therefore, dumped at every stage of the process until the final extraction. However, in the case of nation-mining, there is nothing pure to be gleaned because the idea of a homogenous community is merely a totalization of the patriarchal family, wherein supposedly nothing can disturb the absolute security that is founded on blood ties. Ultimately, race, religion, and nation are attempts to recreate that mythic heaven of patriarchy: absolute sameness and total transparency.[6]

In the process of nation mining, actual human beings become mere waste. Starting from the Armenian genocide and the Holocaust all the way to the recent Yazidi and Rohingya genocides, nationalism in both its secular and religious forms was bound to eliminate anyone whose existence contradicts the alleged naturalness of the nation and pollutes national purity. The nation-state has had a violent birth and life. It certainly will not die without committing the maximum amount of violent destruction it can on human society and its habitat.

Still, it is worth noting that by virtue of drastically changing material conditions of life, catastrophes can create a moment of historical rupture, a fleeting space of discontinuity that allows for grand realizations across societies. Those moments are the most unique chances we get to denormalize what has been normal for ages and see ourselves and the world in a new way. The current moment is potentially one such point in history. If domination, the most definitive aspect of capitalism, is problematized on larger societal levels and nationhood is demystified, a grand historical shift or revolutionary turn is not improbable, even if its full manifestation takes a whole century.

Conclusion

Here is the brutal truth right in front of all of us: we live in a system that is never short of bullets and bombs wherever wars are fought but faces a deadly shortage of medical masks and gloves to meet a global pandemic. Health workers died in the thousands precisely because they are not considered as valuable as soldiers and, unlike soldiers, lack basic protective gear. In the leading democracy of the world, a citizen could purchase a machine gun in any town but not a germ prevention mask in all fifty states. There are enough bombs in a few nation-states to eliminate life on the planet several times over, but somehow industry is incapable of meeting basic public health needs.

Does not any of these basic facts suffice to shake a rational human being to her core? Only the stupefying spell of a dominant ideology is capable of preventing people from knowing how irrational and death-driven the existing order is. We face a historical moment at which, if a powerful cosmopolitan movement of emancipation does not emerge, engineered violence will continue its course of totalitarian massification across the world. In many ways this moment resembles 100 years ago (Ahmed 2019a), when humanity stood at the crossroad between cosmopolitan emancipation and fascism, except this time around, the human race cannot afford another century of nationalism and capitalism. A course of continuity will amount to catastrophes far beyond what we have witnessed so far, given the irreversible destruction that is already being inflicted on the very web of life on this planet. Those who were not alarmed by the rise of fascism in the 1920s were not shocked by the trains that carried millions to the gas chambers either. Today, those who tell us everything will be alright again—that we should be grateful, that the market will take care of everything (again)—comfortably mandate a group of superstitious politicians (whose emergency priority is setting a National Day of Prayer) to determine the fate of entire societies. Such idealists are too possessed by their fanatical sectarian ideologies to realize that the walls they are building are for death chambers, and that the twenty-first-century camps are already continental in scope.

The coronavirus outbreak, like the ongoing ecological crisis, instantaneously invalidated everything national borders claim to be. Nonetheless, every nation-state's immediate response to the pandemic was, once again, to close borders—the only thing they know how to do. Except this time, they tried to keep the capitalist market intact, even if it meant risking public health within the territories of their governmental authority. As every refugee knows all too well, borders have always been closed. So far, the same forces that created refugees have used refugees in every possible way, whether as slave laborers, herds of mercenaries, or an imaginary enemy with diabolical destructive powers. However, for nation-states to sustain their hegemony they must keep borders wide open for the flow of capital and commodities. The border is the ideal revolving door to allow capital and commodities to move but at the same time not allow the humans who produce both the product and profit on which capitalism stands to pass through. "We just want your labor; you stay where you are, in your own country," is essentially what the world's most exploited laborers are told by both nationalists and "globalists" in the West. In Žižek's words, "Today's liberal tolerance towards others, the respect of otherness and openness towards it, is counterpointed by an obsessive fear of harassment. In short, the Other is just fine, but only insofar as his presence is not intrusive, insofar as this Other is not really other" (2008: 41).

Ultimately, without the revolving door function of borders, the international division of labor would not be possible. Commodities are produced through the exploitation of both labor and the environment to guarantee the maximum profit possible. Completing the loop, the garbage that most commodities eventually become is often shipped back to the laborers' home countries. "Stay in your own country. You see, we do not invade your country. If we visit, we do so legally. You are welcome to visit our country too, but only legally," they are told. The Other is of course not hated if they stay where they are and as they are, the faceless and nameless sustainers of what culturalists in the global North call "our way of life."

If the free movement of commodities is stopped, the entire "way of life" is under threat. National parties understand what that would result in. It would result in the globalization of the third-world version of poverty. The rest of the story is no mystery either: wherever there is poverty, there is unrest and violence. Nation-states are always prepared to keep their populations in check through the use of armed forces. This time, the threat was not a bunch of refugees on the other side of the sacred border but those inside the borders. Nationhood and nationalism may be useful demagogic tools to mobilize people to go to war or sanctify the leader's endless abuses, but they do not substitute for food and shelter. The moment the invisible hand loses its ability to exploit the faceless and nameless Other, "our way of life" vanishes and the entire order implodes, leaving this revolving door like Dali's melting clock as proof of horrible times. Yet this horror has been ongoing; Covid-19 has only exposed some of it across classes and continents.[7] Nation-states have already entered a stage where their very existence is at stake and will use various strategies to maintain their authority. Today, even a conservative organization as the UN repeatedly tells its nation-state parents that unless something urgent is done, the catastrophe is inevitable (IPCC 2018). This was stated before the coronavirus in reference to the ecological crisis. Now that the nightmare is here, to continue to rely on nationalists for protection would be the worst form of self-deception. Giving in to fear and withdrawal, giving unlimited obedience to the guardians of capital, will amount to complete disempowerment.

CHAPTER FOUR

Capitalism and the Ecological Deadlock

"Climate change," "global warming," and "climate crisis" are depoliti-cized and neutralized references to capitalism's systematic destruction of the conditions of life on earth. It may be little wonder that we obscure the driving role of capitalism in bringing about this crisis, given that even much of the scientific community seemed apt to attribute the earth's ris-ing temperatures to natural fluctuations well into the twentieth century.[1] We now have insurmountable evidence of a human-made catastrophe on a planetary scale. There is even a term, Anthropocene, for this geological epoch in which human activities have had a decisive role in the future of the earth system. With the mid-twentieth century considered its starting point, the Anthropocene has seen comparatively rapid changes in temperatures, sea levels, ocean acidification, and habitat loss, among other environmen-tal detriments (Anthropocene Working Group 2019). In terms of global temperatures, an increase of more than 1.5°C is dangerous, more than 3°C would be "catastrophic," and more than 5°C would have consequences of "unknown" magnitude "not experienced in the last 20+ million years" (Xu and Ramanathan 2017: 5). Making headlines around the world in October 2018, the United Nations Intergovernmental Panel on Climate Change (IPCC) called for urgent action to dramatically reduce carbon emissions by 2030 if we are to avoid global warming of more than 1.5°C (IPCC 2018).[2]

It has become relatively standard for such scientific reports to turn on all the red lights to signal that the train must stop and change direction imme-diately if we are to have any chance of avoiding the fast-approaching cliff. Yet, these reports rarely hold the train operator responsible for taking the current route and deliberately dismissing numerous warnings. In fact, most do not even name the train operator, thereby normalizing the apocalyptic language as though falling off the cliff is somehow metaphysically deter-mined or that we are all simply sleepwalking toward it. If anything, scientific impartiality should demand pointing out that the operator is capitalism, the survival of which is actually dependent on driving the train forward as fast as possible, regardless of what has been happening and what will happen to those of us who are unfortunate enough to be seated in the economy-class cabins. In the cheap seats, we are already seeing the terrible human costs of climate change, and yet the train races on with capitalism at the controls.

Decades of scientific studies and reports have repeatedly failed to inspire the kind of system-level response to this problem that is needed. Particularly in the United States, climate change remains a subject of debate, with some denying that it is happening or maintaining that it is the result of inevitable climate fluctuations. These positions, however, will not be the focus of this chapter. The chief aim here is to interrogate the two dominant approaches among those who acknowledge the impending climate crisis. On the one hand, there is an optimistic approach that reduces the crisis to an ethical one, while the more pessimistic approach has accepted the doomsday as an almost inevitable matter of fate. The first assumes that we could regain a reasonable balance of life on earth through individual lifestyle adjustments, and the second embraces apocalypticism, under the assumption that the problem is simply too far gone. In either case, capitalism goes unchallenged—and often unnamed—as the main cause of the ecological crisis. Refuting both accounts, I argue that the only rational response to the ecological crisis is one that resists capitalism head on.

Capitalism versus Science

What we now know beyond any doubt is that we are fast approaching the "planetary boundaries" (Stockholm Resilience Centre 2019), and there is a consensus among most scientists that immediate and comprehensive action must be taken to avoid ecological catastrophes. Missing from these assessments, however, is the fact that capitalism is inherently eco-imperialist because of its elemental dependency on the exploitation of so-called natural resources. If capitalism ceases to be eco-imperialist, it will cease to exist altogether. As such, there is nothing better for the ruling capitalist class than the prevailing wisdom that the ecological crisis is simply a matter of predetermined fate or a question of ethics. The current state of discourse on this subject presents capitalists an easy out, whereby they can engage in eco-philanthropy while continuing their destructive business practices as usual.

If one does not buy into the hype surrounding recycling or simply questions whether lifestyle changes would be enough to stop this runaway train, the hegemony of capitalism makes it difficult to see beyond the apocalyptic image of an inevitable doomsday. In either case, the problem is the lack of a holistic, interdisciplinary, and daringly critical knowledge of our reality as well as the potentialities of the future we are creating. The dominant reductionist modes of knowledge production are rooted in the fanatic division of labor, whereby even scientists are deprived of a critical sociopolitical viewpoint that could enhance their modes of perception. Otherwise, what most scientists have concluded over the last few decades regarding global warming and the need for a drastic change is an assertion of what eco-socialists have long asserted, namely, a revolutionary alteration of the existing dominant system is imperative to avoid a breakdown of the earth system. As the scientific discourse continues to be apolitical, governments are exacerbating the ecological crisis. Currently, we have at our disposal enough scientific research, including studies conducted by UN-affiliated scientists, to conclude beyond any doubt that the existing global order is driving us toward an ecological abyss. When it comes to the conditions and future of life on the planet, capitalism's diametrical opposition to solving the crisis is now more pronounced than ever.

Of course, those who are in favor of continuing with the status quo want us to believe that as long as we make certain reforms here and there, which mainly come down to more consumption in the name of green choices, there is nothing fundamentally wrong with the existing order. The absurdity of this consumerist green discourse becomes only too clear when viewed in relation to the exponential increases in the extraction of raw materials throughout the capitalist era. Reductionist, abstract accounts of the ecological crisis dismiss the fact that capitalism in its totality is inherently eco-imperialist, and, as such, irredeemable. In 2017 alone, 92 billion tons of raw materials were extracted from the earth, amounting to 240 percent increase compared to 1970 (Material Flow Analysis Portal 2018). Of course, there is an enormous disparity between the global South and North when it comes to the benefits and damages directly caused by the extraction and flow of raw materials; but for the purpose of this argument, if we divide the raw material equally by the global population—which reached nearly 7.5 billion in 2017 (Kaneda and Dupuis 2017)—the result is approximately 12.266 tons per capita. Let us assume that neither the extraction of raw materials nor the population would increase further. In a lifetime of, say, seventy years, the average person would be responsible for more than 858 tons of raw materials, the equivalent of the weight of over 430 (large) cars. Obviously, we are not each equally responsible for this extraction, however much we may enable it through either direct or indirect consumption.

The reality is that those who are least responsible for the deterioration of the ecosystem are most affected by it. In a 2019 UN report on poverty and human rights, the term "climate apartheid" was used to indicate that the poor will suffer from the most devastating effects of climate change, including wars and famine (The Special Rapporteur on Extreme Poverty and Human Rights 2019: 14). However, if we look to the aforementioned IPCC report that warns climate change will reach a catastrophic tipping point by 2030 unless drastic changes are made, the "political action" being called for falls far short of challenging the capitalist system responsible for the imminent collapse of the conditions of life on earth (2018). Perhaps we should not expect the members of the IPCC to give advice beyond their areas of expertise. Yet, it must be acknowledged that the magnitude of the crisis is now such that it cannot be dealt with in terms of individual ethical choices, such as buying local, embracing a vegan diet, installing solar panels on one's rooftop, purchasing an electric car, or "acting green" in whatever other fashionable way. Any non-fragmental and serious consideration of the nature of the crisis would clearly realize that the survival of capitalism will inevitably amount to the destruction of the ecosystem, and vice versa.

Socialism as an Alternative?

Most of the reformist solutions that are offered to avoid the catastrophic worsening of the ecological crisis miss the point because they do not stem from a universal awareness of human activities and history. Both moralist and positivistic accounts will necessarily continue to fail to perceive the magnitude of the crisis. Moreover, remedies that are based on reductionist assumptions of the ecological crisis are, if anything, more likely to worsen the crisis. One of the most crucial lessons we learn from the Frankfurt School's Critical Theory is that capitalist modernity's mode of reason is instrumental reason, which is at the heart of all socially engineered and scientifically perfected monstrosities in recent memory, including the Holocaust. The common fetishism of efficiency is the direct outcome of the capitalist modes of production, and because the normalized instrumental reason is framed by standards of efficiency, the ability to perceive any aspect of the crisis in its totality is rare. Because we fail to conceive the crisis both in its inner dialectical complexity and its inclusive magnitude, any talk of comprehensive solutions is necessarily irrelevant at best, and harmful at worst. The way out is the revolutionary negation of capitalism as a system, and that may put us in a position to be able to gradually imagine and build the alternative. Moreover, a holistic critical philosophy is a prerequisite for the necessary awareness that could comprehend the crisis well enough to be able to, in principle, consider a way out in terms of a revolutionary negation of capitalism.

Socialism would be incomparably more viable than any form of capitalism, but there is a century of misuses and abuses of socialism as a notion. During the long decades of the Cold War propaganda, socialism suffered doubly. The Soviet Bloc states claimed socialism to attribute legitimacy to their oppressive authoritarian regimes, and the Western Bloc attributed socialism to those regimes in order to delegitimize socialism as a viable alternative to capitalism. Caught between the pseudo-socialist and anti-socialist propaganda machines that continued to operate throughout the Cold War, socialism is often associated with illiberalism, or more specifically with totalitarianism, especially in the West.[3] We might not know how socialism would look in practice, but we do know what it would not look like. It is not what took place in the Soviet Union and other self-proclaimed socialist or communist countries. The collapse of the Soviet Union can be used as evidence of the failure of a state-controlled economy, but that must not be equated to the failure of socialist modes of production, which had no place in the Soviet Union within a few years after October Revolution. Thus, if anything, the Soviet Union's collapse amounted to the failure of one version of a capitalist economy in favor of another. This is not to say the version that has survived so far is successful; for how could it be given the impending ecological catastrophe to which it has given rise? An economic system that leads to the fatal destruction of the very conditions that sustain life cannot rationally be considered viable, regardless of one's political stance.

While we do not have a positive and comprehensive account of Marxian socialism based on Marx and Engels's body of work, we can comprehend it negatively. To Marx and Engels, socialist modes of production are defined in opposition to the capitalist modes of production and private property, and that is precisely why they emphasize the significance of the historical development of capitalism as a necessary condition for the transition into socialism. While the capitalist modes of production are centered around private property and the private ownership of the means of production, essential to socialism is the negation of private property and the private ownership of the means of production. Under all forms of state socialism that have been attempted thus far, the private ownership of the means of production was not negated. Put differently, in all cases of state socialism to date, it was the state and party elites, not the public or workers, who controlled the means of production. Of course, these elites claimed to represent the interests of the proletariat, but that makes no difference in terms of the actual ownership of the means of production, and, thus, relations of production, which remained economically exploitative, socially alienating, politically oppressive, and ecologically devastating. In such state-dictated economies, the proletariat were not less disempowered than the proletariat in market-dictated economies. Workers in either case have been free only insofar as they freely choose the only option the system would give them, namely to sell their labor. This, in turn, greatly empowered the ruling class both nationally and within an international regime of antagonistic nation-states, thereby further dividing the proletariat across the world.

Another crucial point to keep in mind is that the failures of the Soviet Bloc must be looked at as failures of the Stalinist experiment, as opposed to failures of socialism qua modes of production, simply because socialist modes of production have never been actualized. Even for an orthodox Marxist such as Lenin, it is inconceivable to establish (Marxist) socialism by means of state bureaucracy. For the most part, Lenin's *State and Revolution* is a justification of the proletarian takeover of the state, as opposed to advocating its immediate abolishment, per historical materialism (1978). Lenin, as a historical materialist, was well aware of the fact that a "communist state" is an oxymoron. Thus, with reference to Marx and Engels's works, focusing on those relevant to the Paris Commune, Lenin makes a case for the urgency of proletarian control of the state as a means of completely uprooting the bourgeoisie and, in turn, putting an end to class oppression. Once that goal of uprooting the bourgeois power is safely accomplished, "the state withers away." Still, Lenin's account makes no attempt to validate the existence of state bureaucracy under any circumstances. On the contrary, throughout the book, it is only mockingly that he refers to ministers and other government officials, including those who consider themselves Marxists. However, under Lenin's party, the Soviet Union quickly fell under the control of a new bureaucratic hierarchy that invented various methods of securing total control over the proletariat and the rest of the society. Arguments regarding whether Lenin or Trotsky would have prevented the reemergence of the state bureaucracy or may have actually laid the grounds for it are not relevant to the aims of this book.

In all cases, and regardless of whether socialism is the solution or not, viable or not, realizable or not, we do not know of any system that is as disastrous, and, thus, as dysfunctional, especially ecologically, as capitalism. Emphasizing the desperate need for a revolutionary replacement of the capitalist modes of production is simply a restatement of what most scientists call for in terms of the need for immediate and drastic changes to avoid ecological catastrophe; however, the very language of most scientists is deliberately apolitical, even when they try to alarm us about the imminent danger that the ship of humanity is sinking (for reasons that are nothing but political insofar as dominant politics are the politics of the dominant class, the politics that prioritize and normalize whatever is necessary to sustain the bourgeois hegemony, especially the endless accumulation of capital, which, in turn, is ensured first and foremost through the perpetuation of the existing relations of exploitation of both labor and nature). More to the point, scientific discourse itself essentially operates at the heart of the ideological hegemony of capitalism. In other words, there is a contradiction in waiting for the scientific community to declare that capitalism is the problem. For only when capitalism is no longer the dominant system will there be a scientific community (with a recognized scientific authority) in which the majority could make such a declaration; on the other hand, when capitalism is no longer the dominant system, such a declaration will be neither necessary nor accurate.

Negation: A Critique of the Conformist Positions

Many eco-socialists, social ecologists, and various anarcho-ecologists, among other anti-capitalists, recognize the need for replacing capitalism as a system. However, the two most common positions in relation to this question illustrate the degree to which even the system's staunchest critics have internalized the hegemony of capitalism. In the pessimist camp, it is not too uncommon to recognize the inherent connection between capitalism and the ecological crisis, but what is increasingly uncommon is imagining a revolutionary project that could put an end to the domination of the capitalist modes of production. While it was once anticipated that the proletariat would be the ultimate liberator of human society, today it is the looming ecological crisis that is most often seen as the "grave digger" of capitalism, but only at the expense of life as such. The revolutionary subject has thereby been rendered superfluous. Refuting that common assumption, I argue that the impending ecological disaster is and will continue to be another profit-generating crisis for capitalism. For instance, as water as an exploitative natural recourse becomes scarcer, it will only become more commodifiable, generating increased profit for monopolies. A recent study shows that four billion people, mostly in the global South, already face a severe water shortage (Mekonnen and Hoekstra 2016).

Thanks to the demise of the left, the end of capitalism, if anticipated at all, is often associated with an ecological catastrophe that would threaten human existence altogether. However, it is more accurate to assume that the ecological crisis, though a common doom for the majority, will only render capitalism more dominant unless progressive international revolutionary action is taken to change the conditions that now make such a crisis inevitable. Those are the conditions that are reproduced by capitalism and on which capitalism thrives. By the same token, the common approach to the ecological crisis as an ethical crisis is both misleading and ineffective because it dismisses the systemic anti-ecological nature of capitalism.

The fact that capitalist modes of production will inevitably lead to more and more ecological crises should be common knowledge by now even though there will always be deniers, some of whom even deny the sphericity of the earth. The unlimited competition among individuals, corporations, and states for gaining profit at the expense of natural resources will continue to destroy life and its fragile conditions on earth. Having access to clean water and air is already becoming a privilege on the global level. If the poor have struggled to secure food and shelter so far, now hundreds of millions have to struggle for clean water as well. The primary international actor in today's world is still the state, whose sovereignty was legitimized by ideas of the mid-seventeenth century. Even two centuries later, there was barely any consciousness of the ecological system, let alone the ecological crisis that will result from industrial capitalism. Today, even climate change deniers are aware of the fact that a factory may have an environmental impact on everyone everywhere. Yet, in the best cases, only the government of the country where the factory is located has leverage over it.

In a capitalist world, it is only natural that each state would aim at maximum attraction of capital with minimal regard for the ensuing environmental damage. It makes little sense for a country to compromise its development or place in the capitalist race for the sake of the planet when every other state pushes forward or has been pushing forward full-steam toward the maximum accumulation of capital. While we tend to point fingers at corporations and governments for not adopting stricter environmental policies, as individuals we behave more or less the same way. How many people would voluntarily diminish their own daily comforts for the sake of protecting the natural conditions of life on the planet? Of course, that is not to say all lifestyles are equally bad or that there is no way out. The point, rather, is that the ecological crisis is a systemic crisis of capitalism, as opposed to an ethical crisis that could be solved through adjusting lifestyles. Just as "wrong life cannot be lived rightly," to quote Adorno (2005: 39), capitalism cannot be lived ecologically. The outcome of this should not be nihilist resignation, but, on the contrary, an act of negation. To negate the system in its totality is the only meaningful response to the ecological crisis of which almost all of us are integral parts, and from which almost all of us will continue to suffer.

Capitalism Cannot Be Managed Ecologically

Given the ideological hegemony of the bourgeoisie, the laws of capitalism are naturalized, which is precisely why they are perceived as the laws of nature. To Marx there is nothing natural about the laws of capitalism; they can and *must* be abolished. However, some Marxian perspectives on the ecological crisis are strongly influenced by Marx's belief that capitalism will ultimately destroy the conditions of its own sustainability. What is less often mentioned is Marx's insistence that revolutionary action is the ultimate progressive way to abolish capitalism. Marx was not of the opinion that progressives should sit idly by in anticipation of capitalism's self-destruction. For the only force that can set the course of history on a progressive path is the revolutionary will of human beings. Human existence is by no means separate from nature; through our modes of existence, we form and re-form the so-called human nature. That is to say, the emancipation of life on earth from the destructive forces that have thus far shaped history hinges almost entirely on revolutionary negation.

What is certain is that global capitalism will not demolish itself in order to prevent more catastrophes. John Barry explains that capitalism is parasitic in two ways, both of which will lead to its own collapse. First, capitalism is "parasitic upon the *non-capitalist social world*" (Barry 1999: 263, emphasis in original). As Marx and Engels write, in a capitalist society those "who work, acquire nothing, and those who acquire anything do not work" (1978: 486). Second, capitalism is "parasitic upon *the non-human world*," that is, the environment and the natural world more generally (Barry 1999: 263, emphasis in original). Because capitalism is driven by the endless accumulation of capital, the natural environment is regarded as nothing but an exploitable source of raw material and a space for depositing industrial waste. Whatever can potentially generate profit is exploited and transformed through manipulated labor. The result of this is an inevitable and ever-worsening destruction of the ecosystem, all while the capitalist ruling class remains fixated on neutralizing any threats to the production cycle due to the scarcity of raw materials. To overcome such problems, capitalists seek out more land, water, and air to exploit, contributing to the catastrophic metabolic rift between humans and the natural environment (Foster 1999).

The capitalist system continues to use "displacement strategies," wherein ecological problems are shifted from one form to another, one place to another, or from the present to the future (Barry 1999: 254–5). As an embodiment of "ecological imperialism,"[4] displacement strategies are used to minimize the damage inflicted on bourgeoisiefied societies at the expense of marginalized societies. Capitalism is unjust even in its distribution of injustices. It causes endless inequalities not only through its exploitation and division of labor, but also through its unfair distribution of industrial waste (Barry 1999: 265). To take one example, while some and often all raw materials for manufacturing electronic devices are extracted from natural resources in the third world, these same devices are eventually shipped back to the third world, where they end up in "digital dumping grounds" (WGBH Educational Foundation 2009). In effect, the environmental abuse is committed twice: during the production process and during the disposal process. In 2008, Americans threw away 130,000 computers every day and more than 100 million cellphones over the course of the year (Castillo 2011). In 2010, the United States generated 2.44 million tons of e-waste, of which only 27 percent was recycled (US Environmental Protection Agency 2011).

There are two main material factors that have made the North the core of capitalism. First, the core North has been extracting raw materials from the periphery South for centuries (Foster and Clark 2004: 194). Capitalism's endless demand for raw materials has led to the destruction of most pre-capitalist societies as well as the elimination of entire peoples, as Rosa Luxemburg argued (Luxemburg 2004: 71–111). Of course, ecological imperialism also triggered a global ecological imbalance, which has only continued to worsen with time. The second reason for the North's capitalist rise, as Foster and Clark argue, is its high consumption of fossil fuel, which has largely instigated the climate change crisis that primarily impacts the South (Foster and Clark 2004: 194).[5]

The ecological crisis is inseparable from the ongoing social inequalities under capitalism as a world system. To elucidate this point, Foster and Clark borrow *Accion Ecologica*'s definition of ecological debt, which is "the debt accumulated by Northern, industrial countries toward third world countries on account of resource plundering, environmental damages, and the free occupation of environmental space to deposit wastes, such as greenhouse gases, from the industrial countries" (Foster and Clark 2004: 194). Citing a report by Christian Aid, Foster and Clark write, "the ecological debt owed by the North to the South in terms of carbon emissions alone amounts to an estimated $13 trillion per year" (2004: 196–7). Two decades ago, the carbon emissions of the United States and Europe amounted to more than 3.5 billion metric tons, comprising more than half of the world's carbon emission in 1996 (Foster and Clark 2004: 195). In 2013, the population of North America was 579,024,000, or 8.27 percent of the world's population of 7 billion, but the CO_2 emissions from North American fuel consumption accounted for 22 percent of total global CO_2 emissions from fuel consumption (GMF 2017).

The Totalitarian Invisible Hand of Neoliberalism Is Visibly Disastrous

It is not inconceivable to assume that capitalism will not only survive the ecological crisis in the foreseeable future, but it will also thrive on that very crisis. Capitalism has grown stronger not despite but because of crises that have for the most part been self-inflicted. Far from weakening capitalism, the two world wars of the twentieth century resulted in the normalization of capitalism as a necessary condition for (liberal) democracy. Even the war on terror has been an extremely profitable enterprise; global military spending increased from 0.78 trillion USD in 1999 to 1.676 trillion USD in 2015 (Stockholm International Peace Research Institute 2016).

Naomi Klein has famously argued that neoliberalism has been relying on crises and disasters to impose its global monopoly. In *The Shock Doctrine: The Rise of Disaster Capitalism,* Klein shows that crises are precisely what made imposing neoliberalism on different societies throughout the world possible (2007). She termed the unhindered capitalism that began to become dominant in the 1970s under the influence of the Chicago school's ideologues, especially Milton Friedman and his followers, "disaster capitalism." Very much like apocalyptic religious fundamentalists who see the complete destruction of the world as the ultimate way out of this sinful form of existence and the entry to God's kingdom, the fanatics of neoliberalism see devastating disasters as cleansing flushes that wipe out all that could be an obstacle for the unlimited rule of "the invisible hand." Needless to say, to neoliberals, as extremist Adam Smith followers, the invisible hand is the only hand that can bring about both perfect order and liberty. In their belief system, the exchange principle, the rule of capital, is the one and only principle that can and should shape social and political relations among individuals and societies. Any social and political force that might oppose the rule of capital is an obstacle to true human freedom. Any intervention in the so-called free market is inherently against the realization of humanity's potential. Thus, for decades they have been using the most powerful institutions in the world, such as the IMF, the World Bank, WTO, and the government of the United States, to *impose* their free market system.

However, they realized over and over again that under relative stable circumstances, where people can exercise some degree of their political free will, most would oppose the abolishment of collective ownership and regulations that restrict capitalist monopoly. People in the South and North would oppose submission to the totalitarianism of corporations under which capital enjoys unlimited power over everyone's lives. Thus, the neoliberal version of freedom, which entails unlimited freedom of corporatism, can only be implemented when and where a society is so paralyzed by a political or natural disaster that it would be unable to practice any form of resistance. Military coups, devastating wars, and environmental catastrophes are the kind of shocks that strip societies of the capacity to resist the new order. As Klein shows the Chicago boys' most successful task has been making sure the new order is imposed discreetly and quickly with the help of local elites during times of disasters. In the name of liberty, the Chicago boys habitually rely on authoritarian political elites to impose corporate totalitarianism. In Chile, the Chicago boys worked directly with the Pinochet regime after the military coup d'état that ousted Allende's democratically elected government. Friedman even worked as Pinochet's adviser (Klein 2007: 7). Two decades later, in Eastern Europe, the unlimited control of the ruling communist parties was replaced with unlimited control of corporations, bringing about the era of global neoliberalism, which to Francis Fukuyama (1992) was the ultimate triumph of liberal democracy as the most advanced historical stage humanity could reach.

Like devastating wars, environmental disasters provide ideal circumstances for ruling capitalist elites to swiftly implement neoliberalism and/or make massive profit. Under disaster capitalism, total or near total destruction translates to maximizing opportunities for both reshaping everything in accordance with the neoliberal model and boosting capital. Klein makes the case that the Iraq war was planned to bring about such disastrous circumstances that would make the implementation of corporate capitalism as smooth as possible. Universal privatization and market deregulation were prescribed by the neoconservatives as the most effective treatment for all Iraq's problems following the war, which was supposed to numb the society for the duration of the change-of-blood operation. From Chile, Bolivia, and Argentina to Poland, Russia, South Korea, and Indonesia, the Chicago boys since the 1970s have always been on the lookout for any disaster to apply their shock therapy represented by unlimited privatization, which in turn amounts to the totalitarian rule of corporates. In every single case, Friedman's shock therapy took place with the support of military and/or political elites who suppressed democratic demands of the society in question (Klein 2007). Where that was not possible, IMF and the World Bank have been instrumental in imposing neoliberalism.

Friedman's shock doctrine has reached a point of popularity such that the formula of disaster-followed-by-unfettered-capitalism does not even require any Chicago boys to play the role of genius economic curers. Take Turkey, for example. Erdogan has been applying the formula repeatedly, which is precisely what made him the darling of the West until his discreet alliance with ISIS and other Islamist groups made him somewhat untrustworthy. Whenever there is a disaster, such as any of those caused by the Syrian civil war or the 2016 coup in Turkey, Erdogan makes full use of it to further neoliberalize the economy and deepen his Islamist hegemony in Turkey and beyond. Other times, he creates disasters to generate the right conditions for more neoliberal monopoly and Islamist hegemony. Since 2003, through his neoliberal policies of privatization of formerly state-owned firms and expanding construction and energy corporations, he has created an Islamist capitalist elite, including members of his family, who effectively control both the economy and politics.

In 2014, Erdogan started a politics of systematic destruction of entire towns in the Kurdish region in Turkey (Burç 2016). Noticeably, the regime emphasized that everything would be rebuilt better than before. Although it is important to bear in mind that Erdogan's political party and family are heavily involved in the corporate monopoly in Turkey and so they are the immediate beneficiaries of the cycle of destruction–reconstruction, I think the main drive behind Erdogan's politics of total destruction in Kurdistan is to allow neoliberalism to accomplish what militarism alone has failed to accomplish. The goal is both breaking the Kurdish spirit of resistance and boosting the Islamist-neoliberal enterprise in Turkey and the Middle East at large.

Neoliberalism's shock doctrine enabled authoritarian regimes to accomplish what otherwise they would have never been able to accomplish. From Pinochet to Erdogan, the third-world dictators learned that opening the doors for foreign investment and privatization leads to (i) weakening people's political potentials by impoverishing the most oppressed and (ii) winning the West's unconditional support. One could argue that the main reason regimes like those of Saddam Hussein and Bashar Al-Assad become targets of regime change policy but the Erdogan regime does not is that the first group resist the neoliberal order whereas the second group embrace it. Issues of human rights violations under the Turkish regime are rarely a subject of any criticism as far as Western governments are concerned. Enjoying both unconditional Western support and monopoly of capital, third-world neoliberal regimes evolved their authoritarianism to a higher level of totalitarianism.

Capitalism has long been in crisis, and thus far as the ecological crisis is concerned, it seems to be just another profitable crisis. Precisely because of pollution and droughts, the commodification of water will become the norm. Sales of bottled water in 2011 compared to 2010 increased by 23.9 percent, 17.8 percent, and 15.8 percent in Indonesia, China, and India, respectively (Zenith International 2012). Globally, the consumption of bottled water since 2007 has almost doubled (Zenith International 2014). The wealthy are able to move to cleaner, more secure places while continuing to make more profit from the miseries of the poor wherever and however they can. It is quite common for ruling elites in the periphery and semi-periphery to send their children to Western schools, invest their capital in the rich Center countries, and freely move around the world, while semi-slavery conditions are imposed on workers in their own countries. Such is the model that will play out wherever environmental conditions become unbearable due to climate change. Immigration laws in the core countries openly favor and, in many cases, even attract foreign capitalists and their capital. It is therefore not climate change that will ultimately threaten capitalists and their manipulation of human society at large. Only the rise of the disadvantaged would have the power to put an end to the systematic destruction of the environment.

Ideologically, the working class in the core countries has mainly been bourgeoisified.[6] It is difficult to imagine the disconnect between workers in the North and those in the South being more pronounced. While the annual income *per capita* in Afghanistan was 561.86 USD in 2016 (IMF 2019), the average American lower- to middle-income consumer spent 69–82 USD (averaging 76.23 USD) per day from July 2016 to July 2017 (Gallup 2017). This means that over eight days a typical American consumer would have spent more than the equivalent of the annual income of an average Afghan citizen. If we look at holiday shopping, consumers in the UK spent an average of 732 GBP (about 1,082 USD) in 2015 (Rubicon Project 2016), about 2.35 times the annual income of an average citizen of the Democratic Republic of the Congo, which was 460 USD in 2015 (World Bank 2018).

Thanks to the international division of labor, third-world workers are trapped in periphery regions where they continually pay the price of the economic prosperity in the core countries. How could workers in Canada find enough common ground with workers in India to inspire both sides to unite in a single struggle against capitalism? On the one hand, capitalists treat the world as one unrestricted space for accumulation; on the other hand, there are endless barriers that prevent workers in technologically underdeveloped countries from forging political connections with the rest of the world. As long as capital dictates international communication, there will always be an expanding economic gap between the periphery and the wealthy core regions. The larger this gap becomes, the more fragmented the working class will become.

The Widespread Nihilist Conformity Is Idealism without an Ideal

Though the proletariat has long been dead as a revolutionary subject, the death of the proletariat should not cause us to conform to the existing order as the only possible world. Nor should the anticipation of the downfall of capitalism lead us to political passivity. Gorz analogizes the relatively popular leftist discourse of the ecological doomsday to the religious hatred of modernity and the ensuing desire to witness the world's ultimate demise (Gorz 2012: 7). He writes, "[S]ince there is no social or historical subject capable of bringing this utopia into being, the theory of the inevitable collapse of capitalism is reworked in an ecological version … . In that version, capitalist civilization is moving inexorably towards catastrophic collapse. There is no longer any need for a revolutionary class to overthrow capitalism: it is digging its own grave, and that of industrial civilization in general" (Gorz 2012: 6–7). The belief that the ecological doomsday is inevitable might in some cases be rooted in the desire to completely submit to the existing order, despite the superficial anti-capitalist rhetoric on college campuses in the West. It is a revolt without rebels, and idealism without an ideal.

While there is sufficient reason not to be optimistic about the ecological crisis, the roots of the apocalyptic tendency definitely go back to ancient mythology that is embodied clearly in religious views. Just as a hurricane or drought is believed to be God's punishment for sins people committed, ultimately God will wipe out everything, as he did with the great flood, the only survivors of which were those on Noah's ark. In Mesopotamian and Greek mythology, total salvation and total destruction are recurring prototypes and, if anything, they indicate the outline of the childhood of humanity, the stage where personality fluctuates between the two primary emotions, love and ire, in the face of an overwhelming mysterious world. The constant sense of powerlessness inevitably leads to neurotic reactions. In helpless situations we naturally tend to picture an immediate future that is either complete salvation through a miraculous supernatural intervention or total destruction to put an end to the suffering altogether. This is precisely why people often turn to faith when faced with hopeless situations. Thus, the psychological motives behind the invention of heaven and hell are the same, so it is hardly surprising that heaven and hell appear together in religious scriptures.

Submitting to the will of the father figure is the ultimate escape from the open-ended anxiety that is inherent in the curse of being free and, thus, responsible for the future. The psychological necessity of the father figure is partly tied to the need to replace the problem of future with a sense of fate, an open-ended horizon of unknown possibilities with a predetermined ending orchestrated by a higher being. The system of reward and punishment is the primordial formula that eternalizes the dictating role of the father figure. Ultimately, the system aims at total purification through putting a definite end to everything that is between heaven and hell. Thus, for the most part, religious imagination has already normalized a hopeless, unredeemable, world that functions merely as path to higher form of existence. The Abrahamic religions have deepened the belief that this world is meant to end catastrophically because it is inherently bad. Being born amounts to a regrettable accident of being separated from the state of idle existence in the mother's womb, the first form of existence, paradise. All that follows is a fall, and all one can hope for is an end to the fall. The longing for the pre-thinking stage of existence is one and the same with the apocalyptic tendency. A world that is so painful deserves to end in a universal catastrophe. Such an apocalyptic ending amounts to the purification needed for the return to the first place, to become one with the creator.

In the twentieth century, after the short-lived age of Enlightenment during which we had a chance to grow into the age of reason but did not, pessimism became an intellectual and artistic badge of honor only under a secular disguise. Surrealism, Dadaism, futurism, and existentialism are some of the most known examples of the European reincarnation of a much older apocalypticism. The dialectical antithesis of that kind of popular mood gave birth to various brands of new-ageism, self-help, and so on. After all, theological dark views were balanced by the comfort guaranteed in the act of faith. The universal peace new-ageists allude to is, of course, real insofar as it completes the cycle of answers, the fatherly care, which is rewarding even when it is punishing. From the 1960s to the end of the 1980s, there were multiple waves of popular movements that commodified Eastern cultism in search for the "inner peace." Popular culture became the ultimate sphere of the industry of happiness. Today, happiness is arguably the most profitable cultural industry, and that is so precisely because depression has become an epidemic.

Once the bourgeois bohemian revolutionary persona took over the stage in Europe, after the bitter defeat of the anti-fascist anarcho-communist revolutionaries in Spain, even "revolution" became a production of the culture industry. The moment politics were handed back to the fathers in suits, bureaucrats, and drug consumption coupled with popular music became an act of dissent, capitalism secured its hegemony for several generations. Once the anti-capitalists became hand-holding vibe-seeking petit-bourgeois consumers of the culture industry, apocalypticism became as present in cafes as it has been in religious spaces for centuries. Thanks to the rise of populist conservativism, now the sources for obtaining self-assurance among the positive left are plenty. For instance, mocking Donald Trump would suffice to exempt one from further political responsibility. Even the "99 percent" discourse functions more as an escape from political responsibility than an anti-capitalist front formation. It is ultimately an easy psychological exit from much more serious political deadlock. While we are all directly participating in rolling the capitalist consumption-profit wheel, identifying with the virtual 99 percent functions more as a moral bailout.

Instead of negating their own bourgeois conditions that prevent them from imagining more effective forms of resistance, intellectual elites morally permit themselves to engage in the capitalist way of life under the pretext of utter hopelessness as they await the impending catastrophe. Today's bourgeois bohemians are nihilists who have turned revolutionary discourse into another risk-free discourse within the broader profitable culture industry.

Meanwhile, the revolutionaries are left alone to face their regional fascist enemies along with the capitalist relations of production that have long deprived them of the means of knowledge production. As a result, even criticism of the existing order is a privilege of the rich who make it to the centers of knowledge production in prestigious universities and mass-media giants.

Apocalypticism, if anything, is responsible for normalizing and eternalizing capitalism. As Jameson noticed, people tend to imagine the end of the world but not the end of capitalism (2003: 76). One of the reasons that, albeit wrongly, led many to reject Marxism was the assumption that Marxism predicted the end of capitalism in the triumph of socialism. The triumph of capitalism and fall of the Eastern Bloc could only mean that Marx was a false prophet. Thus, even in Marx many wanted a father figure who could lead them to the promised heaven. They read into Marxism messianic promises of total salvation.

The whole assumption should be turned upside down for the sake of an accurate reading of Marx and an actual emancipatory perspective. It is Marx who historicizes every consciousness, including theological ones, and it is equally crucial to Marx that without the human consciousness of her own freedom, she neither can be free nor make historical progress to end the conditions of unfreedom. That is to say, being conscious of the human historical will is a prerequisite for historically activating it to materialize progress toward emancipation. Of course, every historical consciousness is also shaped by material conditions, but Marx would add that we are at a historical point where we can realize our determinate role. Marxism itself is the kind of historical consciousness that makes progressive revolutionary movement possible. On the other hand, choosing to see capitalist liberalism as the end of history, as many have, inevitably will eternalize capitalism, and thus our unfreedom. As such, ecological catastrophes indeed become inevitable. Whether seen as the best possible world or the inevitable dark last chapter of humanity, capitalism is normalized and eternalized by the majority who refuse to reject what is imposed on them.

Essentially, widespread apocalypticism can only lead to apocalypses, unless a negative cosmopolitan social movement emerges that will be capable of constructing both a horizon of new possibilities and a revolutionary subject committed to negation as a way of being under all circumstances of unfreedom, not merely those measured by an identitarian principle or cultural fetish. The new revolutionary subject will transcend the proletarian, feminist, and environmentalist, crystalizing a cosmopolitan personality compatible with today's challenges both in terms of consciousness and revolutionary strategy. Who is faced with the compound oppressions in their totality or semi-totality? Just as the Bolshevik proletarian revolutionary appeared on the margins of Europe, contrary even to Marx's own anticipation,[7] it is more probable that the new cosmopolitan revolutionary subject will emerge in the margins of the margins, where the brutality of capitalism is experienced in most of its forms. It is only the multilayered oppression experienced by Kurdish women in Syria and Turkey, having been faced with capitalist imperialism, old-form colonialism, ultranationalist fascism, and reactionary religious fundamentalism as well as extreme societal sexism that could have given birth to the Rojava revolutionary subject we have been witnessing since 2012, even though they had been active for many decades prior. However, regardless of its complexity and multitude, oppression is not sufficient for the creation of a revolutionary subject. The formation of a revolutionary philosophy within those same circumstances is essential to provide the necessary biosphere for the birth and growth of the new revolutionary subject. Such a philosophy has had a powerful presence throughout the liberation movement in Rojava. In fact, under the worst imaginable violent circumstances, their academies continued to operate. Without such a philosophy, oppression can only create more oppression, especially within the oppressed society itself, so we need to be careful not to romanticize or idealize the oppressed merely for being oppressed. Of course, the Rojava revolution is only an example of a movement that commits itself to an inclusive cosmopolitan conception of liberation. The Zapatista movement is another example, which also had to emerge in the margins of the margins in order to have a compound conception of freedom.

There Is No Green Way of Living under Capitalism

One of the most common assumptions is that the ecological crisis is the result of an ethical crisis. Therefore, the environmentalist discourses often try to appeal to moral sentiments of consumers and corporate capitalists thereby naturalizing both consumerism and corporatism. In addition to premising the capitalist modes of production as irreplaceable, such discourses in fact depict capitalists as moral agents capable of solving the problem on which their very existence depends. Furthermore, the environmental moralists shoot themselves in the foot by placing morality as such within the capitalist frame of reference. That is to say, even the ability of being environmentally/morally responsible comes down to the power of capital itself. That is exactly why we are being bombarded with advertisements that allure us to buy more stuff that would supposedly guarantee elevating our way of life to the level of environmentalism. In the capitalist world, the more environmentally friendly one wants to be, the more one must spend. Ultimately, only the very rich could afford what is supposed to be an ideal green lifestyle. Who would refuse the choice of a house in the midst of pristine natural surroundings with clean water and air as well as organic food guaranteed? Except, there are two subsequent questions one must keep in mind: first, how much environmental damage one must do to be rich enough to afford such a luxury, and second, even if in some magical way it were possible for all to afford the luxury, would there be any pristine piece of land left? The simple truth is that there is no such thing as a green product or green development.[8]

Reducing the ecological crisis to an ethical problem is inherently anti-ecological, simply because ethics is an individual territory, whereas the ecological crisis is systemic and anonymous insofar as it is created by the capitalist modes of production, as opposed to evil intentions of certain individuals, including the so-called 1 percent. The appeal to moral discourses of right and wrong is meant to portray the ecological crisis as a matter of lifestyle solvable within the bourgeois limits of civil society, by means of minimal (liberal) political effort. The ecological crisis is intrinsically an outcome of the capitalist modes of production and is concealed through the hegemonic ideology of liberalism, which does not have an ecological perspective or doctrine of social justice. Therefore, neither voting for center-liberal parties nor taking shorter showers will prevent environmental degradation.

There is no lifestyle under capitalism that is not ecologically abusive. The notion of ecology inherently implies an interrelationality of truth within an organic whole. Ecology is arguably the most inclusively dialectical system we could think of. Thus, ecological consciousness should, by definition, defy every illusion of abstract morality, ahistoricality, and absolute individuality. If anything, the ideological diffusion under which the ecological crisis has been realized and perpetuated is itself a norm of morality. After all, morality is the most effective ideological apparatus to maintain the existing state of affairs, and this is especially true in the case of advanced capitalism. Under advanced capitalism, everyone, including capitalists such as Bill Gates and Bill Clinton, can be on the right moral side, which is the new religious redemption on which capitalism in the West relies to continue accumulating profit. We are made to believe that it is possible to live happily under capitalism as long as we are virtuous. To live virtuously, all one needs to do is to purchase certain commodities and, on a more general level, live the right lifestyle, which is of course obtainable as long as one can afford its cost.

A revolution without revolutionary act works best for both sides: the fashionable morally superior leftists who are desperate to keep their progressive persona and the dominant bourgeois bosses who are desperate to keep their democratically consented totalitarianism. It is the ideal marriage between two sides that conceal each other's corruption through betraying their own bad faith. Talking environmentalism and living an ecologically destructive life is not merely the result of false consciousness. For no longer can we claim that we do not know where our interests lie, not only as a social class but also as a species. The capitalist modes of production have naturalized a form of monad individualism that is centered around the notion of private property. At its core, the identity of an individual, in the capitalist social world, is nothing but ownership and capital. Therefore, being aware of the universal state of life on earth at best could enhance the discursive performance that merely justifies one's own privileges. This is the ultimate nihilism that colors the entire public sphere that bridges subjectivity with the social world.

The ecological crises we will continue to face are inseparable from the capitalist systems of domination and exploitation. By the same token, there is no unrevolutionary way out of the capitalist hegemony and there is no liberal way of being revolutionary. For bourgeois ecologists, green politics functions as the new age's religion, and like all other religions it serves to absorb the negativity of the potential forces of dissent by channeling them into illusionary spheres of salvation, which offers the best possible space for the dominant regime to normalize its hegemony globally. Even if the ecological crisis could put an end to capitalism, the ensuing system will necessarily be more disastrous if the historical shift does not come as the result of a progressive revolutionary enterprise.

Our modes of perception and conception are not independent from the capitalist modes of production, so despite whatever sentimentalities we may claim, we fail to even conceive of nature. We may find comfort in simplistic illusions of how to choose the right individual lifestyle, but the bitter truth is that, under the domination of capitalism, we simply do not have the option of living in oneness with nature. "Environmentally friendly" forms of consumption could be presented as moral options, but precisely by presenting the ecological crisis as a question of morality the consumer–citizen is made complicit in the capitalist system. Conceiving the ecological crisis as a moral question naturalizes the existing order by shifting the focus to the individual. In fact, often for selecting moral lifestyles, the individual would have to contribute even more to the system of accumulation, thereby aiding the perpetuation of capitalism and further destroying the ecological system. In 1986, echoing Rosa Luxemburg's plea for anti-capitalist action, Murray Bookchin said, "[E]ither we will create an ecotopia based on ecological principles, or we will simply go under as a species. We have to be realistic and do the impossible—because otherwise we will have the unthinkable!" (quoted in Biehl 2015: 18). As evidenced by the lack of solidarity for today's revolutionaries, the crisis we face is not only the absence of the revolutionary subject, but also the normalization of an anti-revolutionary perspective. In short, the international left has become so hopeless that the leftist discourse seems to reflect a furtive desire for the end of the world as the only way to topple capitalism. The psychological grounds for embracing Thanatos aside, the revolutionary truth remains the same: only the revolution of the oppressed can put an end to oppressive systems. If anything, the looming ecological catastrophe only renders revolutionary action against capitalism more imperative and urgent.

Hope does not exist metaphysically. It is rather something for which the conditions must be created. There is an urgent need for a postnihilist philosophy that has the courage of both admitting the hopelessness of the existing order and the will to move beyond it. Effectively, this philosophy has always been at work among those oppressed of the oppressed who choose a final stroke of rebellious act grounded in a hopeless reality and the courage to choose life nonetheless. Philosophies that are not prepared to face the darkness of the historical moment and those not ready to identify with the struggle of the hopeless ones are doomed to fail and fail us. Only such a postnihilist philosophy can face the scale of the ecological crisis and react without falling back into the rich tradition of false redemption and apocalypticism.

CHAPTER FIVE

Culturalism as an Ideological Crisis

Universalism and the Philosophy of History

The philosophy of history fundamentally comes down to the theorization of history around whatever thematic concept or concepts deemed most vital for making rational sense of what we assume to be some form of intelligible dynamics in the temporal continuation of the human existence. Despite the inevitable eventual disintegration of every generation, there are various cross-generational continuities of production, accumulation, and transformation. Of course, there are frequent discontinuities as well, but that is exactly why history is not the aggregate of temporal units. The philosophy of history, we could say, is the study of whatness of history. Because the whatness of history is also the subject of history, the relationship between philosophy and history, as two fields of inquiry, is similar to the relationship between two mirrors facing each other. Each mirror is caught up in endless reflections of reflections.

The analogy is, of course, inaccurate if we leave it at that, that is, without further qualifications. First, either mirror to the other is the existential Other that both complements and diminishes it. They are similar in their way of being lost in the maze of that which is both the essence reduced to appearance and appearance reduced to something else that is key to all these cycles of the impossible escape, and that something is perception. However, a subject is the prerequisite for perception, any perception, to take place.

The gaze is not part of the game, yet it is absolutely essential for the game to happen on any level. The gaze gives the spatiality of the two mirrors a tangible reality, for there can be no spatiality without the subjective experience. It is that subjective experience that makes spatiality something other than space (just as it makes history something other than mere linear passage of time—which is the point of this ongoing interpellation). The gaze of a subject transforms the mirrors from the realm of existence to being, which not only preserves existence but also entails becoming.

The two mirrors exist before and after the gaze, but the *happening* of the relationship between them, the reflections, presupposes a sensing–cognizing subject, that is, it is completely dependent on the gazing subject. Without a gaze, there are no reflections. Reflection is already perception. To rationally examine this hypothesis, it is likely that you, the reader, have just imagined two mirrors in an otherwise empty place. You may have immediately concluded that "there are endless reflections in the two mirrors; it is pure physics." Yet, it is not pure physics. It is pure phenomenology. The only way one would be able to conclude that the reflections are there in the mirrors is through imagining the state of the two mirrors. And the trick is located here: in imagining the state of the two mirrors, one already imagines examining them, and this inevitably involves the imagined gaze. All the physical conditions for the reflections to happen are present, but the presence of a gazing subject is a necessary condition—not in the Berkeleyian sense though because the claim here is not about the existence of the mirrors but reflections in them. Reflection is not even sensory data, but sensory data that has been processed. I am tempted to say *cognized*, instead of processed, but then we run into a serious difficulty pertaining the so-called artificial intelligence, which has to be delayed for now. However, there is the scenario of adding a camera in the room where there are two mirrors. That would prove the reflections, yet photography is essentially the technology of the spatial extension of the human gaze *and* the temporal freezing of the gazed scene in the form of a two-dimensional reflection, which would allow discontinued continuation. This takes us back to the original statement regarding the endless projections between philosophy and history.

Both philosophy and history are obviously human attempts to discover some sort of laws or at least patterns in terms of happenings in relation to *being* human and *being* human in relation to happenings. In the case of philosophy, the objective is conceptualization of the dynamics. In the case of history, the goal is more descriptive. Philosophers' end goal is the construction of theory whereas historians see theory as a method, a means, to write history.

In both cases, however, the human subject claims the possession of an objective sensor, a sensor that can report back across time and space to the philosopher or historian, who in turn would engage in complex processes of inductions and deductions to arrive at some form of knowledge. The sensor is never objective, because its creator is also situated within historical and philosophical particularities. Therefore, the philosophy of history is always already ideological. A philosopher or historian that denies ideological biases is even more ideological for the simple fact that the objectivity claim, at best, that is when it is honest, implies complete internalization of the hegemonic ideology. Essentially the difference between philosophies of history comes down to the sides they take at least insofar as it is imbedded in the questions they construct.

Given all that, we are fully justified to read history through the lenses of social antagonisms, which is precisely what Marx does. By the same token, zooming in, we could read history in terms of the struggle toward the realization of human freedom. Such a struggle is framed by the antagonism between two opposing poles and everything in between. The biases of philosophers or historians manifest themselves in their depictions of progress and regression, and locating particular events and movements on that divided line.

Taking this metatheory down to the level of theorization itself, we can make the following normative claim: history can be comprehended as the history of the conflict between chauvinistic tribalism and egalitarian cosmopolitanism. In fact, the above claim can directly be grounded on both Hegel's philosophy of history and Marx's theory of society. Hegel's *Geist* at the end of the day is the highest form of reason and freedom in an inseparable unity (each inevitably necessitates the other). History, to Hegel, is a progressive movement toward the realization of *Geist*, with each major civilization we have come closer to the realization of our universality. The Hegelian totality must be understood in the negative sense, that is, as the absence of obstacles. In this sense, through the totality the subject, the singular, becomes free, and only through the free subject can the totality be actualized. That is the reason Hegel tries to classify each canon according to its recognition of individual freedoms. For instance, he considers Occident Christianity more advanced than Islam, and Lutheranism more than Catholicism (Hegel 2001: 374, 435–46). Hegel measures historical progress on the basis of intellectual capacity for abstraction and, thus, the recognition of the free human subject.[1] Every violence against a singular is violence committed against the process of the actualization of the universal. Thus, the Hegelian totality should be seen as the antipode of totalitarianism, and the Hegelian teleology as the negation of theology whose orientation is inherently backward and whose end goal is to return to the prehuman—readmission to the pre-fall realm that stands outside historical time. Hegel's enthusiastic endorsement of Napoleon is grounded in his universalist philosophy of history, the basis on which he celebrates the state, as the rational guarantor of the universality of individual freedom.

However, Hegel's philosophy of history is not Hegelian enough. That is, it was still operating in an idealist orbit situating itself outside the laws of gravity. Marx's critique of the Hegelian philosophy of history could be interpreted as a spatial critique of a system that lacks spatiality in every sense. In his lectures on the philosophy of history, Hegel spends most of the time comparing cannons and religious traditions without an actual critique of religion as such from the point of view of a philosophy that is conscious of its own temporospatial limitations, and Marx blames Hegel's disciples for further absolutizing Hegelian idealism (Marx 1994: 27–31).

Hegel breaks history into stages of the realization of *Geist*, ending with German Reformations and the Prussian state, while for Marx class is the central concept, allowing for a universal history that is incomparably more concrete than the Hegelian system. Hegel and other German idealists and theologians were caught up in a virtual world entirely of the creation of their own fancy. The more they engaged in philosophical projects to appropriate their predecessors, the more sophisticated their self-created maze became. Feuerbach asks the basic question of "why should I not be able to start from Being itself; i.e., real Being," as opposed to "the notion of Being or abstract being?" (1972).

Feuerbach's critique of Hegel is also a powerful exposure of the metaphysical nihilism that shapes all religious belief systems and most of philosophy since the demise of the Ancient Greek world. This nihilism takes off the moment "nothingness" comes into the language as an essential subject of metaphysics, including pantheist metaphysics across theologies and philosophies. The term "nothingness" was employed within thought systems that are necessarily based on representation, so it has been used as if it designated something or an actual state of being even though the idea is that "nothingness" is the negation of being. Absence or lack is a sensual state that is more descriptive of the subject than the world outside her mind. Yet, nothingness is comprehended as absence or lack. That is not to say, it is possible to think of nothingness in any other way, and that is the problem. The moment we think we are thinking nothingness, we are thinking of something, which is not nothing.

Not only did entire traditions from Buddhism to monotheism fall into this fallacy, but also metaphysics across ages and traditions got caught up in this *duality* of existence and nothingness. This duality is presupposed in the Hegelian dialectics from the first moment. It is also presupposed in the myths of creation, reincarnation, divinities, and all that falls under monotheism. Feuerbach creates a powerful disruption allowing for a return of philosophy to reclaim all its theologically occupied territories. "Nothingness is the limit of reason," Feuerbach states. That is exactly why, he argues, when we say someone "knows nothing" we simply mean the person *does not know anything*. To think nothing can only mean no thinking. Every attempt to think of "nothing" is already thinking of *something* (Feuerbach 1972).

Feuerbach concludes, "And what after all is nothingness if not a ghost haunting the speculative imagination? It is an idea that is no idea, a thought that is no thought, just as a ghost is a being that is no being, a body that is no body" (1972). The problem of the idealist self-delusion is located here. The imagined is confused for a more-than-a-mere-mental-existence of an entity. When challenged, the entity's existence in the imagination is used as proof for the objective existence of the entity. Over the ages, layers upon layers of complexities are added to imagined entities and their imagined worlds. Philosophy too was caught in this business of manufacturing representations that do not represent anything, but intersubjective hallucinations communally sustained and ideologically perpetuated in the interest of a system whose survival is dependent on the irrationality of people, a system of rationalized irrationality and justified injustices. The existence of God is absolutely necessary for the existence of entire social systems of enslavement. In fact, colonialism would have been impossible without utilizing religion in the campaigns to submit the colonized, and, as we all know, colonialism was essential in creating the global system of capitalism and sustaining it for so long.

Marx writes:

In truth, Hegel has done nothing but resolve the constitution of the state into the universal, abstract idea of the organism; but in appearance and in his own opinion he has developed the determinate reality out of the universal Idea. He has made the subject of the idea into a product and predicate of the Idea. He does not develop his thought out of what is objective [*aus dem Gegenstand*], but what is objective in accordance with a ready-made thought which has its origin in the abstract sphere of logic. It is not a question of developing the determinate idea of the political constitution, but of giving the political constitution a relation to the abstract Idea, of classifying it as a member of its (the idea's) life history. This is an obvious mystification. (1970: Part 1a)

In Hegel's philosophy, Marx adds, "the philosophical moment is not the logic of fact but the fact of logic. Logic is not used to prove the nature of the state, but the state is used to prove the logic" (1970: Part 1a).

The state is the universality of religion matured, for Hegel. For Marx, the state is the alienation entailed in religion re-idealized. As for the dead God, money is the perfect replacement, the new God in terms of both the fetish and the power of purity (as abstract value) and purity of power (as capital). Therefore, for Marx, while all critique starts from the critique of religion, critique must focus on the state. In every step, Hegel ends with the ideal; to Marx the human is the root of the human, and the universality must be driven from concrete reality, not metaphysics. Thus, it makes sense that Marx replaces the idealist and tribalist notion of nation with the materialist and universalist concept of class. "Nation" is the outcome of a mentality that has been theologized, mystified, for ages whereas "class" is a concept created by an anti-theological philosophy, a rebellious philosophy of praxis aimed at revolution to change the material conditions of life and thought, to emancipate the human potential for imagination and transform it from an enslaving subjective power to an emancipating force.

Marx's appropriation of Hegel's philosophy amounts to putting everything in sociological terms or translating the philosophy into concrete and concretizing praxis as it takes place in the actual living circumstances of actual humans. In claiming that the history of humanity is the history of class antagonism, Marx simultaneously secularizes history and universalizes thought. With Marx, philosophy declares independence from theology by emancipating its subject matter from the mazes that had been formed throughout generations of monks entertaining themselves in their isolated social spaces. Of course, that is not to say philosophy has actually been emancipated. Most philosophers have chosen to be anti-Marxist, just as most scientists chose to be anti-Copernicusian for more than three centuries after Nicolaus Copernicus's death.

The Marxian move essentially overcomes the gap that had separated theory and practice ever since the human society was divided between those who work and those who manage working and its fruits. If human history is the history of class antagonism, then the only meaning of rational progress toward freedom is the movement toward the abolishment of all that prevents the opening of the human horizon in its full potentiality for actual human subjects. These actual human subjects are themselves the only actors capable of actualizing their freedom through negating all that walled them in a space of tribal/national existence. The realization of freedom simultaneously implies the negation of imposed limitations and the creation of a new reality allowing for forming personhood.

Accordingly, social movements can be situated within a continual line of struggle that goes back to ancient history. One of the manifestations of that struggle has been the enduring conflict between mentalities that gravitate toward the prototype of an antagonistic tribe and those that operate on the grounds of a more universal, which is to say broader and more inclusive, world. The only possibility for the negation of oppression is moving away from irrational-oppressive social structures toward the universality of freedom, and, therefore, in their struggles to free themselves, the oppressed simultaneously advance the historical realization of reason and human emancipation as such. We should recall Walter Benjamin's philosophy of history, as in his thesis XII:

The subject of historical knowledge is the struggling, oppressed class itself. Marx presents it as the last enslaved class—the avenger that completes the task of liberation in the name of generations of the downtrodden. This conviction, which had a brief resurgence in the Spartacus League, has always been objectionable to Social Democrats. Within three decades they managed to erase the name of Blanqui almost entirely, though at the sound of that name the preceding century had quaked. The Social Democrats preferred to cast the working class in the role of a redeemer of future generations, in this way cutting the sinews of its greatest strength. This indoctrination made the working class forget both its hatred and its spirit of sacrifice, for both are nourished by the image of enslaved ancestors rather than by the ideal of liberated grandchildren. (2006: 394)

The main point here is that contrary to Hegel's idealism it is precisely the absence of the *Absolute* that compelled human society to create a false metaphysics, mythical realm, for justice. This movement eventually led to monotheism, which in turn further delayed the universal realization of freedom and reason by taking history astray, further into a savagery that has endured from the fall of the Roman Empire to this very day. Today the violence is catastrophic on the planetary level thanks to the instrumental reason administrated by modern pragmatic politics of chauvinism embodied in nation-statism. In the absence of a universal front of the left and the rise of both Christian and Islamist fundamentalism in the form of imperial powers, we should expect the intensification of violence for a long time before human society is forced to grow out of this irrational phase. Of course, it is illusional to assume human society eventually makes the progressive move as a whole. As always, the struggle for freedom will be led by the oppressed of the oppressed.

The Marxist view of historical progress entails the dialectics of oppression and freedom. For the revolutionary subject is born out of absolute necessity, and her creation of spaces of freedom is an outcome of her previous state of unfreedom. The oppressed is left with no choice but to invent a space for life and in that invention the horizon of freedom is also crystalized. The human subject as an end in herself was not born until the Enlightenment. The realization of the universality of the singular, the individual, and the singularity of the whole, human society, is arguably the most advanced stage of humanism. If we ascribe this realization to universalism, then it is born in the Enlightenment, but the newborn is still in a critical state. While the bourgeoisie was the pioneer of the Enlightenment thought, it also became the obstacle to the realization of the Enlightenment as a cosmopolitan project of human emancipation. The bourgeoisie was the first to betray the universality of reason as freedom in favor of the universality of (instrumental) reason as capital. Two points need to be kept in mind here. First, the industrial-technological applications of reason for the sake of the continual accumulation of capital and fortifying class institutions, such as the state, diametrically contradict the universality of reason, on which the emancipatory aspect depends. Second, holding on apparatuses of oppression, regardless of the degree to which scientific methods are employed, necessarily fragments reason in both form and content, universality and emancipation.

From its historical formation starting in the sixteenth century, there were two determining, and for the most part opposing, lines of evolution within the bourgeoisie. The first one is capitalist through and through. In other words, all the social and political changes it brings about are driven by the maxim of capital itself. That is to say, whatever is needed to ensure the continual growth of capital is deemed necessary socially, politically, morally, and even metaphysically. The expansion of the so-called free market, development of the means of transportation to and from sources of raw materials and cheap labor, modernizing military, socializing literacy, democratizing political administration are just a few broad examples of changes put in motion by the requirements of the capitalist political economy. Indeed, we see all these changes starting to take place in Britain and pioneered by the British long before other places, including France. In fact, the strictly capitalist component of the bourgeois revolution, the brutish line of modernity, can justifiably be called British.

The second defining line of modernity or the bourgeois (r)evolution, on the other hand, is primarily French and it is centered around fidelity to political liberalism or republicanism. Undoubtedly, the French Revolution of 1789 is the most definitive moment of the historical triumph of the bourgeoisie's *political* revolution. Of course, the bourgeoisie in both Britain and France share the same worldview and enterprise insofar as feudalism is concerned, but the British–French conflict throughout modernity can be interpreted in terms of the conflict between the two poles of the bourgeoisie: the first is motivated by capital but also adopts policies of social and political liberalization; the second is motivated by political emancipation but also adopts capitalist policies. Here it is worth quoting Eric Hobsbawm on the French Revolution of 1789:

> In the second place it was, alone of all the revolutions which preceded and followed it, a mass social revolution, and immeasurably more radical than any comparable upheaval. It is no accident that the American revolutionaries, and the British "Jacobins" who migrated to France because of their political sympathies, found themselves moderates in France. Tom Paine was an extremist in Britain and America; but in Paris he was among the most moderate of the Girondins. The results of the American revolutions were, broadly speaking, countries carrying on much as before, only minus the political control of the British, Spaniards and Portuguese. The result of the French Revolution was that the age of Balzac replaced the age of Mme Dubarry. (1996: 52)

For the British version of the bourgeois world, the market is sacred whereas in the French formula of the new world it is the republic that embodies the will of the people. Even in their colonies, the distinction is clear. The British concentrated on putting in motion the most efficient systems of extraction and transportation of raw materials and labor by all means possible including colonialism and slavery. The French, even in their bloody wars of colonialism saw themselves as missioned revolutionaries of the Enlightenment. In this regard, one cannot help but notice the vast Napoleonic projects of constructing systems of information and socialization of knowledge. However, we should be careful not to exaggerate the significance of this bifurcated aspect of the European bourgeoisie if for nothing else because eventually each line implies and imposes what the other stands for. Nonetheless, I think making this distinction may shed some light on continuities and discontinuities, potentialities and deadlocks, horizons of freedom and dams of totalitarianism, universalism and nationalism that are entailed in what Horkheimer and Adorno (2004) called the "dialectic of Enlightenment." In addition, the conclusion I want to underline is that the French Revolution represents a leap in revolutionary action insofar as it realized the inherent universality of reason and inevitable rationality of emancipation. At its brightest moment of truth, it was a universalist enterprise in the precise sense of rejecting chauvinistic frames of reference which were on the rise as the Christian hegemony and its claim of universality were deteriorating, allowing for the formation of new, fragmented, identities.[2] The Enlightenment as a revolution was the exact antipode of what became Eurocentrist imperialist ideologies that, whether implicitly or explicitly, are premised on global tribalism.

Global tribalism is sectarian and reactionary, but it imposes its in-group as the neutral and historically most sophisticated human being. It presents its tribalist application of violence as a strategy of human emancipation. Just like Christian and Islamic claims of universality, it abstracts its in-group as "the human" and the "enlightened" as opposed to out-groups who have failed to meet the criterion of the universal, the human proper, the saved or enlightened. Augustine starts his *City of God* with a long account explaining the fall of Rome as something that was bound to happen because of the Romans' false gods. For instance, he begins Chapter 32 with the following words, "If, then, there remains in you sufficient mental enlightenment to prefer the soul to the body, choose whom you will worship" (1871: 44). Similarly, in his *Confessions*, Augustine frequently defines absolute truth in terms of God as "true Light." Therefore, to Augustine faith is essentially the universal criterion for and the goal of the human elevation. Augustine writes,

> But the Word, who is himself God, is the true Light, which enlightens every soul born into the world. He, through whom the world was made, was in the world, and the world treated him as a stranger. But I did not find it written in those books that he came to what was his own, and they who were his own gave him no welcome. But all those who did welcome him he empowered to become the children of God, all those who believe in his name. (2003: vii)

In the Islamic tradition, the pre-Islamic history of Arabia is called "the age of ignorance" (*al-jahiliya* in Arabic). Also, those who are not members of "The nation of Mohammad" are considered "ignorant" by definition simply because enlightenment would entail believing in Mohammad's message, the message of universal light. Indeed, the Quran uses the Arabic word for light, *nwr*, in reference to knowledge, goodness, and most importantly God's revelation of the divine truth to the world as in *nwr li-al-alameen*. There, dichotomy of light versus darkness occupies a symbolic yet obvious referential role as the locus of all the other signifiers of the metaphysical bifurcation of truth–falsehood or good–evil.

While the "light" symbolism is easily traceable to Christianity and Judaism, we should keep in mind that there is an older history of the light–truth–goodness metaphysics that dates back to Zoroastrianism, the first known monotheistic theological system where light is in fact the most central symbol. In fact, the name of the Zoroastrian God, *Ahura-Mazda*, already contains a variation of the word fire—*Ahur*. Some Kurds still use that word for fire while other Kurds use *Agir*. In Hindi and Urdu it is *aag*, Punjabi *aga*, Persians *Atash*. Azeri belongs to a different linguistic family than that of the languages mentioned above, yet its word for fire is even more central. In fact, *Azer* is the word for fire, and Azerbaijan, literally means the "land of fire." It is also worth mentioning that the Zoroastrian temple is called *atashgah*, which literally means "fire-place." In most of the Zoroastrian archeological sites the *atashgah* could easily be recognized.[3]

Of course, it was, and still is, a long way before we revolutionize the material conditions for the actualization of human freedom, yet it is worth noting that it is the French Enlightenment to which Marx, Engels, Lenin, Trotsky, Mao, Che, and other Marxists would speak. In fact, it is the French Revolution that gave birth to modern "left" and "right," not to mention the modern concept of revolution. It was the first moment in Europe's history when the miserable actively and consciously mobilized to change the course of their own history qua human beings entitled to dignity and freedom. Of course, the bourgeoisie played a leading role in the revolution, but it became the counterrevolutionary front to limit the transformation and, most importantly, produce what would become modernism's bloodiest ideology, which is nationalism. At its birth, the republic is a revolutionary project of emancipation. Then, it becomes an empire backed by popular mobilization inevitably entering an existential war against the old regimes in Europe. The tension persists even after the French conquests are undone from Russia to Italy. Hobsbawm (1996) is justified to call the fifty-nine years that separate 1789 and 1848 "the age of revolution." In fact, even the 1848 revolutions could be seen as the continuation and ultimate spread of the 1789 Revolution across Europe. Just as the progressive movements that emerged from the marginalized in Europe were struggling against the new ruling groups, those who were most brutalized by the French colonizers and enslavers outside Europe created a decisive struggle for emancipation. More specifically, in St. Domingue, later Haiti, where a slave economy had been established under the French rule, the first true universalist revolution took place. Thus, the Haitians should have been credited for the first universalist revolution to abolish domination unconditionally and uncompromisingly. This is also the main thesis Eduardo Grüner advances in his book on the Haitian Revolution (2020). Grüner does not stop at drawing attention to this significant omission in the history of the Enlightenment, but rather he sets out to investigate the ideological/racist reasons behind the omission (2020).[4]

By the mid-1800s there were already multiple fronts of a bloody conflict between various forces, new and old, imperial and national, right and left.

However, one thing became very clear: the torch of Enlightenment project was in the hands of the radical left who had been in a decisive struggle against not only the imperial dynasties but also the nationalists, not only the Christian influence across the continent of Europe including Russia but also the powerful bourgeoisie that was about to reshape the world through complex enterprises of bureaucratization of the state and standardization of the social space. Just as Marxist communism was about to emerge in Europe with its famous declaration of the immanent collapse of capitalism (per the *Communist Manifesto*), bourgeois imperialism was taking off in all directions. In the meantime, even before the proletariat learned about its name, not to mention its revolutionary task, romanticism provided nationalists and all local chauvinists with what would function as a new religion, another virtual space for salvation, another opium to push the newly born masses into a mental spider net for generations to come.[5] The republic is reborn at a vivid moment in 1871 as a "social republic." Most importantly, the Paris Commune aspires to accomplish the ultimate goal of emancipation, yet immediately the bourgeoisie intensifies its efforts and former enemies, the Prussian state and the Versailles government, join arms to bury the first proletarian revolution right at its birthplace.

Romantic philosophers such as Fichte operate within a nihilist-idealist orbit that carries the same mental symptoms of religious nihilism: xenophobia in the form of extreme narcissism and irreconcilable distrust toward the world qua a space shared by the different Other, the obsession with the threatened in-group purity, and a neurotic rage against all the dazing pluralities embodied by the expanding metropoles. Therefore, the emergence of nationalism as a reactionary outcome of the Enlightenment is not any less disastrous than the emergence of theocracies at the beginning of the dark ages. Nationalism was growing in the decaying flesh of the empires just as theocracies were formed on the dead body of the Roman empire. Except, this time around the historical fall-back into sectarianism and tribalism was not completely inevitable because there was a cosmopolitan movement struggling to shape a radically different horizon in accordance with the emancipatory potential of the Enlightenment.

Universalism and Culturalism

In Europe, 1848 was the turning point between the cosmopolitan movement led by the marginalized, who were aware of the fact that the only possibility of one's emancipation is the emancipation of the human subject as such, everywhere and forever. The birth of the Marxian communist project from the end of the 1840s and its growth to the end of the century and into the new century is something unprecedented in history. In 1848, things could have taken a different direction, but the reactionaries prevailed for the most part and nationalism leaped forward in terms of its hegemony. The loss of the Paris Commune was arguably inevitable, but it marked another tragic setback to the other dream, the dream of the Enlightenment taken into its full realization. It would take another generation before hope is born again, but this time under even more hopeless circumstances, in Russia and the Ukrainian plains that have always been on the farthest margins of Europe. From 1842, when Marx first starts publishing at the age of twenty-two, and 1940, when Trotsky is assassinated, something extraordinary takes place. A cosmopolitan, secular, and egalitarian revolutionary movement challenges the entire social and political compositions of hierarchy across societies and continents. This communist movement refuses to recognize any borders put in place by ruling groups, whether among states, racialized categories, sanctified mythologies, traditions, social castes and classes, fields of knowledge, or mental versus physical labor.

While the Enlightenment thought that had led to the French Revolution was for the most part shaped by thinkers who were accustomed to the salons and the privileges of intellectual life, Marx and Trotsky were of a very different caliber of intellectuals. As otherwise two nameless men who were born into marginalized Jewish families within the margins of Trier, in the Prussian Rhineland and Odesa, in the Russia-ruled Ukraine, respectively, both of them were always uncompromisingly against nationalist ideologies, imperial hegemony, and religious actual and imaginary authorities. Both died in exile. Both occupied positions of leadership and relative fame but continued first and foremost as uncompromising revolutionaries seeing emancipation as inherently universal.

The same historical period can be described as the most catastrophic age, the age of imperialism, colonialism, nationalism, fascism, and countless genocides that have continued ever since. By the second decade of the twentieth century, nationalism in Europe and Anatolia reached its fascist stage of evolution culminating in the Armenian genocide between 1915 and 1922, which would set a model for the Nazis to design their "final solution" in the 1940s.[6] However, in the interwar period, the cosmopolitan project finds itself at another historical crossroad after the 1905 and 1914 failed revolutions in Russia and the 1917 October Revolution, which was immediately confronted by the Western powers, the Ottoman Turks, and the Japanese empire. Between 1919 and 1939, the confrontation between the communists and anarcho-syndicalists, on one side, and nationalists, including fascists on the other side, was at its peak. All we need to remember is some of the confrontations in different parts of Europe, including Italy, Hungary, Spain, and Germany.

When Trotsky was killed, the fascists had already won the war in Spain; Stalin had wiped out all the influential leaders of the 1917 October Revolution, and the Nazis had already constructed the Auschwitz camps. In the post-Second-World-War years, it became clear that between Stalin and the Western powers, there was little hope for the cosmopolitan project to be victorious, but that was exactly the time when the struggle exceeded the borders of Europe to reach Africa, Asia, and Latin America. Wave after wave of communist revolutionary movements were reinvented by former colonized peoples from China, westward, to Chile. These movements were not restricted by any means to certain societies with particular cultural or religious backgrounds. The communist movement was just as strong in the Muslim majority Indonesia as it was in the Catholic majority Cuba.

However, wherever the communist movement emerged, liberal capitalist countries spared nothing to crush them. The anti-communist policies of the West were direct contributors to the rise of both nationalist and religious fascism from Indonesia, Pakistan, and Afghanistan to various parts of the Middle East including Iraq, Iran, and Syria. It is common knowledge now that the United States regularly supported military regimes against left leaning movements and governments, including but not limited to Pakistan, Afghanistan, Iran, Turkey, Iraq, South Africa, The Democratic Republic of the Congo, Mexico, Cuba, Chile, and Guatemala. Of course, the Soviet Union had its share of supporting bloody dictatorships from its satellite states in Eastern Europe to the Baathist Syria and Iraq, and the Nasserist Egypt. In fact, a case could easily be made that Stalin's regime alone murdered more communists than any other regime, not to mention that regimes that were supported by Stalin also had a major role in wiping out revolutionary communists in their respective countries.

By the end of the Cold War, the communist project had been all but embodied in a universal front. Even worse, nationalism and religious fundamentalism were on the rise while neoliberalism replaced what was left of the universal ideals of liberalism. Since the early 1990s, just as everything started to get much worse in terms of the prospects of equality, the concept of class suddenly began to disappear from the public sphere across regions and societies. As more and more people gave in to the triumph of neoliberalism, a new set of terms were adopted by international organizations, universities, TV shows, daily newspapers, and, even more disturbingly, the activists and intellectuals of the marginalized peoples themselves. As if suddenly the basic needs of people became secondary to all social and political questions and struggles.

At the center of the new discourse in the age of neoliberalism is the term "culture." The danger of the rise of culturalism and the demise of universalism is well expressed by Berardi as he writes, "when relativism becomes culturalism, when belonging is mistaken as the foundation of law ('memory is right'), when workers' internationalism is defeated, modern universalism dies, and Humanism dies with it. Only the global, idiotic proliferation of particularities remains: crime and suicide" (2015: 129). Everyone is talking about culture as if that mysterious term explains people's lives, histories, behavior, goals, and whatever else one could not understand. In fact, there is barely any need to try to understand anything about "other" societies; all one needs to do now is to recognize that they have their own cultures. Even liberation movements are now depicted, at best, as movements that demand "cultural rights." Even those who are impoverished and systematically criminalized based on their racial identity adopted the language of culturalism. The spokespersons of survivors of genocides, such as native Americans and Australians—the majority of whom had been Christianized, impoverished, criminalized, and socially devastated due to the ongoing colonial policies—speak in terms of cultural identity, for example, "our culture." If all this shows one thing it is the degree to which the dominant ideology has been internalized by the dominated. Therefore, the ideological crisis of the present moment is just as problematic as the ecological crisis. In order for any hope to be concretized, this ideological crisis needs to be addressed head-on. In the rest of this chapter, I will give a concise account of the absurdity of culturalism and the ways in which culturalization of non-whites are committed by both whites and non-whites.

Culturalism is an essentializing mentality that perceives humans as homogeneous groups classified based on their "cultures," in the anthropological sense of the word which has typically been used in relation to non-Europeans/non-white peoples. It is a normalized ideological form that commits racist dehumanization of the Othered using a seemingly humane (non-racist) language. Culturalization can therefore be defined as the discursive processes of essentializing and anthropologizing the Othered other, denying her personhood insofar as being a person entails autonomous capacities, such as free will and reason, that is, individuality. To culturalists, a set of perceived cultural practices are ontologically definitive of the identities of all the members of the taxonomized population, which could be as small as a "tribe" or as large as the inhabitants of an entire continent.

Culture is an ambiguous term, but the ambiguity fades away in the racial context of the discourse. When it is used in reference to white people, it refers to the aggregate of artistic affluence of, say, a city or a region. It could also be used in the gentlest possible sense to refer to refined palate, artistic literacy, and civilized manners. It is all that has to do with appearance such as learnable, improvable, actable forms of speech, clothing, and bodily manners in harmony with the particularities of the social space.

On the other hand, when the term "culture" is used in relation to a non-white people, the exact opposite of the first meaning is intended. It refers to a set of taxonomic characteristics that are prehistorically or ahistorically determined, eternally determining, and internally homogenizing.

Because culture is assumed to be the most determining factor of the identity of a non-white population, non-white individuals are treated as if they lack personhood. That is to say (presumed) homogeneous cultural practices are thought to be ontologically definitive of the identities of all the members of the entire population. What is this black box that both mystifies and oversimplifies the perceived identity of a population sometimes as large as the inhabitants of an entire continent? Culture is depicted on other perceived collective identities, such as national, racial, and religious, which are themselves extremely problematic as mythologies constructed for hegemonic purposes. Culturalization, in short, is an ideological tool utilized for the purpose of dehumanizing the othered Other through processes of homogenization of societies, essentialization of perceived values, and depoliticization of all that is political.

Culturalism: A Form of Racism

Just as "race," in its modern sense, was invented by Europeans to perpetuate and legitimize various forms of inequality, colonialism, and imperialism, "culture" has been universalized as a definitive feature of all non-white peoples. This prompted some critical theorists to coin "cultural racism," to refer to a form of new racism that primarily replaced "race" with culture after the Second World War, when it became too problematic to adopt the notion of "race" as a scientific term (Wright 1998: 10). However, the politically correct move did not come about to end racism but rather to allow for its continuation. This argument is fleshed out very well in several works (for instance, see Balibar 1991; Bonilla-Silva 2003; Žižek 2008b; Lentin 2014; Rodat 2017), but the new form of racism remains extremely dominant in and outside the academy. It is among the most liberally thrown around terms, and for some reason used in relation to the non-white Other. Indeed, Raymond Williams (1983) figured out that culture is among the most widely used words in English. Ironically, the only concrete inference of this study by Williams is that culture does not seem to designate anything given its conflicting and vague uses. Žižek in a book titled *Violence* (2008b) flushes out the ways in which "culture" has been used in the neoliberal era to depoliticize everything that has to do with the miserable state of the world under capitalism especially after the 1980s and the fall of the Eastern bloc. David Harvey too identifies the phenomenon of absolutizing cultural identities as one of the features that defined the rise of neoliberalism (2007: 42, 47, 50).

However, despite these significant critiques, culturalism as a reactionary ideological crisis or as an anti-emancipatory neoliberal enterprise has not been problematized widely enough to be delegitimized at least among the left. Effectively, culturalism has been incomparably more devastating than old racism in terms of weakening internationalism. Recall, Lenin's Asianic family background was barely an issue for the internationalist revolutionaries of the first half of the twentieth century. If Lenin emerged in our time, early twenty-first century, his revolutionary project would be culturally reduced into something easily dismissible (if not criminalized, echoing what right-wing historian and Nazi apologist Ernst Nolte did). The irony is that in the name of recognizing differences, culturalism has particularly targeted non-whites and effectively tribalized everyone thereby, by default, racially attributing the universalist quality to whiteness (more on this later in this chapter). Zygmunt Bauman touches upon this covert aspect of culturalism:

Identification is also a powerful factor in stratification; one of its most divisive and sharply differentiating dimensions. At one pole of the emergent global hierarchy are those who can compose and decompose their identities more or less at will, drawing from the uncommonly large, planet-wide pool of offers. At the other pole are crowded those whose access to identity choice has been barred, people who are given no say in deciding their preferences and who in the end are burdened with identities enforced and imposed by others; identities which they themselves resent but are not allowed to shed and cannot manage to get rid of. Stereotyping, humiliating, dehumanizing, stigmatizing identities. (2004: 38)

Thus, culturalism is essentially a Eurocentric invention aimed at preserving the myth of white supremacy using discursive tools compatible with the post-Nazi democracy in the West, whereby race is affirmed, and racism is denied, instead of a climate in which race should be seen as a fiction and racism as a reality in need of confrontation. The racists of the Jim Crow era openly discriminated against non-whites and defined whiteness in terms of the pureness of blood, which in turn designated every Black ancestry as an irreversible case of biological contamination (resulting in the loss of the purity required for the status of whiteness). The Nazis, similarly, divided the world according to their dichotomy of Aryan versus non-Aryan. In both cases, culture was seen as a subcategory of race, and racial superiority entailed cultural superiority as a matter of course. In the post-Second-World-War era, "culture" proved to be the best candidate for democratically maintaining the racist discrimination against all non-whites. The discursive move is not complicated on its fundamental level. Namely, the taxonomical term of race lost too much of its currency to be used as an essentialist "type" for deducing categories of hierarchical human classification; instead, "culture" could function perfectly for that purpose. Consequently, instead of speaking as if race determines the essence of human groups and therefore their values, mental capacities, civilizational potentialities, and so on, today's racists from liberals to neo-Nazis use "culture" as a taxonomic class for essentializing Othered populations. Muslimness, for instance, functions better than Arabness to essentialize Arabs in a politically correct manner. In fact, a cultural label even further simplifies the task of categorization and essentialization for the sake of Othering. To stick with the same example, Muslimness is used as well to swiftly group many other peoples who would otherwise, that is, under the rules of racial racism, necessitate more subcategories of non-whites, such as Iranians, Turks, North Africans, and so on. Of course, thanks to this simpler form of racism, not surprisingly, in today's West, Muslimness is seen exactly as a race, as an identity determined by birth and ancestry. In fact, it is common for the highly educated in the West to confuse between Arabness and Muslimness, an "ethnicity" versus a religious belief—not that "ethnicity" is any less problematic than "race," but I simply do not have the space to go into that.

Sherene Razack, a professor at the University of Toronto, explains the racist function of the paradigm of culture very well:

Indeed, the notion of culture that has perhaps the widest currency among both dominant and subordinate groups is one whereby culture is taken to mean values, beliefs, knowledge, and customs that exist in a timeless and unchangeable vacuum outside of patriarchy, racism, imperialism, and colonialism. Viewed this way, culture maintains "a superautonomy that reduces all facets of social experience to issues of culture." (2001: 58)

Another excellent account of cultural racism is that of Philomena Essed:

This difference in the application of cultural determinism is not an ad hoc phenomenon. It is highly functional in the culturalization of racism. *To proceed from "race" to "culture" as the key organizing concept of oppression, the "other" must be culturalized. In that process the concept of "culture" is reduced to (perceptions of) tradition as cultural constraints. Cultural hierarchies are constructed and sustained, but the dominant culture is never made explicit.* Instead dominant group members appeal to the higher order of "ethos" and "knowledgeability" to assert that their version of reality is superior because it is not affected by any cultural constraints, such as cultural bias. (1991: 171; italics added)

Susan Wright provides a brief historical overview of the emergence and development of the current anthropological notion of culture in the academy. The following passage from Wright's article is of utmost significance:

Although anthropologists have developed new ways of thinking about "culture," these "old ideas of culture" have percolated out from academic discourse and, as will be shown below, are still in widespread use in public parlance. The main features of this, still-current "old idea of culture" are:

- bounded, small scale entity
- defined characteristics (checklist)
- unchanging, in balanced equilibrium or self-reproducing
- underlying system of shared meanings: "authentic culture"
- identical, homogenous individuals. (1998: 8)

We should also keep in mind Wright's following observation:

New Right authors seem to agree with the idea that the world can no longer be seen as a mosaic of discrete cultures, and that migration and diaspora have generated populations with multifaceted differences. They appropriated the anti-racist language about the need to respect cultural difference. This did not mean that they rejoiced in cross-cutting differences and fluid identities, or celebrated the creativity inspired by such hybridity, as Hall enjoined (1993). Instead, *they inverted this meaning of "difference."* They opposed the dilution of separateness which Hall relished, and *turned difference into an essentialist concept to reassert boundaries: the distinctiveness of Englishness must be defended.* (1998: 10; italics added)

Culturalism is not merely the continuation of racism with good intentions; rather, it is advanced racism with ideological and political consequences far more advantageous for Eurocentrism. After the Second World War, many European elites realized that "race" is no longer a viable concept because of an array of both political and scientific reasons, but they did not stop believing in it. The belief that there is a fundamental division between Europeans and non-Europeans had been so deeply rooted in their perception of the world that they could not question the validity of racism or simply stop perceiving the world in terms of the white versus non-white dichotomy. Thus, neither epistemically nor politically has any improvement taken place due to replacing race-talk with culture-talk. In fact, the new form of racism has been extremely more effective in mystifying and dehumanizing the Other and thereby denying her every attribute of human personhood, including the capacity to autonomous reasoning and pursuit of freedom and prosperity. Above all, culturalism, unlike racial racism, is impossible to invalidate. Racial racism was a scientific hypothesis, so its invalidation was bound to happen as soon as the disadvantaged put their hands on some means of conducting scientific research and knowledge production. Refuting cultural racism, on the other hand, is as impossible as proving the inexistence of any superstitious entity, such as demons, angels, God, and so on.

To demystify culture, along with many other bourgeois means of ideological hegemony, a return to Marxism is imperative. Any serious Marxist or constructionist should know that the notion of "race" was invented in order to justify Europeans' exploitation or elimination of others, whether through colonialism, slavery, or genocide. The process was of course not so direct and simple. The dominant creates its sciences and truths according to its modes of knowledge production within the same historical process of the reproduction of its domination. To be dominant is to have the power to determine the very standards of truth, good, and beauty. Therefore, every normalized system of moral values must have a much broader, and a much less visible, epistemology at work. In order to act as if the sky is blue as a matter of fact, it is not enough to perceive the blueness of the sky. Rather, we need to live in a social world in which the blueness of sky is continually and normally assumed. The factuality of "race" therefore had to leave the stage of theories and become part of the very dominant mode of perception before it could be useful as an ideological tool for perpetuating and reproducing European domination.

To prepare for denying the Other their right to life, dignity, and land, first their humanity needs to be denied, an order of superiority–inferiority is established so that the rank of the privileged within the social order is itself the moral and rational immediacy of entitlement. The simple taxonomic formula to divide the humankind into subgroups based on their "evolution" was not a Nazi invention by any means; rather, it had been a normalized European worldview by the end of the nineteenth century. This ideology was not even an invention of politicians. In fact, as Immanuel Wallerstein explains, the academy founded an entire field of research to do just that, namely, to study non-European societies as categorically different from Europeans. That is the sole reason of the birth of anthropology. Because the premise of anthropology is racist, it only made sense for it to form theories that are inherently racializing and reach conclusions that reaffirm the racist worldview. Anthropology borrowed "race" from biological taxonomy to create its most fundamental notion even before setting out to study primitive populations that resided outside Europe. As for the races that had proved to have evolved beyond savagery at some point in their history, such as Egyptians and Chinese, Orientalism was founded while anthropology stayed crucially relevant in those cases as well (Wallerstein 2006: 7–9). Thus, "race" was forced into being for the express purpose of designating non-European groups vis-à-vis Europeans as a group/class.

"Culture" too, in its newer sense, is a product of anthropology even though the first anthropologists who adopted it did so precisely to refute the earlier anthropologist accounts that viewed non-Europeans as savages, that is, culture-less when "culture" is used to mean valuing arts and literature and possessing refined taste and manners. The founder of cultural anthropology, Edward Burnett Tylor, published his *Primitive Culture* in 1871 to tell the world a primitive tribe indeed has its own culture, only with a limited evolution. This thesis was received to be groundbreaking in its humanist motives and potentiality. However, instead of de essentializing the Other, an essentializing meaning was assigned to "culture." Culture began to become a dominant paradigm to encompass the entire value system, way of being, way of life, belief system, or in one word, "identity" of any human group perceived by white elites as a collective, which could be as small as a "tribe" of a few hundred members or as large as the population of a country such as China, a region such as the Middle East, or even an entire continent in the case of Africa.

Thus, "culture" became a term with two opposing meanings: the old socio-aesthetic versus the new essentializing meaning. In the first sense, it is used to designate the unique effort to sublime, to rise above nature. The second sense, on the other hand, is closely related to nature, rawness, primitiveness. The first emphasizes uniqueness whereas the second de-individuates, collectivizes, and homogenizes. How are we able to tell which sense is intended in any given utterance? There is no ambiguity in the context and the rule is extremely simple: the racial context determines whether the term "culture" is used in the first or the second sense. If the subject is white, the term is used in the first sense. In all other cases, usually the second meaning is intended.

The term culture in this anthropological sense gained currency during the same decades when human zoos in Europe and the United States were extremely popular. To Europeans, observing the appearance and behavior of caged individuals, couples, families, and in some cases, an entire village, must have felt like looking back in time with the same curiosity one has about any animal that appears to have something slightly more sophisticated than instincts. As a matter of fact, zoo goers today would give us a very good idea about how human zoos must have been a subject of fascination. It must be added that today's fan of cultural events is the contemporary version of the human zoo goer. As well, cultural tourism is nothing but today's version of the European "explorer" who used to go on journeys supposedly to learn about "primitives" or the Orient.

The Nazis constructed a political vision on those grounds that had more rigorous organizational aspects in terms of both scope and details than other European enterprises to colonize, exploit, enslave, and so on. Overall, social Darwinism is one of the most retrogressive steps taken by European elites who emerged directly from the womb of the Enlightenment only to reverse the brightest aspect of the entire project to a mythology no less fictitious than the superstitions of the dark ages, only empowered with steam engines and the utilitarian formula of total control. It took the Second World War to take human zoos out of business, but it is extremely naive to assume that the Eurocentric perception of the non-European has changed drastically just because the Nazis lost the war. For the most part, the same racist worldview has endured—only the term "race" is replaced with "ethnicity" or "culture" and the explicit claims of hierarchy are made less often in the public sphere as a matter of political correctness. Nonetheless, the old anthropological and orientalist lenses are still at work in the academy and beyond. What further solidified cultural racism are two main factors. First, the internalization of the culturalist assumptions by the many non-European elites, including scholars, who then played a key role in disseminating culturalism in their societies of origin as well. Second, the conservative and reactionary movements from the global South who found in culturalism an effective tool to justify their anti-Enlightenment sentiments in the name of resisting Western hegemony. That is to say, they adopted the worst reactionary ideological creature of Western hegemony precisely to legitimize their rejection of everything that is emancipatory whether within the Enlightenment project or beyond. No wonder the stars of nationalist fascism and religious imperialism speak the same anti-imperialist language of the dogmatic left in the West. No wonder many Western leftists are allying with the fatal enemies of the left in the Middle East and North Africa, in the name of resisting American imperialism.

The same mentality makes it almost impossible for a Westerner to imagine feminist movements from the Middle East that are non-Islamic or anti-Islamic—even though if we take Iran for instance, almost all militant opposition parties reject the Islamic gender roles and in many cases are card-holding atheists with a strong women presence in their ranks. The most popular movement of resistance among Kurds in Turkey and Syria adopts a feminist philosophy called jinology (jin means woman in Kurdish), which is openly atheist in its theory of history and system of education.

We need to keep in mind that not all racists were Nazis, which is to say not all those who bought into the objectivity of "race" as a biological concept were guilty of evil doing. Nonetheless, they were all committing the same fallacy. That same fallacy is still committed, but under another illusionary notion: culture. Today's white-supremacists, neo-Nazis, and neo-fascists are culturalists. Therefore, it is another illusion to think culturalism would solve even the moral problems of old racism.

The most fundamental problem with old racism is the factual falsehood. Therefore, even if we make the naive assumption that ideological hegemony of capitalism has nothing to do with racism, the moral problem is a consequence of the false perception/depiction of reality. In fact, the moral justification of forms of subordination during the eras of modern slavery and European colonialism was grounded on the assumed factuality of "race." However, the paradigm of "culture" has accomplished the ultimate goals of racism much more effectively than the biological notion of "race."

It was precisely the scientific claims about race that made its refutation feasible (on scientific bases). By grounding itself on biology, racial racism made the task of exposing its fictionality quite inevitable. Namely, all we needed to do to refute it was to turn to biology itself, that is, by conducting good biological research on the human genes. The same thing cannot be said about cultural racism. How can "culture" be refuted as a fictional notion? The fact that culture is a product of the so-called social sciences makes it impossible to refute. We could prove that there is no correlation between skin color and mental capacities of humans, but how can we prove the same thing about a loose notion such as culture?

There is hardly any way to prove the fictionality of "culture" because it is in the first place based on a fictional foundation borrowed from old anthropology and orientalism. The culturalization of the entire regimes of knowledge production has neoliberal capital behind it directly hegemonizing the paradigm of culture across societies. In today's Western universities, arguing that culture is a fiction, a pseudo-scientific notion, that it designates nothing other than an illusion in the minds of those who take it for granted, is analogous to arguing against biblical astronomy in the Medieval universities of Europe. Nonetheless, as part of the same long struggle against superstitions, revolutionary critique remains to be essential for defeating the irrational regimes of truth. By the same token, emancipatory movements should squarely reject the tribalizing paradigm of culture as inherently colonial, racist, and reactionary.

Neoliberalism recognizes a form of diversity, namely cultural diversity, that is inherently homogenizing and, thus, exclusionary. If the identities of all Chinese are reduced to a single cultural identity, every Chinese person is effectively denied subjecthood, that is, the entitlement of being an autonomous subject. When the Chinese, along with, say, Indians, Arabs, Africans, Mexicans, and so on, are included via representations of their assumed cultures, all Chinese peoples, along with Indians, Arabs, Africans, Mexicans, and so on, are in effect being excluded through false inclusion. The moment the left bought into this neoliberal totalitarian method of *inclusion through exclusion*, universalism was fatally betrayed in the West. The Western left's betrayal of universalism, in turn, has resulted in endless cycles of ideological crises and disastrous alliances with retrogressive forces across societies, as explained in several contexts in this book.

Some Social Symptoms of Cultural Identitarianism

The culturalist identitarian assumes that those who are defined by their collective homogeneous cultures, the non-white populations of the planet, live according to values fundamentally different from the values of the white West. For instance, it is typically assumed that the non-white Other does not care much about individual freedoms, gender equality, or even prosperity, as if non-whites do not mind being subjected to poverty, torture, and diseases. The weirdness of such presumptions held by culturalist identitarians does not invoke the need to check the accuracy of their own views of the Other; instead, the presumptions are perpetuated in an environment of performative respect. The film *Borat* (Charles 2006) is phenomenal in exposing the boundless stupidity of culturalism and its imbedded racist assumptions. Contrary to the common assumption, the movie should not be perceived as mocking the non-white Other, a man from Kazakhstan, a Central Asian country rarely mentioned even in the news. Indeed, the point the movie proves so vividly is the utter racism that hides beneath culturalism. Borat, played by Sacha Baron Cohen, repeatedly pushes the boundaries of what could reasonably be expected from a Kazakh, which could be the cultural identity of any non-Westerner as far as the tricked Americans are concerned. Repeatedly, his character is taken for a real person. What should have shocked the world is the existing prejudices among Americans. One would think there is no way on earth Borat's behavior could be believable, yet the absurdity goes on for the entire duration of the movie proving beyond any doubt that the non-white image is so weird in the culturalist ethos in the United States, no absurdity coming from the Other—including, say, defecating in a bag and bringing the shit to a dining table—would be unbelievable. The behavior might be shocking, but the shock is absorbed thanks to the black box that "culture" is imagined to be. It is worth noticing that the movie's subtitle is *Cultural Learnings of America for Make Benefit Glorious Nation of Kazakhstan*. The use of "cultural learning" could not have been more appropriate in the irony.

The problem, as seen by the conservative identitarians, is that the non-white Other represents an existential threat on the white "way of life" and resources. The nicer, more tolerant, liberal culturalist identitarian abides by the same worldview except she is tolerant of the different Other. She would say, "I like Africans" in the same way she would say "I like orange juice with my breakfast." She would say, "I love India" as if India were a cat. The problem surfaces when s/he meets the first, say, mean African or dishonest Indian. Then, the whole image of the Other is shaken. The logic at work is utterly simple. Because they are all one species, if one of them acts in a certain way, it must be indicative of the whole culture, which determines their behavior. When she knows about a criminal who happened to be an immigrant, the whole assumption about the cuteness and harmlessness of the Other starts to crumble.

When the entire non-white world is seen as a handful of species with fixed nature, it is simply outside the pool of mental possibilities to perceive the non-white Other as an individual capable of being nice, mean, honest, dishonest, conservative, progressive, and so on. Culturalism denies the othered Other any space for personhood. It is only the white who thinks and acts as an autonomous person. The Other follows the collective rules, just as an animal has a predetermined nature. One could always predict how a cat, any cat, acts in a certain situation. Similarly, the culturalist assumes the Other's behavior is collectively defined depending on where she is from.

To that degree the dominant ideology of culturalism is racist. Whether the culturalist is a liberal, libertarian, conservative, or cardholding neo-Nazi, she does not have the intellectual capacity to see non-whites as persons. Thus, prior to being a moral problem, racism is a problem of stupidity, of the intentional refusal to cultivate a basic sense of the reality. You cannot be non-racist simply by being nice to non-whites. Strictly speaking racism is an intellectual deficiency; it is just stupidity nicely packaged in various boxes depending on the marketing context.

A typical packaging of this racist stupidity is common discourses of diversity as college advertisement. If you randomly check a North American university website, it is very likely that on the main page you will see a photo of a group of students that includes different skin tones. The objective is, of course, to market the school as a diverse one. This in itself would not be problematic, but in the context where every Black person is seen as a representative of all Black people, every far Asian is seen as a representative of all Asians is inherently racist. Such diversity does not solve the problem of racism. In fact, it normalizes it.

The Other Is Deprived of Personhood

The common false belief that Westerners are individualistic as opposed to other societies, who supposedly adhere to communal values, is another manifestation of this (racist) culturalist mentality that attributes personhood only to white individuals. Because of the simplistic nature of the culturalist categories, often a white person who spends, say, a few months in an Asian or African region assumes a sort of expertise on almost everything about the people of/from that region. The unspoken assumption here is that one will fundamentally know all of "them" if one knows "their" culture. Thus, living among "them" for some time is considered sufficient to grasp how best to demonstrate respect for their weird cultural beliefs. For just as there are rules about how to behave in order not to anger a bear, there are rules regarding how to avoid offending the Other, who, like a bear, is perceived as being prone to violent outbursts if provoked. According to the culturalist mentality, those rules are all coded in culture (because culture is naturalized).

More often than not, culturalism is not based on bad intentions, but it is nonetheless always false because it is essentialist and reductionist. Even if motivated by good intentions, culturalism has two problematic tendencies: self-aggrandizement and the deprecation of the Other. The culturalist self assumes the role of a God-like subject who objectifies the Other, collectivizing and stripping "them" of their subjectivity and individuality. A statement such as "I love India" (again, as if India were a cat) is obviously made with good intentions, but that does not change anything about the fact that there is a condescending mentality behind it. The real emphasis of such statements is on the God-like, benevolent subject, who is able to love the irreconcilably different, helpless, miserable, and otherwise unlikeable Other. Such a statement reduces the individual worlds of over a billion persons to the object of the speaker's love.

Another common example is the common fixation on "helping Africa," which is arguably one of the most common missions or quests for moralist college students. Behind the presumed selflessness of the person who goes to Africa to help, there is a deep-seated self-image of the colonizer as the one who saves lost souls, civilizes savages, and enlightens minds. Africa is also imagined as the space for a quest that transforms the subject through its mysteries and adventures. It is a mythical world that the culturalist enters as an ordinary person and comes out as a hero. It is a place for exploration and exotic experiences that provide the bored tourist with personal stories to repeat for the rest of her life.

Ultimately, culturalism is an attempt to attribute an inalterable "nature" to the collective Other, just as cats and dogs have inherent natures.[7] The Other's perceived culture is assumed to function more or less in the same way as the Other's nature. Meeting a single Thai person is assumed to open a window to the culture, that is, inborn nature, of all Thai people. Learning about the Other's culture is essentially like learning about different animals. There are certain things the culturalist is told to do and not do around people from different "cultures." Again, this is directly drawn from the idea that there are specific ways to domesticate different wild animals or train different pets, because all the animals of a certain species are thought to share a nature. The culturally sensitive person who is educated by other culturalizers is taught formulas of, for instance, body language in order to send certain message to the Other, who in turn is believed to react in a certain way. In 2003 and the following years of the American invasion of Iraq, the American army hired "cultural guides" to help its soldiers deal with Iraqis in culturally appropriate ways. Thus, soldiers were told things to do and things to avoid among Iraqis. One does not need to see those lists to figure out how disturbingly Iraqis had been reduced to an oversimplified collective with the same cultural essence. It suffices to mention a few examples from *Soldier's Handbook to Iraq*, which must have been distributed to American soldiers in Iraq during the invasion. Its third section is titled, "Arab Costumes and Culture," and it includes lists of dos and don'ts in several different settings. Below are examples of two lists:

CONVERSATION

DO: Open conversation with small talk and pleasantries.

DO: Talk to an Iraqi as an equal.

DO: Maintain eye contact, but don't stare down your host.

DO: Follow the Arab's conversational lead and discuss what he brings up.

DO: Place your feet flat on the floor if you are sitting on a chair, or fold them under you if you are sitting on the floor.

DO: Attempt to use any Arabic language skills you may learn. Your attempts, however crude, are appreciated and demonstrate your willingness to adapt to a new culture. If you can recite a poem or a tongue twister, you will win esteem for your skill.

DO: Avoid arguments.

DO: Avoid discussions on political issues (national and international), religion, alcohol, total women's liberation, abortion, and male–female relationships.

DO: Bring photographs of your family during conversations.

DO: Look for subtle or double meanings in what an Arab says. Arabs often answer

indirectly.

DO NOT: Show impatience or undue haste, for example, looking at your watch when participating in discussion.

DO NOT: Ask direct or personal questions, especially about female family members.

DO NOT: Criticize an Iraqi directly. This will cause him to lose face and respect for you.

DO NOT: Patronize or talk down to an Iraqi, even if he does not speak English well.

DO NOT: Say "no" when an Iraqi asks a favor of you, or admit you do not know the answer to a question. Instead, respond with a "maybe," e.g., you'll look into it, or you need to talk it over with your superiors.

DO NOT: Move away from an Iraqi who stands close to you during conversation. It is customary for an Arab person to stand about one foot away.

DO NOT: Lose your temper and publicly embarrass anyone.

DO NOT: Try to convert a Muslim to your faith.

DO NOT: Be offended when an Arab shows great interest in your social, personal, professional, and academic background. Arabs do not enter personal or business relationships casually or lightly as we do in the western culture.

MEETINGS

DO: Arrive on time, not early.

DO: Shake hands with everyone on entering and leaving the room.

DO: Drink at least one cup of the offered beverages.

DO: Start meeting with small talk. Maintain eye contact.

DO NOT: Be totally business oriented.

DO NOT: Ask yes/no question.

DO NOT: Point the soles of your feet to an Arab when you are sitting with him. To do so implies you are placing him under your feet—an insult.

DO NOT: Expect or ask an Arab to uncover his head. (1st Infantry Division, 3.8–9)

Notably, the handbook includes historical and statistical information about the population of Iraq, which includes Muslims, non-Muslims, Arabs, Kurds, Turkmen, Assyrians, and so on, yet "Muslims," "Arabs," and "Iraqis" are used interchangeably in the section about culture. Each one of these instructions is laughable, but among the striking ironies is that it instructs its addressee to "talk to an Iraqi as an equal," as if that is also a cultural specification of Iraqis, and as if abiding by that principle does not undermine the very idea of the lists of instructions as well as the culturalizing mentality behind it. The American soldier is also being instructed not to lose his/her "temper and publicly embarrass anyone" or "patronize or talk down to an Iraqi." Would not this imply that (at least in some) other cultures it is okay to embarrass, patronize, and talk down to people?

Then there are more nuanced instructions such as, "do not Point the soles of your feet to an Arab when you are sitting with him. To do so implies you are placing him under your feet—an insult." It is not clear whether that applies to "Arab women" as well, but the exclusion of women here, and in many other instructions, might be due to the assumption that they would never be present anyway. Yet, the problem exceeds culturalism and exposes the authors' sexist chauvinism against women for they use the masculine third person pronoun to refer to "an Iraqi," which makes it clear that the authors not only abide by the perceived cultural practice of not treating women as persons but also fully accept it as a simple fact; otherwise, there would be no need to omit the female third person pronoun in a text that is meant to address other fellow Americans.

The issue of not pointing the soles of one's feet has been emphasized so often, as part of the cultural education, it is very rare to see an American official crossing legs in any picture where Iraqi men are present. The ridiculousness of this cultural education aside, apparently it did not occur to the American officials that Iraqi men and women who abide by such a cultural interpretation would also be able to realize that Americans are not Iraqis and, therefore, are not expected to know or abide by the same symbolic practices. It is equally astonishing that the instructors and decision-makers seem not to have recognized that like Americans, Iraqis would not appreciate being occupied, ordered around, interrogated, and so on. Being so obsessed by the cultural creature, the human creature in all sides is tragically violated. Thanks to such beliefs about the Other, Americans not only violated lives and dignities of millions of Iraqis but also inevitably violated their own humanity in the same process. Such violations of humanity as such evidently cause irreversible damage to the identity that goes far deeper than all patriotic or cultural identities.

Obviously, the decision-makers in the American army had been taught culturalism and were trained as culturalists in schools. School teachers and university professors are arguably most responsible for the dissemination of culturalism in the American army and beyond. Later in this chapter, I analyze a very recent example of a text written by a college professor and intellectual who virtually takes the best possible stance within culturalism, which nonetheless is a racist stance because culturalism is racism. Culturalists may respect some perceived cultural practices, but by virtue of collectivizing, essentializing, and presuming the Other's identity, they inevitably violate the core of the Other's dignity, which is first and foremost her personhood as a human subject. All that could be harmful to anyone from anywhere is only harmful insofar as it is associated with her personhood as a conscious human body.

What does not occur to the self-assured culturalizers is the possibility of the Other to have a personal take on such and such social norms, practices, beliefs, and such, which is of course always the case. Ironically, culturalizers, who are culturally sensitive people, do not know that when they treat the Other in such a simplistic way, they betray their own ignorance. Even if the culturalizer is the prime minister of the second largest country in the world, she would stand out as a fool when she attributes a cultural identity to millions of people and acts accordingly—recall Justin Trudeau's $1.5 million trip to India in February 2018, when his attempt to show cultural respect made him look more like a Shakespearian clown minus the sarcastic wisdom. Such ridiculous assumptions put culturalizers in ludicrous situations, because they have it in their minds that certain behaviors culturally guarantee the same predetermined meaning. Many have learned to brush off such weird situations created by a culturalist with some friendly laughter, even though, ironically, it is the culturalist white who treats the Other like a little child whose intentions are simple but not necessarily comprehensible for an outsider. Thus, often when a culturalist white meets a non-white, a reoccurring scene is that of both sides laughing loudly to cover up some sort of awkwardness. On a closer look, it is easy to realize the irony involved; namely, the non-white would be putting on an artificial but friendly laughter as an attempt to save the white from feeling stupid whereas the white would be laughing to make it up for messing up a proper cultural practice. The culturalist ethos is the world Borat has exposed.

In all cases, the non-white Other is assumed to be a member of a homogeneous collective with a single cultural identity, whether that be a noble-savage, authentic community living closer to nature or one of the victims who deserves sympathy. The culturalist, on the other hand, is always the provider of solutions, the benevolent moralist subject, who merely by speaking to the Other demonstrates the white virtues of modesty and open-mindedness. Of course, there are certain things, such as Yoga, that must be learned from the exotic Other, but those things are perceived as belonging to the mysteries of the East. The tourist goes for a quest and they could come back with new and exotic abilities. An acquaintance told me, "I am from India. I spent most of my life there, and I do not know what nirvana is. Yet, a white man goes to India, sits on his ass for a week, and says he reached nirvana."

The white culturalizer "loves" the Other, not because the Other deserves love, but because love (particularly undeserved) is a teeming virtue of the white. However, even when "loved," it is very important that the Other always maintains the relational order that preserves the racist white's myth of superiority and the image of the Other as a biological category. In other words, as long as the Other plays the predetermined role of a cultural bearer lacking personhood, and thereby feeds into the culturalizer's sense of self (and thus the privilege of the racist white), the culturalizer thinks of them fondly as a sort of obedient pet. On the other hand, if the Other were to show any sign of personhood, autonomy, or free individual will, this would be disturbing, and possibly threatening, to the culturalizer. Imagine the case of an immigrant who answers the question "How do you like Australia?" by stating something along the lines of "I don't like it very much. I am here because of the same reasons that drove you, your parents, or your grand or great-grand parents here."

Genuine plurality requires recognizing every individual's right to their personhood, not grouping all non-whites under cultural labels. Culturalism is deeply Eurocentric, so it cannot be a remedy for Eurocentrism. In the name of inclusivity and plurality, only whites are treated as individuals entitled to personhood. Another false premise is the assumption that non-whites desire different treatment. No! The problem of discrimination is that it is based on ideologies of inequality, whether adopted consciously or unconsciously.

We live in dark times in terms of universal fronts of struggle and solidarity among the oppressed groups. Now, more than ever we need voices of universalism that unapologetically bring the ideals of human emancipation and egalitarianism to the forefront of the political discourses of dissent. It is not a coincidence that the forces of oppression in the East, West, North, and South, including those who claim enmity toward each other, adopt the culturalist doctrine. Fascists in the Middle East perfectly fit into Western fascists' image of the Middle East, and Western fascists are similarly generalized by their Middle Eastern nemesis to demonize the West and, thus, legitimize indiscriminate violence in the form of religious terrorism.

Regardless of their intentions, those who culturalize what has become known as the Enlightenment values and attribute them exclusively to Europeans in effect deny non-Europeans both subjectivity and rationality. Whether it is done in the name of the myths of white superiority or in the name of "respecting" the uniqueness of non-Europeans, such relativization is in fact nothing but a form of absolutism. Also, it is inherently a racist mode of thought because it racializes the universal. What culturalists from both the right and left fail to realize is that those universal values have always been fought for most decisively in the margins, whether in Europe, Asia, Africa, or the Americas. Moreover, claiming that the Enlightenment values are European because they originate in Europe is not different from claiming that Europeans should not use algorithms or algebra because they were discovered by Persians and Arabs, or, even worse, that writing cannot be universalized because it is a Mesopotamian invention.

To reject the phony paradigm of culture at work in culturalization and its implicit fragmentation of peoples, a return to Marx is precisely what is needed. Obviously, there has been a widespread critique of the traditional interpretation of Marxism (i.e., the base-superstructure view of historical materialism), but it seems that the widespread culturalism and other forms of idealism had led to the other extreme pole: no weight is given to the material conditions of life as, at least, somewhat significant in determining people's ideologies. Hence, to fight off the idealist extremism of culturalism, what needs to happen is precisely a revival of the older interpretation of historical materialism, according to which culture is one of the elements of ideological superstructure, and the material conditions of life, *mainly but not entirely*, determine the ideological superstructure of every society. At any rate, it takes no genius to realize that no culture in the world can make people admire poverty and violence, but poverty and violence, wherever they occur, can affect social values, ways of life, morality, politics, law, philosophy, art, education, and religiosity. Moreover, as Horkheimer and Adorno realized, under capitalism, culture is an industry the main purpose of which, besides profit, is the creation of a totalitarian unity, politically and, a fascist formula of sameness, socially. Even, or especially, the sense of individual autonomy is itself mass produced within the regime of the culture industry (see Horkheimer and Adorno 2002: 32, 94–6, 126).

PART TWO

Negations

CHAPTER SIX

Refuting the No-Alternative Rhetoric

Nihilism and the Fanatic Guardians of Reality

Today, if there is one universal political tendency, it is nihilism. Even the anti-war pacifists are long gone, and the streets and city squares in the West are turned into little more than spaces of totalitarian transparency and undisputed sacredness of private property continually protected by such police apparatuses that would have been unimaginable under any twentieth-century regime. The mantra of no alternative continues to be at the heart of the ideological distortion—except that today it is part of a common denialist position that is the cornerstone of the broader nihilism that made the unlimited hegemony of neoliberalism possible.

The rise of religious and nationalist fascism is incomparable to any moment in the twentieth century if nothing else in terms of the sheer size of the doomed populations considering that India and Brazil are already ruled by fascists, not to mention the unprecedented popularity of far right movements in the United States and Eastern European countries such as Poland and Hungary and the increasing imperialist expansion of Islamism across the Middle East and North Africa all the way to parts of east Asia. "What is the alternative," We are asked the moment we question the intolerability of the existing order, whether in terms of the ecological crisis or the other devastating crises that seem to only increase in number and intensify in devastation. Given all this, a powerful negative philosophy to counter the normalized nihilist worldview is more urgent than ever. What is at stake is the fate of life on the planet as we know it, so there is nothing more dystopian than giving in to passivity in the name of the inexistence of a viable alternative. Those who are upset about the utopianism inherent in revolutionary projects or any postnationalist movement of communism seem to dismiss the following fundamental questions.

What Is It about the Existing Reality That They Love So Much?

Even if we assume that communism does not work (whatever that means), which part of the existing reality works so well, whether rationally or morally? How could communism be more dysfunctional than a system that is rapidly heading toward the destruction of the conditions of life on the planet?

Would they, the guardians of reality, commit to being so fanatically realistic when they think of their spiritualist affiliations?

How realistic is it to hold a book that contains views and claims even a fifth grader would easily refute (outside the mystified realms imposed on her) as the source of absolute and eternal truth?

Granted, Stalinism was a nightmare that resulted from a communist movement; but what makes liberal capitalism removed from the countless fascists it produced? Granted, Mao came out of the communist movement and his party was responsible for the disastrous policies that led to famine and thus the death of millions; but should not liberal democracy be held accountable for famines that are intentionally—not by a dictator's shoddy management—created through economic embargoes imposed on entire populations?[1] If communism is forever delegitimized because of Stalin's crimes, should not liberalism be abandoned due to the fact that the largest liberal democracy is guilty of the indiscriminate use of nuclear weapons, not to mention the large number of wars liberal democracies started?

If we are expected to prefigure an alternative world system before we negate the existing conditions, why is it that the guardians of today's reality fail to imagine the fact that a century from now in this very world, the very existence of humans and millions of other species will be in fatal danger and millions of species will have already disappeared for good, according to the research conducted today by scientists who are neither revolutionary nor utopian?

What is so unrealistic about claiming that capitalism is simply not sustainable beyond this point if for nothing else but that it is rapidly exhausting the ecological conditions of life on the planet?

Why is it that we are expected to provide an irrefutably realistic image of the postcapitalist world before we can be justified in politically rejecting capitalism? How rational would it have been to expect an anti-feudalist in the early to mid-eighteenth century to predict the French republic? Has any preindustrial book, divine or not, been able to predict today's world of machines? How many formulas of electromagnetics, thermodynamics, or biochemistry have believers in the sacred books read in those books? Isn't it worth asking why it is that instead of any reference to what had not yet been discovered, including, say, Newton's laws of motion, every single sacred scripture is geographically and historically limited to the moment and place of its emergence? For instance, the Bible and the Qur'an make reference to donkeys and camels, as opposed to, say, trains and cargo ships. If nothing else, shouldn't these basic observations be seen as evidence for the validity of the Marxist philosophy of materialism, that is, the philosophy that sees history as the history of actual living beings and their actual environment?

Finally, isn't it strange that so many "ordinary" people are trained to act as the guardians of reality? These anti-revolutionary and anti-utopian guardians of reality seem to never fail to react against an egalitarian doctrine such as communism, even while spending a good deal of their time in a state of supposed freedom, numbing every possibility for thinking through the consumption of commodities of the culture industry, such as Hollywood movies, fiction, and so on precisely in order not to face the reality.

One would think such fanatic defenders of reality would have a better appetite for learning concrete facts, at least in the positivistic sense. In November 2020, about 74 million adult Americans, who apparently cannot stand the mention of socialism, freely chose to vote for a man whose respect for basic human perception, math, logical propositions, medicine, and reality as such is next to none. Yet somehow it is the Marxist who is considered utopian and unrealistic. There is not any other philosophy about which so many people have such confident opinions without ever bothering to read the texts that represent it. Everyone seems to have an opinion about Marxism, yet very few have read any portion of even the original texts by Marx.

Social Equality Is not an Ideological Invention but a Realization

Entire state apparatuses, from armed forces to educational and religious institutions, are largely devoted to the defense and management of the existing reality. Whether the arguments put forward are moralistic, political, historical, or scientistic, the ultimate goal is the ontological justification of the way things are. From Leibniz's "best possible world" to Fukuyama's "end of history," the underlined claim is that there is no alternative to the existing world. It is no wonder, then, that progressive rejection of regimes of oppression and exploitation is routinely met by the question: "What is the alternative?" This question is largely rhetorical in nature, most often used to imply that the existing world, flawed though it may be, is the best possible, thereby deflecting any serious criticism of the status quo.

Immediately after the 1990–1 events leading to the fall of the Soviet Bloc, a narrative of the ultimate historical failure of the communist project was generated and generalized. The Soviet Union collapsed inwardly under its own weight, but of course neoliberals acted as if they were the victorious party, especially in terms of writing history as a history of their own triumph.[2] Thus, even though none of the questions that gave rise to communism had been resolved, according to the new narrative, communism became a part of the irretrievable past. Neoliberals would have us believe that just like the Mesopotamian, Egyptian, and Mayan civilizations, communism is now relegated to the history books, but unlike those civilizations it was a peculiar enterprise that was doomed to vanish relatively quickly.

As if a whole canon of concepts and terminologies had been magically wiped out, as if suddenly the question of social equality and political egalitarian struggles had become forever irrelevant, the new liberal era turned out to be an era dictated by the fanatics of capitalism. Thanks to the absolutism of the free market, everything was up for grabs in a world that became a space for unlimited manipulation and exploitation by and for capital.[3] Of course, at the very head of this absolutism is an intelligentsia. Just as millions of worms might attack a body left alone and helpless in the battlefield, armies of opinion makers did everything to delegitimize the communist project. They stormed communism from every possible corner to prove that it had no chance of survival, to normalize and eternalize capital's absolutism. They simply regained full control of the platforms of the public sphere to tell the poor, exploited, dispossessed, and silenced everywhere, including in the West, in endless authoritative ways, that there is no alternative to capitalism. If we were to summarize the bourgeois intelligentsia's totalitarian campaign across academic fields and realms of public opinion making in a few sentences, it would read as something along the following lines aimed at the dispossessed:

> *It's time to wake up* and stop harboring such dangerous dreams: *haven't we always told you to be realistic, that inequality is natural and social hierarchy is crucial for all human societies? To resist capitalism is to resist human nature. Now history has taught you the lesson the hard way. Accept the reality and be happy. For in the end happiness is a state of mind. Only utopians who have no clue about reality and human nature could link happiness to social equality.*

Both the strategy and objective of such a campaign are quite straightforward. The strategy is focused on creating a universal belief about the ultimate failure of communism, and the objective is to ideologically fortify the assumed eternality of capitalism. Of course, ideological domination can neither outdate communism nor eternalize the status quo. What the neoliberal intellectuals did get right is that the endurance of communism does entail an existential threat to capitalism. Among what they missed, or pretended to miss, are two crucial facts: (i) communism is not the only existential threat to capitalism and (ii) movements shaped around some variation of social equality are bound to recur so long as inequality is a social reality.

The collapse of capitalism is not something that could be prevented indefinitely through the bourgeois domination of the modes of perception. Nonetheless, there is a world of difference between a random collapse of capitalism and a postnihilist revolutionary negation of capitalism. The former could be a precarious historical event with an infinite number of possibilities including more regression to tribalism or theocracies, as has been the case, while the latter would amount to historical progress in terms of human emancipation as a rational and attainable political objective. What makes the Marxist philosophy worth defending is precisely its comprehension of capitalism and simultaneous aim to dialectically negate capitalism in the interest of historical progress. Here, it is crucial to emphasize that what has taken place since the end of the 1980s is a totalitarian campaign against the very dreamability of social equality. What has been almost entirely destroyed is not communist societies or states (no such things have ever existed) but our ability to imagine a way out of capitalist totalitarianism and our courage to dream on rational grounds. Nothing was spared after the 1980s to, in Adolfo Gilly's words, "eradicate the idea itself of socialism in the mind and the dreams of human beings" (quoted in Traverso 2016b: 10). Generally speaking, the anti-socialist campaign has been successful so far. Nowadays, thanks to the hegemony of idealism under capitalism, even in the academy it is more acceptable to believe in a system of superstitions than it is to argue for the realizability of socialism. It is as if socialism has been a failed experiment and anything outside the logic of the total hegemony of capitalism is inherently illiberal, irrational, violent, and so on. Nothing is new in this normalized discourse of nihilism that fanatically denies every horizon of possibility for ending the enslavement of classes and societies for the sake of the endless increase of power in the hands of a small number of people. Domination and nihilism are ideologically and structurally intertwined. By the same token, an emancipatory revolution capable of ending domination in all its societal forms is postnihilist, which is to say such a revolution must be centered around perpetual negations of everything that perpetuates the state of hopelessness. While capitalism is a system of up-to-bottom privilege and exploitation of bottom-to-up, postnihilism, as an emancipatory project based on the philosophy of negativity is a democratic system of bottom-to-up across societies negating the existing spatial sanctities from up to bottom. That is to say, what is sacred in the existing order needs to be negated first, not last.

Despite the gloomy implications of the decline of revolutionary thought over the last four decades, the following two arguments, including their premises, are worth emphasizing:

1. In the most basic sense, social equality is not an invention but a realization. It is the state of being free from human-to-human exploitation, and as such its absence gives rise to its revolutionary

affirmation. Therefore, the eradication of communist ideas is simply impossible not despite but because of the capitalist conditions of social inequality. Just as slavery makes the realization and actualization of freedom from slavery inevitable, even if after thousands of years, social inequality forces human groups to realize and eventually actualize equality in the form of a negation of negation.

By the same token and in a more historically specific sense, communism is the negation of negation. It is the negation of a pathological and disaster-ridden social order, which is capitalism. Capitalism renders its own negation, and thus communism, a matter of inevitable certainty. We might swing between various forms of barbarism for a long historical period, but eventually, as a species, we are bound to make the evolutionary–revolutionary move forward unless we as a civilization do not survive the barbarian turns caused by capitalism.

2. Marxism as a socialist movement is first and foremost a movement that emerged under circumstances not of the making of the Marxists. Marxism first appeared as a practical critique and was quickly transformed to critical praxis. Both as a philosophy and a social movement, Marxism loses its power when it is detached from the act of critique. Critique is by definition negative but of course not arbitrary. Marxism as a critical theory always has its feet firmly on the ground precisely because it is a critique of not only what exists but especially what is dominant.

Now, from both lines of argumentation the following conclusion could be reached: negativity is definitive of Marxism. Marxism is constructive in terms of a communist future not despite but because of this negative character. Equally important is to comprehend Marxism's "progressiveness" in terms of its dialectical negation of capitalism. The particularity and precision (of its negative power) fundamentally differentiate it from reactionary romanticism, naïve materialism, or idealist sentimentalism.

Nietzsche's radical intervention in philosophy is his declaration that "truth has a history." The implications of such a proposition, if taken seriously, literally abolish the pillar on which metaphysics, in both theology and philosophy proper, has been standing for ages. For if truth has a history, every question about truth must be situated in particular social contexts, which means the metaphysical abstractions are nothing but mystifications to present a perspective as eternal and absolute. It is precisely this Nietzschean radical declaration that cracked open one of the three wounds in the Western canon, as Foucault (1984) argues. In fact, this is also why Foucault, both as a genealogist and an archaeologist of knowledge, is Nietzsche's most faithful disciple. Foucault took Nietzsche's discovery and deconstructed entire fields of inquiry, including history and philosophy, based on a non-metaphysical premise about knowledge, which made postmodernism possible. The outcome of the Foucauldian revolt against traditional philosophers and historians could not have been more ground-breaking. Thanks to that revolt, now we can speak of knowledge as production, and we can interrogate everything that is societal in terms of regimes of truth. The Foucauldian revolt shed an illuminating light on the long secret affair between power and knowledge on macro levels, philosophically, and micro levels, genealogically.

The other two wounds Foucault mentions are Karl Marx and Sigmund Freud. Marx in fact went much further than Nietzsche by not only declaring that truth is historically constructed and deconstructed within social relations of power, but he also introduced the concept of "production," arguably the most central and critical concept on which the entire postmodernist spectrums of critique and analysis stand. The concept of production enabled us to once and for all demystify history, present, and future simply, but profoundly, place the concrete human and concrete social relations as the only players on all the fields of knowledge. Marx did not need to declare the death of God simply because he placed God where it has always belonged, namely the sociology of truth. He problematized the entire idealist canon that had operated on the assumption of prophecies, revelations, intuitions, and so on. Thus, to Marx, truth is in fact constantly produced and reproduced within actual social relations, which are first and foremost relations of production. The Marxist intervention, therefore, is not merely philosophical, rather it is a critique that is also at the same time a practice. If we were to express the revolutionary essence of Marx's discovery in a few words, it would be something along the following: *both truth and its perception are a matter of production*. The Marxist is revolutionary in so far as she *makes* truth through her own praxis.

Marx discovered that consciousness itself is historically situated and socially formed. That is to say, consciousness cannot have *that which does not exist* as its object of reasoning. Also, every consciousness is a subject's consciousness, a subject who has a concrete, particular, and distinct existence within concrete, particular, and distinct life conditions. Therefore, not only all metaphysical claims are necessarily baseless, but even every claim of a future communist society must remain negative. For knowing what a communist society should be like, we must first create the conditions that make such knowledge possible. Arguably, the largest and most fatal misconception of Marx's revolutionary project is that his materialist philosophy was subjected to an idealist interpretation. The modes of perception that have been shaped to mystify, to search for prophets, to find absolute truths, simply turned Marx to another prophet, which has had catastrophic consequences for both revolutionaries and the marginalized as well as the revolutionary will to negate world systems of oppression. Put briefly, assuming positive knowledge of a communist society is necessarily false because it repeats the idealist fallacy of attributing a metaphysical power to consciousness.

In a letter to Arnold Ruge, the twenty-five-year-old Marx wrote:

> Even though there is no doubt about the "whence," there does prevail all the more confusion about the "whither." It is not only the fact that a general anarchy has broken out among the reformers; each one will have to admit to himself that he has no exact idea of what is to happen. But that is exactly the advantage of the new direction, namely, that we do not anticipate the world dogmatically, but rather *wish to find the new world through criticism of the old*. (1967: 212; italics added)[4]

Communism at this stage can only be negative in terms of both revolutionary approach to political action and the awareness of the not-yet-concretized part of truth. It is the revolution itself that creates the conditions for a communist consciousness step by step as the praxis negates the existing order brick by brick. The revolution changes consciousness through changing its material conditions. What we can know is capitalism, and, thus, what communism is not.[5] To be able to imagine the alternative, the material conditions that render such an imagination impossible must be negated. Marxism is the discovery of formula, of historical materialism, of the fact that we have been the Platonic cave dwellers. That formula is the revolutionary frame that also brings revolutionaries together to form a historical front for absolute negation. In this sense Marxism is neither utopian nor conformist, neither nihilist nor idealist. It rejects a world in which imagining another world is impossible, but this rejection takes place within a universalist project of negation, whereby an alternative world *is made true* materially and historically.

The Marxist critique of what is dominant is meant to give the socialist movement a definite step forward at every actual point of revolution.[6] Instead of offering a prefigurative alternative model to substitute the existing order, Marxism points to the feasibility of a path for revolutionary praxis that transforms the conditions of both practice and thought, thereby building a new reality through the same steps the revolutionaries take for rejecting the existing one, *making* new truths via the same process that negates the old truths. The alternative it offers is not a predesigned model for the future society but a concrete project for a concretizing revolution. The rational approach to the crisis of the lack of an alternative does not lay in taking up the challenge at face value, as if human society could be designed by experts.

Marx's revolutionary subject as well is defined in terms of a negative identity. As Žižek puts it, "what qualifies the proletariat for this position is ultimately a negative feature: all other classes are (potentially) capable of reaching the status of the 'ruling class,' while the proletariat cannot achieve this without abolishing itself as a class" (2008a: 414). By virtue of being propertyless, the Marxist revolutionary subject is already situated in a negative position in relation to the rationalized world of private property. Her revolutionary potential lays first and foremost in her brutal exclusion from the dominant social space because she may be compelled to transform that exclusion to an immediate freedom from private property. It is precisely because of her undeniable unfreedom that she is capable of becoming a free and freeing subject. By negating the forces that negated her subject-hood, the revolutionary sets out for complete emancipation in two crucial senses: first, in the sense of freeing herself from the ideological hegemony of the bourgeoisie and the accumulating norms and values of class society in general, and second, in the sense of uprooting the domination of the ruling groups. Bringing down an oligarchy, theocracy, aristocracy, or a bourgeois party's rule does not in itself constitute a revolution regardless of the noise that may accompany the event. In fact, such events are uprisings that may very well intensify the means of control, unless each uprising is immediately framed within a broader and more concrete revolutionary framework aimed at reversing the totalitarian nature of domination. Marx and Engels thought the proletariat's project of self-emancipation as a class is necessarily a project of universalist emancipation from the shackles of class society. The significance of such a revolution is in its capacity to alter the modes of production, including the production of knowledge, values, and perception. The Marxist philosophy's significance for a postnihilist philosophy of revolution is irreplaceable, if nothing else, for the fact that it overcomes the ultimate and ages-old gap between knowledge and practice, subjectivity and history, existing reality and objective rationality. It pinpoints the ultimate source of alienation in tangible sociological terms, thereby trashing a long history of mystification of life in the name of spirituality and bifurcation of the living human in the name of an irreversible conflict between the supposed human heavenly essence and her eternally condemned body.

Far from being dismissal of the existentialist and ontological questions that occupied several generations of philosophers, Marxism in fact could be considered a radical existentialist philosophy precisely for its capacity to draw our attention to the right direction to search for what has created and perpetuated alienation. Some of the greatest existentialists came very close to discovering the Marxist solution to the existentialist puzzle, but they eventually fell for the irresistible allures of the bourgeois bohemian life-style and space that allows for sinking into the endless sweet sorrows that accompany self-pity paired with the satisfaction of universalizing despair as a metaphysically fixed situation inherent to being a human in the world. All this also allowed for the abyss of alienation to be anesthetized and philoso-phized by some French bourgeois philosophers and then sold as commodi-ties of the culture industry to some of the most miserable in the world. No wonder the phenomenon of hippie nihilism spread around the world within a couple of decades. In the name of ultimate ontological wisdom, disturb-ing forms of narcissism and apolitical bourgeois individualism became a formula for the production of the mass individual among social strata that otherwise might have confronted not only fascism but also the conditions that had been giving rise to fascism continually. Suddenly, thanks to bour-geois existentialism manufactured in Paris, despair, drugs, and sensational art became a world phenomenon. What could have been more fitting for an environment in which fascism grows almost unchallenged? And, indeed, fascism has grown in variations and mass quantity to become world crisis while many on the left are busy writing bad poetry about the era of revolutions failing to notice the ongoing revolutions in the margins of Paris and Europe as well as the margins of their margins, where true hope is concretely created out of truly experienced hopelessness.

Very much like bourgeois economists who deduced "laws" from what they witnessed around them and thereby eternalized the bourgeois economy, the French existentialists ontologized the circumstances of despair producing a culture of bourgeois bohemianism and extreme indifference even though many of them were quite honorably involved in the anti-fascist struggle. This is not to say that existentialism's insights were all foundationally false in the sense that theological insights are founded on false metaphysical and epistemological presumptions. Rather, the main problem with existentialism was that it was quickly turned into an alternative to Marxism, draining much of the potential energy of revolt. By virtue of being shaped around orientations of philosophers who were immersed in bourgeois standpoints, existentialism internationalized a bourgeois tendency for a self-absorbing lifestyle despite the fact that some of these philosophers as individuals chose anti-capitalist and anti-fascist politics.

Existentialism had a bourgeoisifying effect on the working class across the world, of course, to different degrees of intensity. Under the ironic banners of radical individualism, substantial numbers of the youth across continents became disenchanted members of a disenchanting mass, burying the prospects of internationalist class politics alive. While each individual may enjoy a sense of heroism entailed in the experience of standing alone in the world not believing in anything, so to speak, these individuals, unknowingly, do produce a mass stance, a politics of collective submission to the dominant systems, which are never indifferent. This also worked out very well for the ruling bourgeoisie in terms of a swift construction of bourgeois totalitarianism through the rapid implementation of the privatization of social space and commodification of everything including the body. The more ontologized depression and anxiety, the more depoliticizing their societal effects become. The more epidemic they become, the more profitable they become for a sector within the very same system that produces them.

We can trace back the beginning of the demise of the public sphere to the same age when the pseudo-rebels of existentialism, the bourgeois bohemians, turned the public space to a replica of the private space. To take one example, public nudity neither emancipated the body nor public space. In fact, it helped in commercializing/commodifying the body and de-politicizing public space thereby turning it to an extension of the bourgeois private space. By the end of the first decade of the twenty-first century, public space in Europe had been dead for so long, the Arab Spring brought back cross-generational nostalgia (not only for the lost public space but also for the political body). Even activists of the Occupy somehow and on some level sensed that there was no longer a public space to occupy or even a body to do the occupation.

Whether in the Middle Eastern capital cities or European and American metropolises, public space along with its political agent and user, the body, have been bourgeoisiefied resulting in the production of a totalitarian space. This catastrophic demise of the most fundamental subject of democracy and democratic space, even in the sense of bourgeois democracy of the nineteenth century, took place for the most part unnoticed. Today, we are all capitalists in everything including our absurd claims of anti-capitalism. We all have a few moralist complaints beyond which we have no way of even articulating, let alone problematizing, our alienation. The moralist tendencies have only further intensified the political disablement of the so-called civil society. Today's liberals and leftists for the most part dwell within a moralist ethos—even though all they need to do to realize the uselessness of the moralist discourse is to consider the fact that a donkey, any donkey, would score higher in morality than any moralist, whether in the left or right, simply because of the fact that a modern human's life causes infinite death and destruction compared to a donkey's peaceful life.

We have all accepted to be consumers of the commodities of happiness and/or substances of anti-depression. We are no longer able to imagine a way out, yet we take this inability as a sign of being eternally doomed. We mistake what we can and cannot imagine for what is and is not possible. Here, it is essential to revisit the negativity thesis in terms of Marxism's true revolutionary potential as opposed to the interpretations that voided Marxism from its materialist core, rendering it another form of idealism, a source for false hope based on prophecy.

At the hand of leaders and intellectuals, Marxism was turned into something essentially anti Marxist, another creature of idealism that presumes the priority of consciousness over life, a fundamental fallacy even the French existentialists warned against, albeit not always using similar phraseology mainly due to their obsession with the Cartesian turn and the Heideggerian abyss. In Marxism's name, a positively imagined alternative world was called communism. This communism that has been falsely attributed to Marx's philosophy has believers, ex-believers, and many more enemies. It is difficult to decide which group among the main camps, which I will identify in more specific terms later in this chapter, are more wrong. What should be clear is that common positions that are taken about Marxism are based on idealist, that is, non-Marxist, modes of conception.

Marxism is a philosophy of negation, but the seekers of a new prophet and a new scripture forced a positive outfit on it. They read into it the picture of an alternative world Marx neither attempted to describe nor pretended to know.[7] To Marx, prefiguring a communist society, beyond general, mostly, negative frames, would have been a terrible fallback into idealism, which he so vigorously criticized even when it was committed by radical materialists, such as Ludwig Feuerbach, or radical communists such as Saint Simon, Robert Owen, and socialist anarchists such as Mikhail Bakunin and Pierre-Joseph Proudhon, among others. The issue at its root, for Marx at least, could not have been confusing. Namely, what we are able to imagine is restricted by the historical and societal conditions in which we live. We may be able to radically expand the limits of our imagination, but we cannot exceed certain historical and spatial boundaries without lapsing into some form of hallucination, arbitrary utopia, and unfounded predictions, speculations, and so on. Even in his masterwork, Marx never gives the reader the illusion of the predictability of the nature of a communist society.[8] Such an attempt would be false by the standards of his own theory according to which all that has to do with consciousness comes after, and is constructed within, the material conditions of life. Claiming any positive prefiguration of the anticipated communist society would reverse the order, rendering his philosophy another text of idealism. Indeed, that is precisely his main critique of Feuerbach.

Marx could not agree more with Feuerbach that humans had created God in their own image, and then mistook this product of their own imagination for a higher, ahistorical, metaphysical being, in which absolute truth, power, and justice are placed. However, Feuerbach repeated the idealist fallacy by assuming that such a philosophical and materialist declaration in itself suffices to correct all that has gone wrong in human history. In other words, Marx thought, God is indeed a product of human consciousness as an illusion, but that consciousness, including its fictive creatures, is formed within existing, material, conditions of life. As long as those conditions are not altered radically, the consciousness cannot be altered radically. The death of God, in other words, can only be accomplished by the negation of the actual conditions that repeatedly produce illusions such as God, human nature, economic and natural laws, and so on, which in turn become part of the ideological institutions that normalize, naturalize, and eternalize the existing relations of domination. This cycle of idealist reproduction of a false world cannot be broken by a philosophical declaration denouncing a false consciousness. Philosophy is, at best, a problematization of a false world. By the same token, in a rational world, philosophy would not be necessary. Philosophers themselves are sustainers of the existing order unless they become revolutionaries, negating the existing conditions of unfreedom devotedly and uncompromisingly.

Marxism, therefore, is not a philosophy of an alternative world, but a philosophy for negating the existing conditions in order to actualize a space in which constructing and imagining another world is possible. It is a revolution to construct an alternative as opposed to an alternative waiting for a revolution. It rejects the conditions that make freedom unimaginable, as opposed to an imagined freedom to be lived in the future. It is also a negation of modes of (un)thinking that assumes revelations, preexisting grand solutions, moral ideals independent of history, and, in short, a realm of ideas above the spatiotemporal realm in which the body exists. It should not be expected from Marxism to provide us with a catalogue of the future communist world. Whether a text is a materialist or not, idealist or not, ancient or not, revolutionary or not, genius or not, sacred or not, it could not exceed the historical limits under which it is produced. The same goes for our interpretation of every text. The meaning of a text changes from a reader to another, a time and another, and a space and another. These changes reaffirm that the only conditions of a text's production and reading are material conditions of actual human beings situated in material circumstances. We do not have a single text of any origin from any time and place in the antiquity that, for instance, mentions trains or emails. That is so for the simple reason that it was impossible for any mind to imagine trains and emails before the material conditions and modes of production changed so drastically as to allow for their invention and actualization. People in the antiquity could and did imagine non-existing entities and worlds, but none of those products of imagination were merely some sort of distortion or combination of certain existing entities. For instance, Mesopotamians imagined winged houses or a serpent with a female human's head, and the Greeks imagined creatures that are half man and half non-human animal, such as horses, goats, and so on. All kinds of divinities and divine knowledge, spirits, and spiritual visions have been claimed across ages, yet none was able to depict what was not knowable in their own respective historical circumstances, which are also the circumstances of their own production. That is exactly why those divinities themselves remain prehistorical even in the imagination of today's believers. Thus, often we hear about religious experiences, revelations, and so on, except, somehow, they all take place in the old (ghostish) forms—as opposed to, say, a letter, an email, or a phone call from God to any of these believers with postal addresses, email accounts, and phone numbers. Somehow, God seems to be unable to leave the golden age of holy donkeys, evil daemons, and deadly diseases, not to mention the fact that this all-knowing and all-powerful divinity's knowledge in any field, from mathematics to basic physics, from astronomy to history, does not surpass basic wisdom from ancient Mesopotamian societies. Nonetheless, every text whose author is claimed to be God, remains to be held as infinitely prophetic and absolutely sacred by its believers. The mentality that desperately projects its mystification on the world and eternalizes absolute restrictions on itself is definitive of idealism. Also, we need to keep in mind that this idealist addiction on absolutism remains to be a dominant norm in today's world.

The archaic mentality of idealism approaches every revolutionary philosophy, including Marxism, in the same way it approaches a mythological system. It projects its idealism on Marxism or neurotically protects its idealism against Marxism. Here we can identify four main groups. More often than not, those who reject Marxism do so because it does not provide an alternative world and those who endorse it do so because they believe it prophesizes an alternative world. In addition to these two main groups, there are two other groups of those who take a position regarding Marxism without bothering to read its philosophical texts. There are anti-Marxists who, of course falsely, claim that Marxism functions as another religion, mistaking the idealist distortions of Marxism for Marxism. Finally, the fourth main camp is composed of former self-proclaimed Marxists who did not find in Marxist texts and movements the salvation they had once believed they would find. Thus, what most anti-Marxists have in common seems to stem from a compound problem of two sides: an idealist interpretation of what is falsely assumed to be an idealist belief system.

Marxism, in short, is assessed on the basis of the feasibility of the realization of a falsely projected heavenly world. How could and should Marxism, or any other philosophical system for that matter, be expected to depict a society that is entirely different before the conditions of such a society begin to take shape? To reiterate, no text could ever succeed in constructing a world beyond the limits of its particular places and times. Even the fictions and myths, the underworlds and heavens, the dreams and fantasies, are easily traceable to what existed, feared, desired, and so on in particular times and places by the existing human beings who lived in the material conditions of those times and places. Take the imagery of afterlife, in any religious text, for instance. How hard is it to realize that they reflect the limits of what was possible to be imagined under their particular historical circumstances? God may be dead, but those who search for a God continue to produce new Gods, and new scripture, for the same old purposes, namely, to find eternal and final answers. Those seekers of God, whether they fall in love with Marxist texts or some ancient texts of wisdom, will continue to rotate within an orbit, which may be full of mazes and wonders, but it is a nihilist, denialist, fictive, and fictionalizing orbit, nonetheless.

Marx aimed to find the scientific formula to capture the dialectics of history. If nothing else, in its most basic foundation, the formula leaves no space for repeating the ages-old idealist fallacies. Also, it may fall out of fashion, but it stays as valid as always. It is absurd for any rational human being to disagree with the theory (historical materialism), just as it is absurd to deny the validity of the universal law of gravity even though the law is named after one person, who happened to be the first to discover it, and despite the fact that the discovery took place a very long time ago (more than three centuries ago). That is to say, Newtonian or not, one cannot reasonably refute the universal law of gravitation. Marxist or not, one cannot reasonably refute the formula of historical materialism. Whether the formula is indeed scientifically valid or not, it is false to subject it to an idealist measure (that is itself soundly refuted by the theory). It is also false to determine the invalidity of the theory based on its false interpretations and applications. We may disagree on the theory's accurate interpretation, but one thing is certain: every assumption about the theory without reading the texts that represent it is necessarily false. Finally, Marxism offers a philosophy of communism only to the extent that communism could be grasped as a negation of capitalism.[9]

What we can and must know is that the existing regime of truth, social relations, and frames of perception can be negated. We can and must know what an alternative world should not look like. Going by the negativity thesis we can take concrete steps, each of which will create an actual new possibility for knowing. A postnihilist project, therefore, continually expands the space of freedom, action, imaginations, and the conditions in which it can grow as an actual force of deconstruction and construction. The negativity thesis I advance here and elsewhere for interpreting Marxism does not indicate or imply an arbitrary form of negation, and in fact no such form of negation can exist. Every negation is particular and concrete, which is what distinguishes negativity from nihilism. Nihilism, at best, leads to a political withdrawal from the world, a denial of the reality and its political implications, and an illusion of revolt that serves nothing and nobody including the self-absorbed nihilist. Contrary to the bourgeois nihilist who is a participant in the relations of domination, the revolutionary subject is herself a negative subject.

The revolutionary subject *makes* truth through a praxis formulated according to her consciousness of the historical context and significance. Therefore, the revolution is a necessary condition for making/imaging the alternative world possible, not the other way around. The point of revolution is to reset the circumstances of objectivity, truth, and what is possible. Revolution does not answer the existentialist questions regarding despair and alienation precisely because the questions themselves are loaded with false premises and are articulated with nihilistic terminology. By the same token, the postnihilist philosophy of revolution problematizes the fetishization of despair as being a means for apoliticizing all that is political, allowing the state ideological apparatuses to psychologize everyday life and pathologize the endless social symptoms of alienation. If anything, the systematic reproduction of despair and pathologization of alienation once more become ideal sources for the accumulation of capital through both the drug industry and the culture industry. The drug industry ensures the containment of the depressed, anxious, and schizophrenic population while the culture industry becomes ever more profitable thanks to its primary role in sustaining the constant entertainment and the culture of (artificial) happiness.

Theses on Feuerbach, whereby Marx leaves the left Hegelians' including Feuerbach's materialism behind, is the turning point in the history of philosophy where materialism leaps out of the idealist dark age. The idealist age in the West assumed the false dichotomy of mind–body from Plato's time, which was then reincarnated in Christianity, and revived again in Modernity on Descartes's hands. Parallel to this split, a gulf between intellectual activity and physical labor, theory and practice, knowledge and action, kept expanding across these dark ages. In turn, far from overcoming the human estrangement (the fetishized subject of existentialism), every increase of consciousness in such a world was bound to intensify alienation. Also, in such a world it is only to be expected that the more one knows, the more paralyzed one becomes in terms of action.[10] By the same token, the heroes, those who excel in action, can be anything but philosophers. Armies of such heroes are easily mobilized by small ruling elites to use as killing machines and policing tools against the marginalized groups and the very class most of the recruits come from. From the time of ancient Greeks and Persians to our day, all crusades have been decided by a few in the ruling groups for the interests of a few in the ruling groups but have been carried out by the miserable against the miserable.

To this day, for the most part, the social sciences, from anthropology to political science, have not been able to adopt the following two basic materialist corrections:

1. The realm of ideas and values does not exist independently, that is, outside the social and historical conditions of actual living bodies; and

2. Reality and truth are a matter of constant perceptions of change and changes of perception.

As a result, the dominant ethos of our age can best be described as "dull empiricism," which is an expression Trotsky used to mean, "the unashamed, cringing worship of the fact which is so often only imaginary, and falsely interpreted at that" (1970: 88). Beneath the "dull empiricism," idealism and pragmatism are effectively at work.[11] The limit of knowledge is determined by pure utilitarian purposes, especially, from the perspective of power. Schools are the main institutions for recruiting "dull empiricists" who are trained to maximize the instrumental efficiency and minimize thought. For any intellectual work, activity that is not invested for pragmatic outcomes such as profit, prestige, and privilege is considered not only unproductive and thus wasted but also potentially counterproductive and thus threatening. Therefore, today's heroes are the fanatic guardians of the existing order who excel in instrumental reasoning and thereby demolish every intellectual space for reason qua understanding, for perception qua grasping the becoming of truth, and certainly for anything that has to do with critique qua negativity. Today's most powerful (or successful), therefore, are power-utilitarians, inductive donkeys, and smart imbeciles, who are exceptionally lacking in autonomous thinking and, at the same time, fully mechanized in terms of power-utilitarianism, rendering them ideal climbers of the ladder of social privilege.[12] Thus, we should stop being surprised by the fact that someone like Donald Trump could climb all the way to the top of the pyramid of power; his clear under-intelligence and insensitivity (compared with the average people anywhere) is not a shortcoming but a merit insofar as the existing order is concerned. In fact, the same thing could be said more or less about the entire global system. That is to say, privilege and power are for the most part allocated according to the ability to not think outside the utilitarian framework of the social hierarchy, which is determined by the duality of power and capital. In today's world of fascist populism, open vulgarity, misogyny, anti-intellectualism, and, of course, racism attract popularity, which in turn accumulates more power and privilege.

Culturalism, the oversimplifying and intellectually undemanding habit of explaining social phenomena as manifestations of culture, is today's widespread idealism. At the other end of the spectrum, the positivistic obsession with data is vulgar empiricism at its purest. Either way, two presumptions are continually reaffirmed: first, prefiguring an alternative is a prerequisite for a realistic rejection of the existing world; and second, there can be no alternative to the existing capitalist world. The embodiment of this bureaucratic mode of knowledge production can best be seen in international relations where the dominant schools take the nation-state as an eternal, natural unit of study.[13] Of course, this conceptual deficiency goes far beyond the field of international relations. The common assumption is that there will always be the nation-state simply because (now) there are only nation-states. On the left end of the academy, we may come across many theories that claim criticality, anti-capitalism, and anti-imperialism, such as postcolonial theories, particularly Saidian theories in cultural studies. However, as I argued in Chapter 5 of this book, more often than not, those who adopt the paradigms of cultural relativism have actively essentialized the non-white Other in their attempts to regain the non-white Other's historical and subjective autonomy. In their effort to free the Other from the West's hegemony, they reduced the Other to a caricature-like reversal of everything that is assumed to be inherently Western, almost biologically white. This is much more catastrophic when we realize that what is attributed exclusively to the white European is everything that is universally emancipatory and potentially progressive (Ahmed 2021). Essentially, there is nothing new about the mentality of culturalism, whether it claims postcolonialism or cultural relativism. The non-European Other to Hegel, for instance, was a non-historical agent who is not aware of her freedom and incapable of abstraction (2001: 31–3, 117, 121–3, 374). Even to Feuerbach, "the Orient" represents the source of the confused imagination that mistakes human consciousness for divinity, which is then represented in religion (2008: 34, 117).

The naive culturalists ended up attributing all that is human to the white and, simultaneously, painted a picture of the non-white as the reverse projection, that is, the "non-human" Other. If individual liberties are an exclusively European value, then it only makes sense, according to this unconsciously racist mentality of culturalism, to assume that non-Europeans do not value individual liberties. By the same token, if secularism is a European invention, the non-European is non-secular; if the industrialization is a European ambition, then the authentic, self-respecting non-European cannot possibly have any industrial ambitions. All this has led the academy to reproduce an extended era of racism, whereby the non-white is believed to be primitively innocent and innocently primitive. A crucial aspect of this unwitty postcolonial reproduction of Eurocentrism is noticed by Balibar:

> It was important to recall this history, albeit very allusively, because it leads us to temper how we view the critique of progress, or at least not to accept all the apparently self-evident aspects of that critique without some caution. The fact that the most recent of all the great versions of Marxist progressivism was an ideology of escape from underdevelopment which was statist, rationalist and populist, should deter us from flippantly declaring "the end of the illusions of progress" *from Europe,* or, more generally, from the "metropolitan heartland" (or the "North"). As though it were once again up to us to determine where, when and by whom rationality, productivity and prosperity are to be sought. The functions performed in the history of the labour movement by the image of the forward march of humanity, and by the hope of one day seeing individual fulfilment and collective salvation coincide, are also topics still awaiting a detailed analysis. (2007: 88; italics in original)

As for the right end of the academy, the Other is assumed to be inherently barbarian and violent, astonishingly standing outside history. The broader ideological reflection of this state of Eurocentrism and neo-Eurocentrism is overwhelmingly present in the conservative–liberal duality in the United States, Canada, Europe, Australia, and New Zealand.

That is exactly why the value system, political ideology, language, and the entire modes of perceptions of the privileged are considered as natural, universal, rational, and super-historical whereas the underprivileged, even when leading an emancipatory revolution, are habitually essentialized, culturized, tribalized, and irrationalized precisely in order to perpetuate their marginalization. There are countless cases of this, a few illustrative examples of which are analyzed in more detail throughout this book. Here, mentioning a few examples in passing should suffice to illustrate my point. Notice movements that used to be called "liberation movements" up until the 1980s are now, at best, depicted in terms of ethnic politics that demand "cultural rights"—as if any human group could be so stupid to launch armed struggle merely to be allowed to wear a certain traditional clothing or celebrate a certain folklore. Not that these rights are insignificant, but wherever the oppressed engage in armed struggle, much more than these is at stake. Wherever liberation movements take place, those involved are well aware of the fact that it is their humanity as such, both existentially and ontologically, that is being denied. Yet instead of recognizing the inherent universalism of such struggles, what we usually hear amounts to nothing but culturalization, tribalization, and mystification of the marginalized group. This ideological distortion of the marginalized is very easy to recognize once the dominant discourse is de-normalized, as I am trying to do here. For instance, if we simply listen to what the marginalized say about the reasons of their protests, uprisings, and revolutions, it becomes immediately clear that their struggles, in fact, represent what is rational and universal as opposed to the dominant order that is irrational and essentially barbarian. Let us not forget the fact that it was the Haitian revolution that truly abolished enslavement by adopting the universal human rights both the American republic and the French republic failed to recognize.

Personally, I have never seen and heard of a Darfuri for instance, claiming that their opposition to the Sudanese government is because the latter does not treat them as Darfuris; to the contrary, the entire problem they consistently emphasize is that they are not treated with dignity as humans. This is true in the case of every liberation movement we might think of, whether in a liberal democracy, such as Black Lives Matter in the United States, or in an illiberal state, such as the Kurdistan Workers' Party in Turkey. This should not be read as claiming the struggling marginalized deny or should deny their singularity. Rather, we should once and for all comprehend that the universal is always embodied in the singular, in the concrete. All human individuals and groups necessarily have their own differences, but the point is not to use those differences to discriminate against them as human beings. In addition, there is no doubt when a group of people are discriminated against as Blacks, Native Americans, Armenians, Jews, Palestinians, Kurds, or Yezidis, some of them will resist as Blacks, Native Americans, Armenians, Jews, Palestinians, Kurds, or Yezidis. Liberation movements above all else struggle for the realization of the equality and freedoms they are entitled to, which is by definition a universal right, the basis of liberalism—except liberalism even on the ideal level undermines itself.

Liberalism undermines itself through its betrayal of its universalist origins in the Enlightenment. In the name of cultural diversity, neoliberalism has established a totalitarian regime of dehumanization, as it becomes clear in the false dichotomies erected between white-European-Western and Other. Today, it is for the most part white liberals, including liberal feminists, who fail to imagine a feminism that is not racially, religiously, or culturally essentialized outside the white West. For instance, the common assumption in the West is that feminist movements in the Middle East are "Islamic feminism," an oxymoron that is simply unheard of in most places in the Middle East, except perhaps from some Islamist apologists. Similarly, in the Middle East, only fundamentalists believe in "Islamic human rights" as opposed to (universal) human rights. Western liberals adhere to this distinction in human rights in the name of respecting the Islamic identity and rejecting Eurocentrism, completely unaware of the irony this entails, for example, the fact that they attribute what is necessarily universal about "humanity" exclusively to the white European. Of course, such racist pseudo-anti-Eurocentrism is often also adopted by non-white elites, and there is nothing surprising about this given that Eurocentrism does enjoy a global ideological domination. This is evident especially among academics who receive their doctoral degrees in Western universities. They internalize the entire means of culturalism, whether knowingly or unknowingly, and further it as a truism through research conducted to gain the approval of their supervisors and institutions. Clear discourses of this kind can be noted among scholars of postcolonialism, but more broadly self-Orientalization is more or less the norm among non-white academics, especially in the West.

Also, "indigeneity" has become one of the latest embodiments of this anti-universal, Eurocentric form of humanism that essentially deprives the non-white from her human identity in the name of recognizing the uniqueness of her cultural identity. Indigeneity has been a white invention through and through, and conveniently it positions the white Western in the moral place of both altruism and heroism. The real crime that is committed against Indigenous peoples is not the elimination of the so-called Indigenous ways of life, cultures, economies, and so on but the elimination of the peoples themselves, which of course led to the total or near total elimination of everything that constituted the various aspects of the victims' societal lives, including language. Indigenous museums are nothing but standing evidence of that crime of mass elimination. Ultimately, from the culturalist point of view, the identity of the dominant is the immediate, universal, neutral, and color-free and so is their politics, whereas all that has to do with the non-white is identity-based, including politics, and identity is defined in terms of (the distance from or dissimilarity with) the presumed universal humanity of the dominant.

Here, the point is not to emphasize the need for moral and intellectual correction of these acts of wrongness and falsehood because this issue is merely a symptom of a much more encompassing hegemony that has been persisting throughout modernity. The neutralization, eternalization, and rationalization of the privileged group's singularity qua universality is built into domination. Breaking down this should be extremely plain: it is the materiality of privilege that makes the ideological hegemony of the dominant possible. Therefore, privilege should not be seen as a quality of whiteness but as actual conditions that are organized in such a way as to reproduce social inequality, that is, to elevate some at the expense of others. In order for wrongness and falsehood to be removed, the material conditions of their reproduction must be abolished.

However, this would still be an incomplete revolutionary philosophy because the act of negation is essentially formed by critique, just as critique is inherently a praxis. This takes us to the broader argument against "dull empiricism," the mentality of the "inductive asses" that have been conducting social engineering, whether under democracies or fascist regimes. A refugee asks another refugee, "how dare you criticize the very country that gave you refuge?"[14] or, even worse, tells the African American to "objectively" examine police data to realize the true criminological explanation for why African Americans are imprisoned in large numbers.[15] Such is dull empiricism: metaphysically paralyzed beyond any redemption and epistemologically chained to the wall in Plato's allegorical cave. The dull empiricist calls for maximum punishment for anyone who dares to question the absolute truth of the shadows on the immediate wall at which she has been staring for her entire life, believing it is reality.

Dull empiricism simply does not have a conceptual sense of power, truth, morality, and aesthetics. For thinking in terms of concepts belongs to a whole different, more sophisticated realm of thought.[16] That is what Trotsky meant by "the general" (1970: 88), and that is also why Deleuze defines philosophy as the creation of concepts. Building on Deleuze's account of thought and sensibility (see Durie 2009: 130–1), we could make the following point: thought renders as its object that which does not lend itself to understanding. When thought faces a deadlock, it does not turn around and give up; rather it calls in reinforcement to overcome the obstacle. The bigger the obstacle to understanding is, the greater the reinforcement becomes. In fact, we have a word for an obstacle to thought that results in more thought; we call it a puzzle. Thought becomes puzzled, and thus stimulated, when it confronts something that is not understood. Adorno's insight is worth quoting here: "The universal tendency toward suppression goes against thought as such. Such thought is happiness, even where unhappiness prevails; thought achieves happiness in the expression of unhappiness" (2006a: 203).

While both secular and religious moralities might, on the surface, disapprove of worldly social norms, essentially, they operate on the assumption that if only people were more ethically conscious, the world's problems would be no more. We can see this in the frequency of moralistic references to the "greedy capitalist" as the root of all crises, as though all would be well if capitalists were not so greedy. This then makes it easy for capitalists to demonstrate their moral superiority through what has come to be known as philanthrocapitalism.[17] They need only to make a highly publicized humanitarian investment such as opening a hospital or school in an underdeveloped African country, funding research for finding cures to certain diseases, or establishing a private foundation in their name to excuse themselves of culpability for the state of the world. Such philanthropic acts represent a pure form of capitalist exchange because they convert the suffering of the Other into a symbolic commodity that guarantees the moral capital of the benefactor. By giving away a small percentage to charities, corporations and business owners appeal to more customers, which, as an effective form of advertisement, is meant to increase profit. Consumerism is precisely what sustains the cycle of exploitation and accumulation of capital, yet the ordinary consumer/citizen need only to recycle or give away a few dollars to a good cause to feel absolved of responsibility. What escapes the naive moralist consumer is the fact that exploitation is the only source of capital. In other words, there is no just way to be a capitalist in the first place. In religious arenas, the moral market is even more advanced because God himself is the broker. The believer must simply pay her dues to the religious institution, and the rest will be taken care of.

What Is Wrong with "What Is the Alternative?"?

Faced as we are with ecological disasters and systematic and institutionalized violence, not to mention the continuation of genocidal acts of multiple forms, it is absurd to repeat nihilism's central rhetorical question, "What is the alternative?" None of the causes of the inequality, oppression, and violence that pervade our daily lives is unavoidable in and of itself, though the causes may be unavoidable outcomes of the existing global system. The main point to be made here is that realizing the inherent wrongness of the status quo is separate from knowing how things should be. That is to say, rejecting the existing order is not dependent on the availability of an alternative. The only sensible morality in a world that continues to allow genocide is the one that is formed through negation.[18] As Adorno said in a lecture on May 7, 1963, "We may not know what absolute good is or the absolute norm, we may not even know what man is or the human or humanity—but what the inhuman is we know very well indeed. I would say that the place of moral philosophy today lies more in the concrete denunciation of the inhuman, than in vague and abstract attempts to situate man in his existence" (Adorno 2000: 175). Echoing this idea of negativity, Max Horkheimer in an interview explained that Critical Theory is "based on the idea that what is good, and thus, what a good, free society is, can't be determined from inside the society that we now live. To this end we're lacking. However, we can speak about the negative aspects of society that we want to change" (2019). This negativity in the broadest philosophical sense is the very framework of Marx's thought. To appreciate this claim, we need to recall that Marx's philosophy is, at the same time, utopian and anti-utopian, realist and anti-realist, deeply and uncompromisingly antagonistic. While he mercilessly criticizes utopian socialists and naive humanists and moralists, the crown of his political philosophy, the single purpose of his life as a political struggle, if we were to put it in one word, is communism. However, by virtue of being a mere idea of the future, communism is necessarily utopian. Yet, unlike the communism of the Saint-Simonians or Owenists, Marx's communism is not utopian insofar as it is based on a theory of history.

Both Saint-Simon and Robert Owen took morality as their springboard toward establishing an alternative world, so their accounts of communism were inherently idealist, reductionist, and unrealizable. They did not account for the determining forces in human society that are not necessarily compatible with the moral right. Therefore, such idealist-utopian forms of communism were bound to fail even before they managed to establish a new norm on any significant societal level. Marx's opposition to such communist accounts had nothing to do with the fact that they were moral; rather, the problem was that they were *moralist*, that is, built on the assumption that morality is the primary determining historical factor. In being first and foremost moralist, those communist philosophies failed to account for more fundamental historical factors that determine social relations and value systems, including morality itself. Their problem was not that they were utopian but idealist-utopian, as opposed to materialist utopian. In their negation of the existing capitalist order, they fell short of exceeding the narrow horizon of morality.

Today's forms of so-called liberation theologies, whether in the Christian or Muslim canons, engender the same confusion. Namely, no degree of moral virtue, sympathy for the oppressed, charity work, and anti-capitalist sentiment would lead to forming a real challenge to capitalism. In fact, those moderate or "leftist" religious movements in some contexts, say, in the Christian Latin America, effectively de-charge social forces of dissent, voiding the energy of the youth for revolutionary rebelliousness aimed at capitalism's totalitarian grip of the world. Even worse, in Muslim-majority societies, those religious movements end up supporting an imperialist and colonialist power in the name of (anti-American) imperialism. That is exactly where both Iranian and Turkish regimes attract most of their Shia and Sunni Islamist recruits, respectively. The writings of the founders of the Muslim Brotherhood and Iranian Shia Islamism are constructed around doctrines of liberation and social justice—thereby deceiving not only gullible religious youth but also Western intellectuals of the stature of Michel Foucault—even as leftist, feminist, and liberation movements across the Middle East are subjected to systematic campaigns of elimination by all means available and at all regional and organizational levels. Therefore, in our contemporary world, the idealist forms of anti-capitalism are at best serving the perpetuation of capitalism. At worst, the so-called liberation theologies impose capitalism without any of its individual freedoms. No wonder some revolutionary communist and feminist figures who had been lucky enough to survive and make it to the West are adamant defenders of liberal democracies. I am personally in touch with dozens of such Middle Eastern communists who live in exile in the West. In my view, a bifurcated personality is the inevitable result of such a bifurcated world of capitalism and pseudo-anti-capitalism. In other words, for many such exiles, being against global capitalism and reactionary forces at the same time creates a split, at least in appearance insofar as superficial dichotomies such as capitalism–liberation theology or West–East are concerned.

Of course, there are also nonreligious forms of moralist anticapitalism, which inevitably end up reproducing falsehood. The rise of the hippie movement and much of the popular culture that accompanied it from the late 1960s until the 1980s are exemplary of bourgeois—that is to say pseudo-anti-capitalist—movements. These movements depoliticized all that is political and politicized what was least political. For instance, suddenly communist resistance became a sort of third-world irrelevance and the Marxist language of critique fell out of fashion, whereas nudity and the use of drugs in the public space became symbols of rebelliousness. All we need to do to realize just how anti-revolutionary the proud 1960s generation was is to look at today's world, which has been run by them and those who were educated by them. Many of the bourgeois bohemians of the 1960s and 1970s, not counting the bad poets and those who make a living out of their nostalgia, became bureaucrats, politicians, and businesspersons in the age of neoliberalism.

The 1960s' most tangible accomplishment was something that, from the spatial point of view, was devastating to every possibility of emancipation from class structures and racist relations of power. Namely, being true to their bourgeois individualistic hedonism, the hippies turned the public space, which is supposed to be the most political space, into an extension of the private space, which has been historically apolitical, to use Hannah Arendt's distinction (1998). One could easily argue that orgies, even if they were performed in all city squares, would not have the slightest negative effect on the fundamentals of the system of capitalism. No amount of peace loving, handholding, sitting on the ground, hot-yoga sweating, or raw vegetable eating would challenge the capitalist relations of production. If anything, today political activism can barely find a place in the public space, rendering it almost completely impossible to initiate or maintain.

From 1968 to 2011, the trajectory of the bourgeoisification of social space and the concept of protest continued creating a climate in which useless protest substitutes actual revolution. The Occupy Movement, for instance, failed not only to occupy Wall Street but also to find a space to peacefully and lovingly exist as a mere gathering of a group of people who had in common anti-capitalist sentiments. Ironically, the demonstration was allowed to take refuge in a private park, after it became clear that it could not exist otherwise (because there was no public space in the first place). The occupiers did not occupy anything, and any occupation of the Wall Street would have necessitated a much broader revolution to emancipate social space as such, to create a public space. Certainly, creating a public space in New York City would take nothing short of a revolution, which is of course not exactly what most of the wannabe occupiers set out to do. In fact, the police system did not let even the demonstrators' own bodies physically occupy (read as take) any space in what is mistakenly called "public space." Thus, thanks to the tolerance of the owner of Zuccotti Park, the actors in the occupation were allowed to erect their tents for a few weeks, reenacting a watered-down version of the legendary events of 1968, which is now considered the golden year of protest.

Perhaps the Arab Spring's immediate appeal among the liberal and left white intelligentsia had to do with the revival of the idea of revolution. The perception was that someone somewhere is creating a revolution courageously. As if the Paris of 1968 had risen from the dead in Cairo, Tahrir Square became the imaginary light that emerged from the Orient to break the total darkness in which the world had been living. The romantics of revolution-somewhere-else did not realize that the Arab Spring was just another event in the same vein of unrevolutionary protests. Of course, there *was* no light as the leftist Egyptians were completely dismissed both regionally and internationally. Within months, sure enough, even the liberal majority that led the uprisings were suppressed by the very soldiers who had been given red roses, hugged, and kissed by the rioters merely for not shooting at them in defense of Mubarak. Even worse, an Islamist became the president of Egypt, pushing many secular artists and popular stars to regret the fall of the Mubarak dynasty. Thanks to another army general who, like Mubarak in 1981, took over, the Islamist regime did not survive. Al-Sisi with the same army and same police put an end to the liberal dream, which had turned into an absolute nightmare.

Thus, once more, bourgeois liberalism proved to be anything but revolutionary, and to the pseudo-revolutionary poets' disappointment in the West, the Springers proved to be just as unprepared for revolution as the occupiers were. The Springers merely had a taste of *a season in hell before* they were forced to accept *the plague* once more as the only season under the sun. Following Occupy and the Arab Spring, the post-communist nihilist age carried on only to become darker. The rise of fascism ceased to shock people. During the last ten years, nihilism has gotten so much worse that the Dark Ages style of enslavement of entire populations, such as the Yezidis in Iraq and Syria, barely provokes any public form of action or debate beyond a few reports by some human rights' organizations. In the United States, a Trump presidency became reality, making George W. Bush look like a highly sophisticated and respectful public figure from another age. The fall of the Berlin Wall that was presented as the beginning of an open and free world turned out to be the opening scene of a world mainly defined by walls and the omnipresent gaze of power. In the new age, the reality is dystopic and most of us have been turned into its nihilist guardians tirelessly maintaining its physical and virtual fortifications.

Capitalism has never been short of chauvinist, moralist, and religious opponents, but none of such reactionary tendencies makes an anti-capitalist philosophy, and without such a philosophy any talk of dissent could serve the capitalist hegemony at best or result in empowering darkagism at worst. There are trends of fascism that virtually advocate various sorts of vague idealism that allegedly oppose capitalism and imperialism, but of course they produce pockets that combine the worst of both capitalism and (internal) imperialism with absolutist mysticism whether borrowed from the Dark Ages or invented within the brands of newagism. Liberation theologies, both Christian and Islamic, are living examples of pseudo-anti-imperialist ideologies that borrow their mysticism from the Dark Ages. What is worth some analysis here, however, is the new-ageist brands of idealism that claim some sort of anti-capitalist liberation.

To encapsulate multiple dimensions of the fashionable idealist anti-capitalist utopia in today's world, let us turn to Ari Aster's 2019 movie, *Midsommar*. Strictly speaking, *Midsommar* sheds light on new-age communitarianism whereby certain societal norms of capitalism may be rejected, but in their place chauvinist, if not outright fascist, norms and practices are established. Religion too may be rejected only to be replaced with another set of rituals and means of hallucination. Ari Aster's movie takes us into a communal world that from outside might look peaceful, all-loving, and intriguingly ecological. The viewer discovers the communal world from the point of view of a group of American graduate students who are leading a typical life of middle-class graduate students trying to deal with their social lives, a few daily means of enjoyment, such as hanging out together, drinking, smoking, and so on. Of course, each one of them is also mildly struggling to fulfil his or her degree requirements. Two of them, Christian, played by Jack Reynor, and Josh, played by William Jackson Harper, will end up in a bitter conflict over the dispute about which one of them had originally wanted to conduct his doctorate research on the closed community. Interestingly, in that conflict the egoistic reality under what otherwise appears to be a nice friendship becomes clear. However, during the journey into the world of the community, in Swidden, all the internal conflicts of the American students become insignificant compared to the horrors they, and we, discover inside the community. The beautiful green landscape, the simple and white outfits of the residents, and the communal peace that impress both the viewer and the American students are soon to be disrupted by the true reality of the communal system. It turns out that systemic murder, rape, and torture are scarcely distinguishable from the rest of the rituals such as those that involve communal meals and celebrations. *Midsommar* is absolute horror in a setting where horror is the least expected. A brilliant touch that emphasizes the conflicting realities and perceptions is the prolonged scene that depicts the experience of drug-induced hallucinations on the very first day of the students' arrival in the village, just before they join the first communal ritual. We, the viewers, along with Dani, played by Florence Pugh, completely lose touch with what is supposed to be the reality in the movie, but the place and the characters we witness in what turns out to be Dani's nightmarish hallucination remain the same. As the students walk to the community with a British couple, guided by their common Swedish friend who is a member of the community, mediocre relational tensions continue to surface, but they are the kind of tensions one may expect to happen in a typical outing of a group of young middle-class Americans or Europeans. Then, gradually the visitors slip into the reality of the horror and the horror of the reality. Overall, Ari Aster does a brilliant job of exposing the problems of so-called localism or communitarianism practiced by groups of people who adopt a tribalist mentality in their attempt to find a morally and spiritually satisfying lifestyle within a local community that is supposedly non-capitalist and, thus, free.

Unlike communism, communitarianism has no issue with the continuation of class society, global division of labor, and so on. These new-age eco-communities combine mysticism, absolute relativism, and aspects of hippieism, especially those that have to do with retaining class and race privilege as if they were completely natural parts of one's life. For them, morally, it is sufficient to claim a passivist position of "peace loving" and resign from the corrupting materialistic lifestyle of urban life. Mild narcotics, organic food consumption, and some sort of pretentious association with Native or Oriental exoticism complete the prospect of this type of (pseudo-) anti-capitalist communitarianism. In terms of the philosophical substance in communitarianist literature, there is not much to speak of other than a collage of fragments from the anarchist tradition of rejecting social hierarchies, secular-sounding religious sentimentalism, and extremely superficial references to resistance usually plagiarized from Marxist phraseology—I say "plagiarized" because Marx is not only dismissed but also often openly denounced by these communitarians. Communitarianism is nothing but capitalist communism for members of the privileged who come together to form their own contemporary tribe, who either designate land on which to establish their village or meet in some rural area to renew their friendship and recharge their dimming desires and sense of political relevance. Aster's *Midsommar* provides a brilliant insight into the horrors of communitarian, spiritualist, pseudo-anti-capitalist communities and their fatal attraction for naive but alienated middle-class youth in the West.

At the end of the day, any such groups that totalize the private space at the expense of public space and adopt certain social and sentimental rules and principles as their trademark, without being political enough to form a political party, naturally form a chauvinistic environment that is perfectly suited for micro-fascism to take root. The most obvious cases of this are the sects that started to diverge from Protestantism in the United States shortly after the European occupation of the American continent. We also have *Midsommer*-like groups, such as the cult groups that became epidemic from the mid-1950s to the 1980s, for example, Peoples Temple, and the Osho (Bhagwan Shree Rajneesh) society, Heaven's Gate, and many others.

Another and incomparably more common class of depoliticized collectives is that of student sororities (and fraternities). These function as apparatuses for absorbing college students' sense of alienation and transforming that otherwise potentially political energy into a sense of artificial belonging. First-year students, especially in private schools, choose a sorority in order to belong to a group, and each sorority has its own symbolism and mini-rituals, which can be as absurd as any ritual, only these are formed with the consciousness of being artificial. In the end, millions of students are socially recruited and provided a sense of political belonging that is completely detached from broader societal politics. In fact, in the world of sororities, the politics of the real world becomes completely otherworldly thanks to the endless social politics that arise within each sorority and among sororities, which can be extremely misogynistic and racist in their actual daily manifestations. Chauvinistic standards of group loyalty are often translated into sheer bullying against individual members, leading to horror stories that are kept secret. Even though cases of suicide are not uncommon, which attests to the magnitude of the horrors experienced in sorority spaces, conveniently most parents and college administrations seem to go along with what once was part of their youth.

Finally, there is the fascism of sports, the analysis of which I am compelled to leave for other occasions in order to avoid further broadening the scope of this book. I only want to draw the reader's attention to two main critical/analytical sides of the subject. First, the sports industry obviously occupies a special place in the culture industry, but arguably more than any arena of the culture industry it aggregates and depoliticizes massive youth energy by channeling it into chauvinistic, provincial, and patriotic expressions, all the while rendering it a gigantic source of profitmaking and, thus, capital. Second, the sports industry naturalizes the spirit of individual competition and group antagonism on bases that are completely irrelevant to anything that could be a worthwhile political disagreement. Sports are arguably the largest and most organized means of mobilized depoliticization. Even the emergence of irrefutably damning studies, such as that of Ward and Strashin (2019) showing that practices of underage sexual abuse in the industry are alarmingly widespread, have not resulted in problematizing the industry as far as the public sphere and education are concerned.

To return to my argument about materialist utopianism, a brief comparison between denial and rejection is in order. A denialist mentally rejects the reality but preserves a political role to act as a conformist if not a reactionary. Therefore, the desirability of monotheism is rooted in the dual functions of religious ideology. On the subjective level, monotheism functions as a psychological shield for protecting the believer from perceiving misery as misery. On the broader, objective level, the religious ideology renders the politicality of the world secondary to metaphysics. All the uncertainties that naturally accompany the passage of time are framed in a set of extra-social rules. Therefore, the state depends on religion as a shock absorber. It is not strange at all that state governments from illiberal regimes, such as Iran and Pakistan, to liberal democracies, such as the UK and the United States, considered houses of worship among the essentials that had to remain open during some of the worst times of the pandemic even though repeatedly it became clear that religious gatherings were super spreaders of the virus. It seems for all these states that it was safer to sacrifice more people to the virus than leave them without the shield of religion, which may lead to more thinking, questioning, and accurate perception of the reality.

The Imperative Negativity of Revolution

Negative consciousness, on the other hand, continually strives to comprehend the sources of unfreedom and, thus, problematizes new dimensions of oppression. With that consciousness, nothing can stop the hopeless from fighting domination. The modern progressive revolutions, from the Haitian

Revolution to the Paris Commune, the October Revolution, the anarcho-syndicalist revolution of Catalonia and Basque country, and the Chinese and Cuban revolutions, were launched by the marginalized. In each case, the moment the middle-class elites assumed authority over the new order, the revolution started to decline. Thus, one of the most significant lessons we should take away from these revolutions is that the reintroduction of bureaucratic politics to a revolutionary movement leads to inevitable failure. The polar opposite of the revolutionary potential of negative consciousness is the banality of the bureaucratic mindset. It is precisely the psychological rejection of any possibility of the realization of another reality that paralyzes negative consciousness, without which there can be no alternative. Therefore, the ultimate purpose of a revolutionary ideology is not to provide a possible alternative but to keep negativity alive. Without such a revolutionary ideology, acts of popular rebellion fail to accomplish any progressive structural change. When insurrections only target the despotic political regime without problematizing the racist, patriarchal, and capitalist relations of domination, they often fail to accomplish even limited political reform.

The Arab Spring, for example, had no chance of becoming a revolution because it lacked a revolutionary ideology, as the left has been extremely unpopular in the Arab world in recent decades due to the rise of nationalism in the 1960s and Islamism since the 1980s. In the absence of a popular left, the student and middle-class activists who led the uprisings of 2011 were mostly inspired by liberalism, their main demands being to bring down the dictatorial regimes and hold free and fair elections. The problem is that liberalism is neither revolutionary at its core nor grounded in a doctrine of social justice. As such, liberalism fails to adequately mobilize people to crystalize a political front with a degree of revolutionary discipline. Thus, it should have been expected that Islamism, by virtue of being militantly organized and having the ideological leverage of religious capital would ride the waves of those popular uprisings.

A counter example is the ongoing Rojava movement in northern Syria, which has been driven by a revolutionary popular ideology from the start, advanced by revolutionary subjects from the margins of the margins of the margins. Notably, that revolutionary ideology was not the intellectual product of institution philosophers. Rather, it was the outcome of a long revolutionary struggle philosophized mainly by Abdullah Öcalan, who has been either inside the Kurdish revolutionary movement or in prison because of it since the 1970s. When the Syrian state nearly collapsed in 2012, Kurds in Rojava did not have a ready-made alternative, but they were prepared to create an alternative based on generations of struggle against various forms of domination. They were aware of what would not work, namely any system that entails power hierarchy, including nationalism, Islamism, and neoliberalism. Additionally, they resolved to negate not only political but also social forms of oppression, such as patriarchy. Kurdish women have emerged as revolutionary subjects committed to cosmopolitan emancipation and radical egalitarianism through advancing a multifaceted fight against the old world. Those at the bottom of the hierarchy of global and regional domination, in what I term the margins of the margins of the margins, are in the prime position for becoming revolutionary subjects precisely because their conception of negation is more inclusive than that of the rest of us. That description fits Kurdish women, who have been placed under oppressive relations by capitalism, global and regional imperialism, colonialism, patriarchy, and religion. Their revolutionary mobilization has left no room for compromise with the power hierarchy, as they have realized that any true emancipation necessitates an absolute negation of the existing reality.

Free and fair elections do not emancipate colonized peoples who became minorities in nation-states. How would you reform a system that denies you political space in the first place and perceives your very existence, as a different Other, as a threat? Those in the upper half of the pyramid are rarely even aware of the existence of those in the lower half. Therefore, they are inclined to perceive the existing world as the best possible and are unlikely to take issue with the pyramid as such. Instead, they may speak of limited political reform, all the while trying to climb a little higher, which is only possible through the exploitation of others. Meanwhile, for those at the bottom, with an intersectional negative consciousness in place, it is the collapse of the system itself that would be most likely to improve their life conditions.

The alternative, then, is a world in which the question of alternative is no longer necessary. Rejecting the normalized world should not be a matter of shopping for options and agreeing to give up the existing world only if the alternative world would be more beneficial. Quite simply, the continuation of the existing order should not be seen as an option. Rather than hopelessly asking, "What is the alternative?" we should view the absence of other options as a reason to pursue greater awareness of the existing crises and cultivate negative consciousness. The alternative is to negate one's own bourgeois conditions, to identify with those in the margins of the margins, where the most progressive revolutions take place. With such consciousness comes the realization that there is no alternative but to negate the existing relations of power. A progressive revolution must first and foremost be seen as a step toward creating other possible worlds, not a transition into a preconceived world. As such, the main task of a revolution is to create and expand the horizon of possibilities, whereby equality would not be such an impossible, otherworldly ideal.

Our understanding of revolution in modernity is shaped mainly around the French Revolution and the October Revolution. Of course, the Haitian Revolution, the two American revolutions, the Paris Commune, the Cultural Revolution of China, and the Cuban Revolution among others were significant in their own right. However, all these revolutions still belong to modernity, and as such they all had in common a philosophy of revolution that would disrupt the continuity of history to reshape the social and political world entirely, thereby preparing for a free and egalitarian world, with variations as to what constitutes freedom and equality.

What is certain is that no single revolution will ever be able to set things right. It is even catastrophic to expect from a revolution to entirely change the world and create a fresh beginning. Such an idea of revolution is not revolutionary enough anymore. In a sense staying true to the spirit of all progressive revolutions amounts to inventing a lifestyle that does not let things descend backwardly. This entails the intellectual ability and political will to negate every form of oppression at the moment of its manifestation. On the same day one might have to negate multiple cases of compound forms of oppression. Living negatively means making such rejections an everyday habit.

The Marginalized and Their Cosmopolitan Episteme of Emancipation

On a January day in Berlin in 1919, at the end of the First World War, a Marxist revolutionary woman (from Polish Jewish background) was assassinated at the age of forty-eight. Her death marks the beginning of the rise of fascism in Europe and the demise of a hopeful era of proletarian communist revolutions. However, thanks to her profound writings and revolutionary activities, she would become an inspiring martyr for generations of revolutionaries across the world. In one of her signature statements, in a speech about two weeks before her execution, she warned, "Socialism has become necessary not merely because the proletariat is no longer willing to live under the conditions imposed by the capitalist class but, rather, because if the proletariat fails to fulfill its class duties, if it fails to realize socialism, we shall crash down together to a common doom" (Luxemburg 2004: 364).

Rosa Luxemburg's genius went beyond theoretical analysis of historical transformations and organizational vision of social forces capable of carrying out emancipatory enterprises. She saw the abyss toward which Europe was marching and concluded that there was only one way to prevent a doomsday even more devastating than the one inflicted on the world by the war that had only just come to an end. To her, the revolution was not a question of choice or a way of life; rather, it was a matter of life itself. Her rejection of the existing state of the world was one and the same with her life confirming will. Her assassination at the hand of a social-democratic (and later Nazi) militia right at the beginning of the interwar period was a sign of an approaching dark age.

About twenty years after Luxemburg's execution, the world lost another Jewish Marxist Berliner, incidentally, also aged at forty-eight. Just over a year after the beginning of the Second World War, stuck on the border between France and Spain, not allowed to escape occupied France, Walter Benjamin killed himself in between histories and geographies that became too small to allow for a universalist to exist. At the time of his suicide, his main concern was the survival of a manuscript he had been carrying around as a stateless refugee. Tragically, the manuscript, along with the auratic existence of its author, were lost in that dark moment of the rise of fascism that would systematically eliminate millions of others who either rejected or were rejected by the world of nation-states. Benjamin wrote, "behind every fascism there is a failed revolution" (quoted in Žižek 2008a: 386).[1] Benjamin's insight is strikingly similar to the idea expressed in Rosa Luxemburg's statement quoted above, except he witnessed the fascist world Rosa Luxemburg and her comrades had done everything to prevent.

The emergence and rise of fascism are historically associated with the era that has become widely referred to as the interwar period, 1919–39. At the very beginning of it stands Rosa Luxemburg, a member of the German Communist Party at the time, articulating in the clearest possible language what kind of historical crossroad the world is at: the essential egalitarian revolution or the abyss of "a common doom." At the other end of the interwar period stood Walter Benjamin, in a remarkable moment of resemblance, asserting the same idea, only from the darker end, at the very edge of the abyss that returned his gaze.

Despite the mysteriousness these few facts might suggest, the resemblance is neither metaphysical qua spiritual access to a nominal (higher level of) truth nor meta-historical as it would have been interpreted within the ethos of the Middle Ages according to which the universe is decodable, thanks to the purported ontological law of resemblance that runs across all that exists, existed, and will exist.[2] The mystery of what appears to be prophetic and messianic can be demystified through the very materialist philosophy that both thinkers adopted and enriched through their works. There is nothing interesting in mystifying the two voices that echoed each other from the two ends of a historical period. Given their social circumstances as marginalized subjects, the two thinkers could not afford denying the historical reality of fascism. They had to look into the abyss of fascism in the eye and uncompromisingly fight its invasion of reality.

The uniqueness of their insight is rooted in their negativity, their refusal to give the fascist project a chance to colonize them despite and because of the hopelessness. Of course, that is not to say that anyone else in the same circumstances as Rosa Luxemburg or Walter Benjamin would have had the same insights. To paraphrase Nietzsche, one can and should make something unique out of what the world imposes on one. Nonetheless, the essentiality of what the world imposes on us, the existing conditions, must not be dismissed in the name of the doctrine of "free will." Outside the laws of gravity, of physics as such, "free will" is just as fictional as dragons breathing fire. The lesson we need to learn from these two revolutionaries is that the scope of the darkness in which we live must be faced courageously, thereby closing all doors of false hopes.

The more totalitarian the fascist hegemony becomes, the more necessary it is to engage in a total struggle of anti-fascism. The darker the horizon of possibilities gets, the more absolute our negativity must become. If it is absolutely certain that the revolutionary project of emancipation against forces of domination will lose the struggle, one should be more certain about the rational imperativeness of the revolutionary stance. Losing a revolution is incomparably more meaningful than letting one's last space of freedom, one's own body, to become part of the space of unfreedom and hopelessness. Revolution and art are both impossible, so their philosophical appeals are infinite. Precisely because nobody seems to believe in something else, because nobody seems to believe in a world where denialism and nihilism are not the norms of everyday life, embodying the revolutionary struggle is the only option with which one is left to reject unfreedom, to prevent being forced into an agent of reproduction of hopelessness. In a hopeless world, fascist forces may be able to determine the end of one's existence, but they must not be given the power to determine one's existence.

Dialectics of Hope and Freedom

On January 11, 1919, four days before she was captured and executed, in a letter to Clara Zetkin, Rosa Luxemburg adds a nota *bene* that ends as follows:

> The severe political crises that we've experienced here in Berlin during all of the past two weeks or even longer have blocked the way to the systematic organizational work of training our recruits, but at the same time these events are a tremendous school for the masses. And finally, *one must take history as it comes, whatever course it takes.*—The fact that you are receiving (*Die*) *Rote Fahne* [the socialist/communist newspaper, The Red Flag] so infrequently is disastrous! I will see to it that I personally send it to you every day.—At this moment in Berlin the battles are continuing. Many of our brave lads have fallen. Meyer, Ledebour, and (we fear) Leo [Jogiches] have been arrested.
>
> For today, I have to close.
>
> I embrace you a thousand times, your R. (Luxemburg 2013, my emphasis)

Rosa Luxemburg was among very few European intellectuals to have the courage to face what was approaching, recognize the decisiveness of the historical moment, and prepare for the worst. The spontaneity with which she utters the statement "one must take history as it comes, whatever course it takes" is itself proof of the inseparability of history and her life, the political and the personal. Like Marx, her dedication to the course of history both as her subject and object was inexhaustible. These revolutionaries did not have the time and luxury to waste on the side roads as history would move on. They dared to know that the totalitarian force with which capitalism is decoloring everything cannot be altered if it is not faced head-on, that is with the kind of movement that is both productive and transformative. Such revolutionaries become the revolution itself as they embody limitless thought and action to the very last moment of their lives.

When Marx was asked to describe the most important characteristic of his personality, he simply replied, "singleness of purpose" (quoted in Fromm 2004: 198). That is exactly what made him a revolutionary. To revolutionaries such as Marx, Luxemburg, and Benjamin, there is an ultimate universal hope, the grounds of which much be created, and that is the only hope that would not ultimately fall back into hopelessness. The hope that justifies their lives is the same hope that justifies their revolutionary activities as historical agencies. Namely, it is the hope for a world in which humans can live meaningfully, beautifully, and freely. Immediate, perpetual, and uncompromising battle against the retrogressive historical forces, therefore, was not even a matter of choice. Their freedom meant nothing without taking on what has historically been predetermined. They realized that the only possibility of being free is to be a determining historical subject, as opposed to a mere determined object of history, and that becoming that historical subject is illusionary without comprehending the immensity of the predetermined. The future is open only insofar as past history is eternally closed, unchanged. That is to say, the human "free will" is neither "will" nor "free" without the subject's full awareness of the magnitude of the unfreedom into which she has been born. That is the reason why each of these revolutionaries was utterly ruthless in subjecting themselves to the truth of and in their historical moments. It was not that any of the four thinkers saw communism as a probable actualization. One of the most common misunderstandings of their revolutionary persona, especially in the case of Marx, is the assumption that they believed in the imminent realization of an egalitarian human society free from all forms of exploitation and oppression. Attributing such a prophecy to Marx is a symptom of failing to grasp the basic philosophical grounding of Marxism.

Marx's philosophy is grounded in the ability to realize the totalitarian unfreedom advanced under capitalism and the courage to grasp the hopelessness that is in the process of being eternalized. It is not despite but because of this courage to know the state of utter hopelessness that Marx fully identified with a single purpose: changing the course of history. There is nothing else he could have chosen to do in the face of such a knowledge of history and, thus, the burden of living in the historically predetermined present moment. He had no time to ask whether he could change the course of history. If there is one thing one learns from reading Marx's biography, it is that it never occurred to him that there will be Marxism, at least in the sense of being the philosophical authority of the communist doctrine as such. That is also to say, as far as Marx the revolutionary was concerned his life could merely have had a negligible effect on the course of history, comparable to throwing one's own body to slow down a tank in a battlefield. Nonetheless, the act itself would remain equally revolutionary at least in the philosophical sense.

Not being a revolutionary would only make one another contributing force of unfreedom. On the personal level, not choosing revolution would render one even more unfree. To a postnihilist revolutionary, the point is not "in such a hopeless world one cannot make revolution but rather something along the lines of "in such a hopeless world revolution" is the only meaningful option." Revolution is to hopelessness, what art is to a false reality. The revolutionary and the artist refuse to abide by the rationality of an irrational frame of reference. They negate a world that is founded on negating the truth of freedom, and by doing so they create a spark of truth whereby the imposed hopelessness and unfreedom are negated. Even if they completely fail to perpetuate the negation of negation in the form of a movement, they succeed in creating a space of resistance. That space for the revolutionary is her own rebelled body, and for the artist it is the artwork. Art is a falsification of a world that is hopelessly false, and revolution is the grand project that spontaneously undoes the reality and constructs another.

The overlap between revolution and art can best be conceptualized as "virtuosity," to borrow Paolo Virno's brilliant concept, and the revolutionary is indeed an artist in the sense of being a "virtuosos" (2013: 248). Here Virno's own description of the virtuosos's activity is worth quoting at length:

> First of all, theirs is *an activity which finds its own fulfillment (that is, its own purpose) in itself*, without objectifying itself into an end product, without settling into a "finished product," or into an object which would survive the performance. Secondly, it is *an activity which requires the presence of others*, which exists only in the presence of an audience. (2013: 248, italics in original)

Virno defines political action as virtuosity, and, in fact, he goes on to ground virtuosity in Marx's own notes on artists whose "product is not separable from the act of producing" (quoted in Virno 2013: 249). There is something Prometheusian about becoming one with the act, aiming at no final product or utility. In fact, the "singleness of purpose" entails the defiance of utilitarian and pragmatic thinking. One is tempted to say that the "singleness of purpose" is the materialist equivalent of becoming one with the divine by losing oneself in it, or the equivalent of what in Buddhism is becoming aware of the big Truth, which necessitates overcoming the illusion of the self. On the personal level, the act is indeed an act of self-liberation precisely through losing the socially constructed identity, the inherently submissive self, the little fascist inside each one of us.

The postnihilist rebel is the person who ceases to be an object of history and a passive user of social space to become someone who acts upon spatiality and history transcending everything around her. Great artists and revolutionaries have the ability to be lost existentially in the act. Precisely in this sense the act is, first and foremost, liberating for the subject. The act itself is like a unique mineral that absorbs the poisonous substances, or breaks the chains, if you will, that pulls one down to the underworld where enslavement is the natural law. The act is directed at the existing unfreedom, but even if it fails, it will accomplish the subjective freedom for the actor. To be free, subjectively, is to have the courage to be lost. The subjective freedom, however, is only an accidental consequence, as opposed to a premeditated objective, because the self is not among the primary concerns of the revolutionary. Indeed, most egalitarian revolutionaries do not waste time writing their autobiographies or they do so apologetically.

It is crucial to note that the postnihilist is *from* the darkest margins at the bottom of the pyramids of power and privilege, knowing too well what hopelessness is. Hope comes into being where it is most absent, and the greatest spaces of hope are created by the most hopeless ones. It is in the nature of unlimited suffering to give rise to a reversal movement, starting with an act of negation potentially leading to unstoppable acts and movements of negation increasingly transcending the spaces of hopelessness. It is the perpetuation of the negations that determines how far the emancipation can go before it is reversed. Revolution is the project that aims to initiate and perpetuate negations until the last space of hopelessness is transcended. No matter how many more revolutions will take place and fall shy of accomplishing their emancipatory goals, revolution will always remain to be the only path out of hopelessness. Here the argument is very straightforward: if and when there are options other than revolution, we are speaking of situations and people that are not hopeless, by definition.

Also, no matter how many more revolutions end up in disappointment, there is a historical movement toward more liberation. It may be true that no single revolution will ever be able to accomplish the human liberation, but it is no less true that no power on earth could prevent progress toward more and more liberation. While we are repeatedly told the human liberation is an ideal impossible to realize, it is incomparably truer to state that it is impossible for the historical process of human liberation to cease to progress. Somewhere in their cognitive systems, conservatives, revisionists, and denialists become aware of the historical truth of progress, so they react obsessively against egalitarian and emancipatory projects. If nothing is left for them to do or say to silence the political projects of the marginalized, they preach on being realistic. Of course, at the end of the day, their fear of a new reality is at the root of all their reactions and denialisms, so they continue to act as the faithful guardians of the existing order.

An objector, whether from the point of view of social democracy or liberal and conservative anti-revolutionary doctrines, may argue that my assertion that *nothing can eternally stop historical progress* itself undermines the historical necessity of revolution. In other words, if historical progress is inevitable, why should we need a philosophy of revolution that aims at forcing drastic change in human society?

On the surface, or abstractly, this anti-revolutionary position makes sense. However, nothing in human lives is abstract. Every unfreedom is a lived unfreedom, and every human's existence, both ontologically and historically, is a finite existence. Reformists are right in asserting that history ultimately progresses toward emancipation, but they are wrong in assuming that such a timeless proposition could in itself make the lived experience of unfreedom any less unjustifiable or less intolerable. Put simply, the marginalized cannot be expected to submit to the existing reality in the name of an emancipation she will not experience. Every human action is just as immediate as it is historical. The simultaneity of the posnihilist revolutionary is rooted in the awareness of both facts: (i) the immediacy of the action at the lived moment and (ii) the historical mediacy of the action in prolonged movements that exceeds the limits of her life. Just as it is impossible to freeze historical progress permanently, it is impossible to rationally justify unfreedom in any particular human life. In fact, what makes theology so inherently anti-emancipatory is precisely its placing of the alleged emancipation outside the believer's life and world. Any ideology that demands postponing the full and uncompromising negation of unfreedom to some other time and place is an anti-emancipatory ideology. Revolutionaries who ask the miserable to postpone their freedom until the revolution reaches its victorious end are despots in the making. The bottom line is extremely simple: no one has the right to ask the enslaved to take it a little longer in the name of whatever the promised land may be. A true revolutionary force is the one that renders historical progress immediate through the constant negation of all that has been constructed around social domination. Here, it is worth quoting Adorno again:

> We may not know what absolute good is or the absolute norm, we may not even know what man is or the human or humanity—but what the inhuman is we know very well indeed. I would say that the place of moral philosophy today lies more in the concrete denunciation of the inhuman, than in vague and abstract attempts to situate man in his existence. (Adorno 2000: 175)

Unlike denialism that is at the heart of nihilism, negativism is necessarily concrete. Also, unlike nihilism it is not centered around disbelief for the sake of preserving the subject's autonomy. Rather, negativism is the faithful belonging to the material spatiality of the world, yet it is a belonging that is entirely framed by a revolutionary praxis, which in turn entails commitment to revolutionizing the world in the *spatial sense of here and the historical sense of now*. The concreteness of negation stems from the absoluteness of suffering.

The Uniqueness of Suffering and the Abruptness of Negation

If there is one proposition that is valid by every philosophical criterion, including metaphysically, epistemologically, ontologically, and ethically, it is the following: *every suffering is unique.* It is precisely this uniqueness of suffering that posits subjecthood as the only universal truth with objective ethical implications. That is to say, moral philosophers who dismiss the concreteness of individual subjects stand on false grounds, and as such they are wrong even when they make valid ethical observations. This is *the* fundamental problem of ethics as a field of inquiry. It assumes subjectivity where there is none and dismisses the only space where subjecthood exists, in the person of an actual living human being. This critique should not be confused with moral relativism because moral relativism remains absolutist in terms of its denial of subjectivity as the only space of moral judgment. Relativism often consumes its critique in an abstract multitude of relations as opposed to negatively recognizing the multitude of uniqueness. Refuting all ahistorical and nonmaterialist accounts, postnihilism maintains that no suffering can be relativized because every suffering is unique. Therefore, a postnihilist revolutionary act is both concrete in its manifestation and absolute in its negativity.

The argument for the historical power of the hopeless ones can now be stated in its full clarity. As much as the social forces of subjugation guard the fences of what is considered real, normal, natural, and eternal, those who are denied a place in history and a time in public space will always be the living embodiments that contradict the existing regimes of truths and perceptions, values and norms, discourses and practices. Just as every homeless person in her very bodily exposure exposes the true fragility of the bourgeois public space in any city from Seattle to Hong Kong, every oppressed hopeless subject, in her very existence, represents a hole in the forehead of the existing reality. To tap in her own revolutionary power, all that the condemned needs to do is to affirm her otherwise denied existence. The choice of the space for the performance is key for the revolutionary impact. For maximum affect she should target the most sacred of loci of public spaces. The regimes of signification that sustain the normalcy of the existing reality are centered around pure fictions, so as soon as they are negated by an action, their metaphysical spell begins to break, so to speak. All one needs to do to expose the lie behind the sacredness of a particular space is to purposely turn it to a stage for a negating act even if for a few seconds. The logic here could not be more materialist. All one needs to prove the actual powerlessness of a totem is to break its taboo. The revolutionary action is essentially demystifying, which is exactly where its historical and spatial power lays. All the armies of the existing reality could not prevent the negativity of a single act of a virtuoso. In this sense, the reality may be claimed by the ruling groups and their mobilized masses, but truth is on the side of the silenced. The ruling groups must constantly construct facades of fiction to sustain the virtual eternality of the existing order, whereas the revolutionary subject can choose any moment to create a hole in the curtain behind which all facades and fictionally sustained regimes of truth production are kept. On the one hand, there is a reality that is in need of so much accumulation of fictions it could collapse any minute under the sheer pressure of its own ideological weight. On the other hand, there is the body of the excluded whose very existence is an existential threat on the lifeline of the existing reality. The excluded is denied a space in the world, but when she invades the spaces of domination, her very existence negates an entire zone within the regime of denialism and, thus, the existing regime of truth. By making her *being in the world* present to the senses of both fellow hopeless ones and the denialists, the excluded makes a postnihilist statement with the potential power to sabotage an orbit within the system of fictionalized and fictionalizing cycles. Depending on the overall situation and the readiness of a revolutionary movement, any such act could spark endless negating acts, each of which in turn could invoke a new series of movements of negating actions.

Let us take the movement that followed the George Floyd murder as an example to further demonstrate the point. There is no doubt every case of suffering is unique and should not be relativized. From the point of view of the prevalent order, however, there was nothing unique in lynching another Black man by a group of armed men sanctioned by virtue of the privileges entailed in their uniforms. The fact that they could commit the fatal violence in the middle of a city and in daylight speaks to both the degree to which violence is normalized and the extent to which the public space is hegemonized by the ruling ideology. We should also recognize the fact that George Floyd was given every reason to react using some sort of physical resistance especially as he was dying, but he maintained his utterly peaceful obedience to the police by not showing any signs of resistance all the way to his last breath. Nonetheless, he was accused of resisting the arrest, according to the police statement that followed the incident. Also, George Floyd was just another silenced being whose death did not come in the context of any form of political resistance. The issue is that from the point of view of the ruling modes of perception and power relations, the excluded is already guilty of existing, so there are multiple layers of historical, legal, and moral arrangements in place to seamlessly legitimize subjecting a member of the excluded to physical violence.

The George Floyd case was just another savage violation of the Black body's presence in public, like so many other attacks that have been committed in so many different ways by the racist system since the 1600s. Essentially, Black subjugation has never ceased for the last four hundred years. At every historical turn, the means and methods of the racist exercise of power have been improved both technologically and legislatively precisely to enable the perpetuation of Black subjugation. Just as it was more or less normal for a

Black person to be brutalized or even killed on any road by a white militia, degrading or even killing a Black person in public is daily practice across the United States. Then and now, the majority of Americans are not bothered enough by the anti-Black violence to de-normalize it in everyday life. Now like then, the public refuses to *see* what takes place in terms of the savagery committed against Blacks. Then, what is the main thing that turned the George Floyd case into an event? The short answer is that the sheer repetition of visually exhibiting the incident literally left the public with no choice but to perceive what it saw. The irony is that what was being presented in that video is the norm; it is an example of an everyday incident in American cities. The public's choosing of not seeing what it saw every day is part and parcel of the normalization of anti-Black violence.

The transforming act took place quietly on the sidewalk when a private citizen did what almost any person with a smart phone could do by simply recording the incident while standing with others witnessing the situation, perhaps in bitterness. Another basic fact is that there have been numerous other cases of filming incidents of police violence against African American men. In some cases, the filming sparked some public reaction, and in some of those cases, the public reaction led to various degrees of de-normalization of the ways in which the police system is perceived in the United States and beyond. In the case of the George Floyd murder, however, somehow multiple moments and circumstances coincided leading to the creation of an initial spark directly caused by the video. The recording, like other recordings by standby witnesses of cases of anti-Black police violence, simply had the potential effect of a momentary negation of the denial that is not only at the heart of the racist system but also definitive of the prevalent racist mode of perception. The representers and defenders of the system simply deny its structural racism, whereas the endless replaying of the unedited video left little room for the public's psychological denial of the visually overpowering truth. As a result, the credibility of the official narrative became a little less unquestionable even by the standards of the numbed conscience of the public. There was a ripple effect. Somehow some of the waves had Doppler effects, and the entire regime started to lose its grip over some elements within the dominant mode of perception. The Black Lives Matter (BLM) was prepared as a movement of dissent to prevent the relativization of the murder or giving in to the overwhelming despair that is understandably felt by many of the silenced African Americans. Even when some privileged African Americans, mainly scholars and politicians, tried to contain the movement by creating a space for it within the ideological apparatuses of capitalism and theology, the BLM maintained its fidelity to the margins, keeping the protests alive for a relatively long period of time. Of course, the next logical question is: why is it that such a moment does not reach the level of revolution? To address this question, we need to conduct a genealogical analysis of colonial hegemony to better grasp its totalitarian grip of the dominated. Such an analysis is crucial for comprehending the scope of the challenge with which an emancipatory revolution is faced. Acts of negation are necessary but never enough in themselves to make up a revolution. Also, changing the reality takes more than destruction. It takes a revolutionary hegemony capable of perpetuating the dialectics of negative reconstruction, which is not possible without de-normalizing the dominant regime of value production. If not abolished, the dominant regime, in a relatively short period of time, will be able to regain its totalitarian control over the vital material and discursive apparatuses. Indeed, even when a momentary negation takes place, the dominant regime finds at its disposal armies of volunteers to de-revolutionize the event and, thus, help in securing a flawless continuation of the existing order.

The Anti-Revolutionary Essence of Liberation Theology

More often than not, it is the elites of the margins who manage to de-revolutionize revolutionary movements of the margins. Typically, such elites use their credibility as members of the marginalized and, at the same time, their relative privileges as members of the ruling groups to enhance the hegemonic capacity of the ruling regime so that the negative potential energy of the revolutionary movement is absorbed. Moral discourses are very commonly used by these ideological double agents to appeal to the ruling system to create a space of inclusion for the marginalized. If the decision makers within the ruling groups are smart enough, they cease such golden opportunities to enhance their hegemony and, therefore, further advance the system's image as democratic, diverse, tolerant, reformable, and so on. When it comes to ceasing such opportunities for totalizing the system's hegemony, liberals have a better understanding of the rules of the game compared to conservatives, especially the fanatics among them. If anything, the extremists among any conservative camp are the system's worst insiders because they simply, albeit unintentionally, expose everything the moralist propaganda regime tries to deny.

Despite all the attempts by both the liberal whites and Blacks, the moralist whites and Blacks, the BLM movement's protests in the months following the death of George Floyd for the most part stayed focused on the problem, as opposed to alleged solutions. By the day, the scope of the crisis became more evident to more and more people leading to a continual increase of the public pressure until, eventually, the authorities, including the police, sacrificed the individual perpetuator of the killing of George Floyd precisely in order to protect the institutional perpetuator. The BLM's struggle will go on as long as it remains faithful to the suffering of the past and resists the false hopes constantly manufactured and distributed by the liberal guardians of the reality.

Fatal campaigns against resistance movements of the marginalized are the gradual ones that are instigated through the means of hegemony. In these campaigns, the elites who come from the margins usually play an indispensable role. What a Black member of the Congress can do against the liberation struggle of the Blacks is incomparably more devastating than anything white elites can do to de-revolutionize the Black movements of liberation. What a Black theologian who genuinely speaks in the name of the oppressed Blacks could be far more damaging to the potential Black revolutionary energy than anything the white members of the moral regime could do.

By the same token, liberation theology is among the most effective hegemonic apparatuses of the colonial subjugation of the colonized. Here before engaging in the political philosophy of this thesis, it is essential to bear in mind that in this particular subject matter, the devil is not in the details but in the broad frame of reference and its relevant history. Limiting the historical implications of any phenomenon to the singularity of the historical events could be as misleading as generalizations that dismiss all or most of those events. Therefore, the thesis presented here is grounded historically but, for the most part, defended philosophically.

Black churches and "liberation theology" are typically understood in terms of appropriations of the Christian theology. The appropriations in question have taken place within the Protestant theology in the case of Black Americans, and the Catholic in the case of Latin American liberation theology. In both cases, the affiliated movements have played undeniable roles in supporting the oppressed by a wide range of means, including militant resurrections and revolutionary terror. From Richard Allen, the most significant founding figure of the Black churches in the United States, to Martin Luther King Jr., the Black Christian leaders more often than not have led, supported, or inspired revolutionary movements of anti-racism. Also, whether they were terrorist revolutionaries such as David Walker and Nat Turner or the majority passivists such as King Jr., they were subjected to (often fatal) violence. What has become known as "Liberation Theology" especially after the publication of Gustavo Gutiérrez's *A Theology of Liberation* in 1971 (1988) has been even more directly associated with the left in terms of international politics, affinity to Marxian phraseology, and open support for progressive movements of dissent across many countries, especially in Latin America. Despite the respective differences in their histories and geographies, both Black churches in the United States and "liberation theology" in Latin America can be labeled under "liberation theology" for our purposes. In fact, even Islamic political movements, including the Muslim brotherhood, Khumenaism, that speak in the name of oppressed or colonized Muslims could be included in "liberation theology."

While liberation theology does appropriate theology, but in the broader historical, political, and philosophical context it is more accurate to say it appropriates the politics of the marginalized to better fit into the colonial system of the oppressors. Such theologies appropriate the minds of the oppressed ideologically to find a place within the existing order, albeit, with a certain degree of accommodation from the side of the existing order. The accommodation, reform, or adjustment that the prevailed system accepts is often counted as a score for both sides, but in reality, it is theologized oppressed that does the ruling regime a favor by enhancing its means of hegemony, by rendering it more durable historically and more appealing morally. At the same time, the oppressed, who are allegedly represented by its elites, are made even less in charge of their voice and discursive means to articulate their deepening unfreedom. The potential negative power in the young populations of the margins is either further denied a space of performance or simply turned into extra positivity in favor of the ruling system. By the time the public space is made agreeable to the presence of the marginalized, the marginalized are fully and more completely baptized than most of the majority. The state of the aboriginals in Canada attests to this. After they have been completely deprived of everything that is theirs, after they have been made impoverished by colonialism, after they have been weakened by every single European social disease such as alcoholism, after they have been securely placed within the regime of private property, and finally after they have been Christianized, they are now permitted in public space. There is nothing left of the colonized nations to be freed. The traces of their world are safely put away in museums to entertain the colonizers and make them feel good about their perfect democracy.

The theological appropriation of the African American revolutionary struggle had already become evident by the early 1800s, at the peak of anti-slavery insurgency. Most of the appeals even by radical revolutionaries who were associated with evangelicalism, that is, Methodists who joined the free Black churches, were moral appeals within the Christian frame of reference. As such, regardless of their commitment to anti-slavery militantism, they had severely restricted their prospects in terms of their potential revolutionary enterprise. To put it plainly, the theological identity of the movements essentially rendered their platforms submissive to the ruling ideology and institutions by virtue of being petition oriented as opposed to being revolutionary in terms of presenting a new philosophical vision of the world capable of negating the broader modes of material and ideological production. The conversion moment of Richard Allen is extremely illuminating of the anti-revolutionary orientation built into theology. Allen and his entire family had been enslaved in Philadelphia by a white man called Benjamin Chew, who sold Allen's mother and three of his siblings to another slave holder, yet Allen speaks of him in very favorable terms. Describing his conversion, Allen writes,

> My sins were a heavy burden. I was tempted to believe there was no mercy for me. I cried to the Lord both night and day. One night I thought hell would be my portion. I cried unto Him who delighted to hear the prayers of a poor sinner; and all of a sudden my dungeon shook, my chains flew off, and glory to God, I cried. (1833: 5)

The dungeon and chains of slavery, of course, continued, only now embraced with gratitude. Speaking of Benjamin Chew, the man who had been enslaving his entire family, Allen writes, "not being able to pay for us; and mother having several children after he had bought us, he sold my mother and three children. My mother sought the Lord and found favour with him, and became a very pious woman. There were three children of us remained with our old master. My oldest brother embraced religion, and my sister." Then he adds,

> Our neighbours, seeing that our master indulged us with the privilege of attending meeting once in two weeks, said that Stokeley's negroes would soon ruin him; and so my brother and myself held a council together that we would attend more faithfully to our master's business, so that it should not be said that religion made us worse servants, we would work night and day to get our crops forward, so that they should be disappointed. (1833: 6)

Allen confirms that his faith now made him work harder in the service of Chew. He was also eager to prove this welcome effect of religion to Chew and others. He writes, "At length our master said he was convinced that religion made slaves better and not worse, and often boasted of his slaves for their honesty and industry" (1833: 6).

It is no wonder that one of the anti-slavery organizations that appeared in that era, namely the American Colonization Society (ACS), founded in 1817 in Washington DC, openly called on the American authorities and African Americans to colonize Africa to "civilize" it in light of the American model, primarily using the Protestant code of ethics. Indeed, within five years of its birth, the ACS established a colony on the West African Coast, which became the state of Liberia in 1848. This is among the most damning proofs of the theological appropriation of the Black struggle, which is typically, and falsely, assumed to be Black appropriation of Christianity. More evidently, the colonization of the different parts of Africa would have been unimaginable without the ideological role tasked to theology, whether during the Islamic invasions or the nineteenth-century division of the continent among a few European powers and the ensuing nation-states that have been perpetuating the European domination in both form and essence. Those who are doubly marginalized, such as the Amazigh or Darfuris, have suffered the most at the hands of their rulers and global capitalism. All this goes to say that the Christian and Islamic ideological apparatuses foreshadowed nation-states' ideological technique of exclusion through inclusion on broader levels. The marginalized were made to feel included only to uproot their capacity of resistance more effectively. They were given spaces of inclusion, but those spaces were nothing but tombs that ensured a slow but sure death. At the end, what is included in a nation-state is a colonized people deprived of the ability to even recognize, let alone express, her unfreedom.

By using Christian or Islamic phraseology to express the injustices of colonialism, the converted Other had already lost the struggle against colonialism. It is no wonder that despite his emancipatory platform and the fact that he was assassinated, Martin Luther King Jr.'s persona was relatively quickly adopted not only as a national hero but also as a cultural icon in the symbolic capital of American patriotism, that is, to showcase the democratic façade of white racism. The reappropriation of Martin Luther King Jr.'s legend by the culture industry was convenient precisely because of the Christian frame of reference King had adopted. Malcolm X went to the colonizers in the Islamic canon seeking support for his anti-colonial fight. He even became a welcome guest of some racist and colonial regimes in the Middle East. While Malcolm X is more difficult to be reappropriated within the American culture industry, he remains to be a more presentable figure than Marxist Black Americans. Revolutionary Black American Marxists stand no such chance of being tolerated in the United States.

It is "liberation theology" that renders the God created by colonialism a worshiping entity for the colonized. It is that immense ideological resource that makes utter and unlimited submission possible in the name of justice. It is also that method of hegemony that could make, and does make, a colonial preacher or a colonial soldier out of a colonized subject. When the value system of any marginalized group is colonized, all their revolutionary movements and hopes are in a serious danger of demise. If we are compelled to designate the relationship between theology and liberation, at least within a philosophy of revolution, the only rational approach will have to aim at liberation *from* theology. Certainly, "liberation theology" is an oxymoron from the viewpoint of the most basic premises of materialism, which is a necessary criterion for a philosophy of revolution.

That said, one can invalidate theology as a potential doctrine of liberation *empirically*. Wherever theologians have succeeded in taking over a revolutionary movement, they have also succeeded in creating a regime no less discriminatory and absolutist than the toppled one. Of course, this might be said about some communist revolutions as well, but we need to keep in mind that there are crucial historical, philosophical, and categorical differences between the two. The communist movements failed to topple down their main enemy, the global bourgeois class. In failing to do so, in each region the movement diverged from the Marxist philosophy of revolution, which is by definition internationalist. The identity of the communist revolutionary subject is based on an objective criterion.

A communist politics can only be a politics of the world proletariat. Thus, philosophically, there is no ambiguity about the fact that when a communist movement becomes national in its politics and aspirations, it is no longer communist. Only when it failed as a revolutionary movement, what had been a world communist movement became something nightmarish under Stalin and other advocates of "socialism in one country." Moreover, the failure of the communist movement in the twentieth century was neither unavoidable nor immediate. It took time and an aggressive international civil war for what had been a communist revolutionary objective within reach to disappear into some unknown horizon.

None of the above qualifications applies to theological movements, whether Christian or Islamic. Christian and Islamic theologies are universal in their totalitarian and imperialist tendencies to tribalize human society, which is the diametrical opposite of "internationalism" or "cosmopolitanism" advanced by communism. To take an example, the Iranian Islamic regime wasted no time to deliberately target national, religious, ethnic, and gender minorities, not to mention the communists. Unlike the materialist camp, the Islamists did not need to diverge from their belief system to wage their genocidal campaigns. There was no time period to separate the moment of authenticity, so to speak, and the moment of divergence, as far as the oppression of the minorities and marginalized is concerned. In fact, Islamist movements, even during their phases of insurgency or opposition, make it clear that they follow absolutist policies of discrimination against women, religious minorities, communists, and such. Whenever they had a chance, they made it clear that they do not tolerate out-groups.

In the Christian world, the oxymoron nature of "liberation theology" can also become evident if we consider the endless bloodsheds committed by Christendom. The intolerance is such that even Christian sects never stopped to victimize each other. While Protestants were the victims once upon a time, who could deny the role of the Protestant sects in the American neoconservative politics of social domination and neoliberal politics of imperialism today? Ordinary Catholics suffered their own share of discrimination in Ireland and the United States, yet at the peak of the anti-fascist struggle across Europe, the Catholic establishment hardly hesitated to choose the fascist camp against the communists and anarchists. Granted that Christian "liberation theology" cannot be held responsible for all that has been committed by the Christian social and political forces over the centuries or even in twentieth-century Europe. Its theological affiliation paired with its claim of liberation as a progressive social force render it a legitimate object for examination based on philosophical criterion of revolution. While the brand name is recent, theology has always seen itself as a force of emancipation and always promised the ultimate justice for the miserable of the world.

Every "liberation theology" is premised on the viability of theology as a potential philosophy of emancipation, and that is what I mean to dispute, not the claim that a theology could be innocent in terms of what has been committed in its name by other affiliated theological versions of the same religion. Within a specific geopolitical context, an Islamic movement may very well appear to fight colonialism or an established fascist regime, and other Islamic movements may concentrate on aiding the poor, refugees, and other victim groups, but none of that makes any version of Islamic theology emancipatory in terms of its doctrines of social justice. Again, what is disputed here is not that Islamic theologies are all equally responsible for the crimes committed in the name of Islam across ages and regions, but rather the claim that any Islamic theology could indeed offer a universalist and inclusive political philosophy. A theology might make a valid moral argument, but it cannot offer a valid doctrine of social justice universally and objectively. Needless to say, valid universalism is, by definition, a necessary condition for any viable doctrine of social justice. The followers of a religious sect could very well be innocent of acts committed in the name of their religion, and they may even resist oppression in certain limited contexts, but their theology remains invalid as a revolutionary project even on the level of pure theory.

However, this is not a mere theoretically constructed argument. To this date, not a single Islamic authority has condemned the Armenian genocide. The genocide of Yezidis, in 2014, not only failed to instigate a public debate around discriminatory foundations of Islamic theology, but in fact it failed to distance even Iraqi Kurds from Islamic authorities and Islamist parties despite the fact that Kurds typically consider Yezidis to be part of the Kurdish (stateless) nation. It seems only the colonizing power of theology could make Kurds turn a cold shoulder to the suffering of other oppressed Kurds who are mass murdered and enslaved. Any Islamic theology has more questions to answer in defense of itself than credible claims to make in the name of being a philosophy of liberation. To this day, for Islamic institutions and authorities, be it Shia or Sunni, moderate or extremist, a minority or a majority, anti-Semitism, gender discrimination, and the Islamic-supremacy myth are unproblematized conventions.

A theological doctrine of social justice is essentially a nightmare for the majority of the members of human society even though the religious canon in question may be reformable to be safely allowed in an inclusive world. Thus, theology is categorically different from communism, whose theory of society and history constantly allows for rational improvement even when it goes wrong and becomes nightmarish. The categorical difference, thus, is between a wrong that cannot go right versus a right that could go wrong, between a belief system that is catastrophic, even if (or rather *especially*) when its foundational principles are followed, and a philosophy, the violation of whose principles could be catastrophic. While either Christian or Islamic theology has had more than a millennium of monopoly of political power, secular and scientific communism has never had a chance to rule. Stalinism, anti-communist liberalism, and fascism produced destruction on catastrophic scales, which together and separately could (and should) be seen as the consequences of the violation of the main principles of the negativity that shapes the core of Marxist communism. Stalinism was a clear distortion of Marxism, and in fact responsible for the murder of the biggest number of communists. Anti-communist liberalism, during the last eight decades, committed unprecedented acts of mass murder, using the most devastating weapons of mass destruction, and has had a major role in bringing about the ecological catastrophe. Finally, needless to say, if fascists have one thing in common across the world, it is their anti-communism. Moreover, as both Rosa Luxemburg and Walter Benjamin were well aware, it is precisely our failure to make revolution that results in barbarism.

Theology is a falsehood that might be tolerable if revised drastically, whereas communism historicizes its own claims and, as a philosophy, is essentially founded on the principle of continual rational improvement. The former sees progress as its death sentence, but the latter identifies with progress. The former claims prehistory as its origin and moment of perfection, whereas the latter is forwardly oriented even for its own doctrinal maturity. The former divides the human society into two unreconcilable main groups, in-group versus out-group, but the latter defines its struggle by its sole commitment to objective, that is, material equality among all humans. Marxism may be lacking a comprehensive account for undoing all forms of discrimination, but theology is never short of discriminatory accounts of humans. Marxism is open for rational improvement to become more anti-discriminatory. Theology may be open for anti-discriminatory reforms in terms of particular groups of people, but it cannot become a nondiscriminatory force of universal egalitarianism given its metaphysical claims and the centrality of metaphysics in relation to its moral, political, and historical claims.

Theology is inherently anti-emancipatory insofar as it situates the only hope for the hopeless world of humans outside the world of humans, while communism is premised on the attainability of a human hope within the spatial and historical frames of the rational. To the theologian the material world is hopelessly false, but to the communist the hopelessness of the world can and must be negated via a materialist struggle. Theology aims to turn the world into a waiting station for another, higher, form of existence that is anything but material. Communism aims to realize egalitarianism within the material limits of the potential, so it does not promise hope but aims to create hope. In the theological system, justice is not something in the making, but rather something that has already been perfectly defined and guaranteed by a divine that is above and outside history.

The communist philosophy of liberation is primarily a philosophy of history, not justice, because it maintains that justice can only be constructed, deconstructed, and reconstructed historically and spatially. Therefore, the communist process of liberation is inherently also a process that aims to emancipate history and spatiality from real, existing, material, forces of domination. Every theological doctrine of liberation is first and foremost a spiritual process. To the communist philosophy, the exact opposite is true in two senses: first, liberation can only be materialist; and second, spirituality is nothing but a means of domination, a false hope based on idealism to maintain a hopeless material reality. Even in terms of the most basic level of the dialectics of hope and hopelessness, the contrast between the metaphysics of theology and the philosophy of communism could not be more obvious. Theology's fundamental truth claims are premised on the eternal hopelessness of the human condition in this world, whereas communism's entire wager relies on the negatability of the hopeless circumstances. Theology is, therefore, most anti-revolutionary when it claims liberation, yet communism is revolutionary to the exact extent to which it is emancipatory.

Despite their potential good moral intentions and political sincerity, the agents of liberation theology are among the most effective double agents of colonialism because their deployment of ideological (including spiritual) means, institutional authority, and discursive strategies in the long run maximizes the process of de-charging the negative power of the marginalized. In effect, marginalized Blacks, especially in the southern states, are systematically mobilized to channel all their frustration and agony into mass songs and dances in Black churches, which have become a part of the political identity of Blackness in the United States. Whatever different interpretations of the phenomenon may be, one thing is certain: while Blacks are denied a fair share in the material wealth they created over generations, their religious leaders have been assigned a share in the spaces of colonial God to appropriate it democratically to suit the Black cultural identity as constructed by colonialism. Yet, there is no real contrast between the material exclusion and the spiritual inclusion. In fact, the spiritual democracy is an effective method for maintaining the material oppression. The damage that has been inflicted on the Black soul by the white God exceeds anything the plantation regimes, Jim Crow Laws, and police brutality on their own could have inflicted on the autonomy of Black resistance. Historically, the theological means of ideological hegemony cannot so easily be separated from the overall process of subjugation, but it is nonetheless helpful to point to the anti-emancipatory role of theology, if for nothing else then to detect some of the points at which resistance begins to go astray as a potential revolutionary project. Of course, we cannot deny the supportive role of liberation theology in the case of the Zapatista Army of National Liberation (EZLN), but we should try to imagine how much more revolutionary the movement would have been without that role. Even more broadly, one could argue that Latin Americanism lost much of its remaining velocity when liberation theology started to take the place of communism proper.

Ideological Double Agents as Agents of Paralyzing Hopelessness

Capitalists who are perceived as being from the margins would sell the members of the margins and their struggle for a price much cheaper than what would be demanded or offered by an ordinary capitalist from the racially privileged groups. The elite members who come from the margins often play the role of ideological double agents who invest in the existing system by exploiting the legitimacy of the struggle of the very marginalized groups they supposedly represent. The privileged individuals who come from the margins may say everything that the worst among the privileged would want to (but does not dare to) say. In the meantime, the marginalized groups are relatively more at ease drinking the regime's poison from the hands of their own members. Therefore, the role of a double agent must be thoroughly problematized.

The ideological double agent, who has access to both the privileged centers of power and the spaces of the marginalized, voids the body of the condemned from all the revolutionary power of negation, rendering it an empty vassal to be used for ideological infiltration of the margins to further colonize them from inside. The Black theologians or Islamist Kurds, for instance, expand the symbolic capital of the privileged and further totalize the spaces of colonialism. They make the colonized Black or Kurd shout what the colonizers do not dare whisper in public. For the colonizer, the sacred space is only a part of a vaster space of privilege, but thanks to the double agents who speak in the name of the marginalized, the very identity of the colonizer and all that is associated with it became sacred. Thanks to such servants of the divinities of colonialism, even when the colonized are stepped on, they may shout that they deserves such a treatment and that the colonizers deserve to be forgiven before it even occurs to them to apologize. To the marginalized who are colonized from inside, the regimes of significance, of love, and of meaning are all defined by the divine symbol that is nothing other than the persona of the colonizer.

An essential dimension of the total hegemony of the dominant has to do with denying the victim even the claim of victimhood because such a claim would imply a contradiction in the moral legitimacy of the domination system as such. To accomplish the point of complete denialism of the victim's victimhood, aside from physical elimination of the victims, that is, genocide and its denial, there is nothing more effective than allowing a selected number of the members of the marginalized to join the centers of political, academic, and religious authority. Once they become club members of privilege, the chances are that they will try even more devotedly to prove their trustworthiness and faithfulness to the established order. Thus, the stage is perfectly set for the selected minority member to voluntarily act as an ideological double agent. Everything could work smoothly thereafter to totalize the ruling group's ideological hegemony over the marginalized group that was unfortunate enough to have a member or more joining a higher-up center of power.

Briefly, here are the immediate effects of such a so-called representation of the minority.

1. First and most clearly, the minority in question will be further denied their claim of being underrepresented.
2. The ruling system will have yet another visible point of reference to emphasize its supposed diversity.

3. The system boosts its image as a democratically formed body of authority.

4. In the person of the double agent, and often directly through her statements, the system makes a point to blame the marginalized for their own misery. The double agent's personal privileges are used as proof of the system's supposed meritocracy (implying that those who try hard enough are prized with the rewards they deserve regardless of their background). How often have we all heard yet another Black or brown brag on TV that she came from such and such poverty and misery, yet, thanks to her hard work and the American system, in which everyone can make it to the top, she is now who she is, famous, successful, happy, and, above all, an example to inspire the millions of the nameless and faceless ones who are suffering at the bottom of the pyramid (implying that the miserable ones are not smart enough, not working hard enough, etc.)?

5. In turn, the victim is reproduced but this time as a victim of her own alleged loser mentality and lack of *will to power*.

6. The expressions of agony that should be associated with living as a marginalized are now not only invisible but also replaced with the big smiles of the happy representative, the selected double agent.

7. As a result, what has been structuralized historically through endless processes of colonialism, enslavement, and imperialism is now not only further depoliticized, but also entirely individualized, thereby rendering the concrete individuals blamable for being victims.

8. An ideal boost to nationalism and patriotism is added to the already self-entitling ruling group. Where else can merit be rewarded so quickly and so generously? Except, the accurate way to put such a statement would be something along the lines of "where else can victimhood be turned into a shiny package to symbolize the limitless kindness of the perpetuators?" Or "where else could the victim be turned into a damning proof against the crime of her own existence and a pure exhibition value to embody the kindliness of the perpetuator?"

9. As a result, the nihilistic social environment is further enhanced in the interest of anti-revolutionary prospects.

10. Thus, potential negativity is increasingly replaced with denialism, and revolutionary hope with passive frustration.

11. In turn, the dialectics of hope and hopelessness is derailed, thereby perpetuating hopelessness as an unchangeable state of being.

12. Therefore, the concrete individuals from the margins are even more alienated, deprived of effective political means, and made to feel personally hopeless.

13. It follows, even when the system of domination undergoes existential crises, there is not a popular revolutionary project to seize the historical moment for creating a new horizon of possibilities.

14. Finally, even when a revolutionary space is created by the marginalized somewhere, the revolutionary moment of hope could be missed by most of the other marginalized groups.

This is not to blame ideological double agents for the entire imposed hopelessness, but their role does indeed embody a point of unique ideological concentration aimed at dissolving revolutionary will. They also create foci for absorbing negativity during historical opportunities created by crises. Again, recall the fact that places of worship were considered among essential places to be opened quickly or remained open during the worst times of the Covid-19 pandemic. Crises are rare opportunities for widening the stage of political performance by the movements of dissent, and the ruling groups are well aware of this, so they rely on institutions of spirituality to function as seawalls in such times. What is actualized by liberation theology, in the long run, is nothing but the absolutism of social domination because the colonizer's regime of truth becomes even more eternalized. This problematization also helps us immensely in articulating what a postnihilist philosophy of revolution is not.

Bad Resistance and the Hegemonic Scope of Domination

We need to step back and reflect on the process of colonialism in its totality and its ontological replacement of subjectivity. The common, non-Fanonian, understanding of colonialism bases the duality of the colonizer and colonized on a plain of diametrical opposition whereby the movement of each pole is directly antagonistic to the other. However, such a conception of colonialism could not be more misleading. For in the process of colonialism, beyond a certain point, the colonized becomes entirely situated within a colonial space whereby there is no longer a subject of the Other, but only one subject, which is the colonial one. This colonial subject is affirmed and reaffirmed by both the colonizer's own agency and the activities of the colonized, including those that are perceived or performed in terms of anticolonial resistance. The colonizer wins the game not through eliminating all forms of resistance but rather through producing an identitarian resistance caught up in the cycle of colonial relationality. It is precisely this relational identitarian form of perception adopted by the Other that crowns the universalization of colonialism's irrational rationality.

As I will elaborate later, the very existence of the colonized in this identitarian sense becomes an affirmative force further actualizing the colonial subject's omnipresence. As hopeless as this theoretical argument may sound, failing to recognize its critical scope could only lead to the production and reproduction of false hope and further frustration for the marginalized. That is also to say, the postnihilist philosophy of revolution is not only a negation of hopelessness but also a rejection of false hope that is at the heart of ineffective and counterproductive forms of resistance. Once more, comprehending the magnitude and depth of the existing hopelessness is absolutely necessary for gaining the ability to go beyond the prevailed reality. Also, recognizing bad forms of resistance is inseparable from the process of cultivating the negativity essential for a postnihilist conception of revolutionary practice.

The agents of bad resistance are not necessarily morally bad. Their premises and preassumptions are just false, and, therefore, they constantly operate on tracks of falsehood, which may, in temporospatial contexts, make certain things better for a certain marginalized group, but overall, they deepen the hegemony of the dominant systems of value production, thereby absolutizing and eternalizing inequality. By virtue of perceiving and presenting particular cases of inequality in a moral language, the moralist further normalizes the false assumption that the system in its essence is meant to be ethical or made ethical. Moreover, every system of domination can very well respond to moral appeals, if for nothing else then precisely to reaffirm the false assumption about its ethical core.

In fact, a fascist system tends to produce a moral discourse not only to gain popularity among their targeted social bases but also because the fascist ideologues and leaders, more often than not, genuinely believe in the moral principles advocated in the fascist platform. It is absurd that most of us seem to never stop being confused when we learn the fact that a certain fascist leader, including the textbook cases, Mussolini or Hitler, had certain humane characteristics. The reason for the confusion is rooted in the false assumption that these individuals had no moral principles and were stripped of human feelings, intimacies, and so on. It is just less disturbing for us to assume that they were pure evil with nothing in common with normal human beings. It is more comforting for us to assume that Hitler had nothing in common with us. However, the truth is extremely troubling, and fascism will not be truly challenged until we gain the courage to dismantle our psychological means of distortion, to actively search for what we have in common with Hitler. Worldviews that are based on some form of good–evil duality tend to not only reproduce mass murder but also deny or justify their own act of committing mass murder. As long as our lenses are moral and based on the dichotomy of good and evil, we will fail to catch the little fascist inside us simply because there is nothing easier for us to be confident than that we are good, and even when we act in a way that might seem problematic, we *know* our goals, intentions, and such were good. Notice most people are morally against violence if they are asked, yet most people partake in violence on more than one level and in more than one sense.

"I am against violence, except when it is used to prevent violence." Something along these lines is what many of us typically tell ourselves. There are many ways to articulate that idea, but the bottom line is that we tell ourselves that our moral rule is "no violence," with one exception to the rule in order to sustain the rule itself.[3] Despite the sense of satisfaction one might have about such a moral stance, ironically, what is common is not only the central idea but also the sense of having a sophisticated moral judgment. The good–evil dichotomy renders moral satisfaction easily achievable for everyone regardless of the kind of politics they may or may not support. The only difference is that the imagined roles are reversed from within persons and groups; the in-groups of course see their side as representative of good in the world. Therefore, every use of violence is considered an exception to the rule, as justified violence, from the moral point of view of its perpetuators. It follows that in reality what is presented as an exception is the rule, that is, all cases of violence are moralistically justified by its perpetuators. People whose fundamental standard for political activity is formed around a good–evil dichotomy are essentially similar in not only their way of seeing the world but also the kind of world they constantly reproduce.

The purpose of my problematization of the moralist approach is not the formulation of a philosophical solution.[4] My claim is that moralism merely distorts serious philosophical and political questions. Since, as Adorno asserted, in a wrong world there are no right options (2005: 39), it only makes sense for ethics as a field of philosophical inquiry to focus on negations and double negations, which would necessitate setting ethics on material and historical grounds. Ethical interrogations should shift their focus from abstract actions (ought to and ought not to) to material circumstances and concrete subjects. In a wrong world, positive ethics will only metaphysicalize wrongness, rending "justice" identifiable with the dominant values and the value of domination.

Thanks to the domination of this moralist mode of perception, it is extremely rare for those who participate in genocide to realize what they are committing. The Other is dehumanized, that is, denied subjecthood, and demonized, that is, associated with evil, before they are exploited, tortured, or killed. Thus, the moralization process almost always takes place whenever and wherever violence takes place. In fact, often the moralization process is inseparable from the procedure of mass murder. Therefore, it is absolutely nonsensical to assume that it is the lack of morality that produces the Hitlers of the world. The exact opposite would be truer.

Also, thanks to this way of (not) thinking, it is ideological double agents who concretize the ethical authority of the colonizer precisely because of their adoption of a moral approach to any given situation, even when their (moral) discourse is radically critical of the colonizer. By assuming that exposing the unjust practices of a regime would lead to satisfactory reformation of that regime or some sort of realization of freedom, critical moralists merely contribute to totalizing the ethical authority of the ruling groups.

Put briefly, the moral discourse, regardless of its content and its authors, enhances the ideological hegemony of the broader system of domination. The colonized should never be under the impression that if she proves her humanity, her subjective depth, her ability to be ethical, and her victimhood of colonial injustices, she would be able to end colonialism. To the contrary, it is precisely that approach that turns her to a colonized being and agent serving colonialism. For it is precisely her humanity, her subjecthood, that is denied by colonialism. The colonizer had already assumed the Other's nonhumanity, lack of subjecthood, before violating her social and political space. By adopting the moral approach, the colonized directly embodies the colonialist hypothesis, which is centered around the ethical authority of the colonizer and the colonial subjugation of the Other. The victim's appeal to the murderer's sense of justice further empowers the latter and deprives the former of the last resort as a spatial subject, of the autonomy of the body. Colonizers do not see themselves as criminals; more often than not, they see themselves as the pioneers of justice and engineers of order in the world. More importantly, they do not see the Other as a human being entitled to life. Rather, at best, the Other is perceived as a savage to be civilized, an ignorant to be enlightened, or merely a resource to be exploited. Therefore, prior to being committed, the colonial violence is always seen as the exception that sustains the rule (recall the earlier analysis of violence). How absurd is it, then, to hope that a moral foundation of what is supposed to be an anti-colonial struggle could actually lead to emancipation?

The agents of bad resistance had fallen into the identitarian mode of perception that is created by the dominant ideology. The dominant ideology creates its own version of Otherness out of the colonized Other. The transformation takes place where it is least expected: in the zone of the excluded. This zone is spatially transformed into a margin of the dominant. It is included in order to be ontologically eliminated as a being outside the space of colonial totality. In the inclusion of the Other, the Other is turned into a shadow, a reflection, of the colonizer's self who not only controls all the motions but also distorts the shadowy figure at will. We know the colonizer is a dominant actor on the stage. What most of us do not realize, however, is that the colonizer is also the playwright who initially created all the characters and the director who directed all the essential aspects of the play. By playing a role in the colonizer's play, all those who are on the stage partake in the colonial project. In fact, the audience are also a part of the play's success.

The only form of true anti-colonial revolutionary project is the one that negates the entire theater in which the colonial play is performed. Reversely, the more we are absorbed by the details, sensations, characters, plot development, and the rationality of the theatrical space as the only given reality, the more hopelessly we are immersed in the production of our own hopeless reality without realizing it. A holistic philosophy of negation is essential for going beyond the absurdity, the nihilism, that frames our spatial activities no matter how genuine, ethical, and antiauthoritarian those activities may be and despite the rationality that is produced within the totality of the system. Therefore, the struggle of postnihilism is a prerequisite for its political praxis. In other words, what matters postnihilistically is not the excellence of the revolutionary role, but the revolutionary, which is a meticulous and holistic, replacement of the world in which we are situated. For that to happen the referential frame of meaning production in its entirety needs to be problematized. Again, a resistance that is motivated by and focused on ethical arguments is arguably the most anti-revolutionary form of action because it presumes the limits of the theater as the limits of existence, epistemologically, metaphysically, and ontologically.

In Plato's famous allegory of the cave, the prisoners who have been chained to a cave wall can only see the wall in front of them where shadows are constantly moving, but they have no way to see that the shadows are not all that there is. They cannot even realize that there are objects and light which together give rise to shadows like those they have been seeing for their entire lives. To them the reality is the moving shadows. One of the prisoners breaks free of the chains around his neck and starts a journey ascending out of the cave and eventually realizes what shadows, light, and objects are. His journey leads him to where the sun shines, where the truth is revealed.

If we assume the prisoners have a language, the shadows would not be called shadows because that would imply knowing that there exists another realm of reality, an alternative world. Also, it is within the rational framework of the allegory to assume that something must happen to intrigue and motivate the prisoner enough to make him break the chains and start his quest for the truth. Something in the movements, sizes, or order of the shadows must be contradictory even by the logic of the cave dweller who has no access to any other place and time, any other order of things. The reality of the shadows betrays a contradiction and that leads to the first realization, which is entirely a negative one.

The prisoner's ascending/freeing journey starts by rejecting the given frame of reference and leads to the realization of the fact that what he had been taking for *reality* and from which he had deduced all his knowledge is nothing but a staged scenario, a constructed reality, an eternalized set of relationalities managed and exhibited as the world in which the real and the possible are determined. His journey to the broader world at every stage produces new knowledge that negates more and more of his former reality. The process of perpetual negations is one and the same with the realization of the alternative, the broader, the truer world. It is impossible for the cave dwellers to imagine what the alternative world looks like unless they undertake the actual journey of negations.

We can very well imagine that in the cave the prisoners have been engaged in endless forms of debates, disputes, politics, and antagonisms, but epistemically all their discourses, political activities, and moral judgments are situated within the limits of the perceived reality. It is not that they all think in the same way about conflicts, justice, fairness, human potentialities, and entitlements; it is not that all of them are submissive to the value systems produced over the years based on the endless movements, order of the moving figures, attributed meanings, produced values, and constant changes in their reality. It is just that their activities are, broadly speaking, determined by the same mode of perception in the same way our activities, including "revolutionary" actions, are formulated based on a particular mode of perception. We are, in fact, the cave dwellers insofar as we do not realize that the mode of perception we operate by, regardless of our self-proclaimed identities, is the dominant one not only in the sense of commonality but also in the sense of being determined by the dominant. We may sense the contradictions and ironies that surface once in a while, but we fail to problematize them and thus create an expanding locus of negativity. We live in the reality but do not act on our ability to seek the truth of that reality in the holistic sense.

We do not realize that we are playing parts in the play, that we are placed within a stage, a theater, where our characters, roles, and horizon of possibilities are determined by ideological apparatuses, bureaucracies, and institutions of privilege and regimes of knowledge production. The regimes of knowledge production do expose pieces of truth but only fragmentally, which in turn perpetuate our distraction from pursuing negativity and attempting to discover the illusions that cover the general framework of the reality in its totality. We do not realize that what we call resistance is a shadow reflected and distorted according to a process of direction and lighting that takes place beyond and above the dramatic details in which we are completely consumed. Therefore, even when some of us make sound arguments or brave moves on or off the stage, we are wrong in our perception of ourselves as potential revolutionaries. For revolutionary negation must stem from a holistic comprehension of the hegemonic scope of domination.

Postnihilist negativity is concrete, absolute, and perpetual, so while it is prompted by singular events and contradictions, each one of its negating actions also functions as a kind of another piece of a bridge to go somewhere else, to expand its spatial occupation, to construct its emancipatory alternative step by step. Thus, an analogy for posnihilist negativity from the point of view of the revolutionary subject is a spider's way of moving around in space, which is also its way of constructing its own space thread by thread. A spider's net is a form of geometrical perfection, but there is no division of labor in terms of design and construction. For a spider, even falling is instantly turned into an act of occupying space and creating a new space simultaneously. By geometrizing every act of moving or every incident of falling, the spider masters double negation spatially. By moving in the air without wings, it builds what becomes a bridge. By building each bridge, it also gets closer to sculpting a new world out of the void. The net is never just a net; rather it is everything. It is holistic because it is the outcome of living and what makes living possible for the spider. Postnihilist negativity, simi-larly, is holistic and relies on singular, albeit connected, acts of negations. Each negation creates an opening that enables the postnihilist to simulta-neously move forward another step and conduct another act of negation. The alternative world is the outcome of the continual acts of negation. The totality of the bridges makes up the alternative world because each bridge will function as another building unit of the emerging space.

Another analogous case to illustrate the postnihilist philosophy of revo-lution is a beaver dam. The dam is structured as it is built, and built as it is structured. The perfection of a dam is accomplished through a form of engi-neering that is inseparable from the act of deconstruction, which in turn, is inseparable from the act of building. Unlike a spider net, the inherent design of a beaver dam does not involve any geometrical shapes; instead, it is based entirely on singular traces, each of which is unique. One of the outcomes is an incredible structure to defy the most devastating river events, namely, floods. Thanks to beavers, trees are in fact protected from the destructive power of floods. Also, thanks to beavers, the forest around a river is nour-ished. Thus, even though the beaver may appear to us as being engaged in constant destruction, with each act, it adds another piece in the production of a new space. As a whole, the dam is never just a dam; rather, it is everything. It is the habitat and the structure of a new world literally actualized through determined, singular, and continual acts of de- and re-construction.

Ideological Double Agents as Manufactured Form of Otherness

Turning the colonized into a mere Other, a depthless reflection, of the colo-nial self is among the final outcomes of colonialism. Colonialism aims to turn the colonized into something defined in terms of the colonial self by replacing the Other's ontological being, autonomous subjectivity, with a manufactured identity. The new identity is centered around a mass-pro-duced difference. Every difference that is manufactured reaffirms the influ-ence of the manufacturer. Thus, the colonized Other is trapped in a fishing net, whereby every movement only reduces her ability to act as a free being until eventually her body as her most essential political space is negated, becoming a vassal hanging in a void, a spatial raw material ready for any colonial purpose at any moment. The Other is not colonized as long as she does not define her identity in relation to the colonizer. Let us suppose that X indicates the colonizer's identity. The moment the Other starts to perceive herself as non-X and formulates her political cognition of the world accord-ingly, the countdown of her dying process starts, and colonialism reaches the beginning of its final stage, whereby it creates a world in the colonizer's own image.

The subjugation of the Other to the colonial power aims at de-worlding and objectifying as a preparation for demolishing her identity as an autonomous human subject. In place of the eliminated subjecthood, another identity is discursively installed to name the colonized. This new identity has a double ontological function. It simultaneously obliterates the traces of the dead subject of the Other and reaffirms the hegemony of the colonizer as the only real subject in (and even above) history. Undoing the traces of the Other prior to being colonized is accomplished within the same project that, in the long run, absolutizes the universal hegemony of the colonizer's subjectivity.

Here, building on the notion of "colonial mimicry" introduced by the postcolonial thinker Homi Bhabha is helpful for further problematizing nonnegative, such as moralist, forms of resistance and the role of the ideological double agents in totalizing the hegemony of the dominant. "Colonial mimicry," Bhabha writes, "is the desire for a reformed, recognizable, Other, as subject of a difference that is almost the same, but not quite" (1984: 126). Bhabha adds that "the effect of mimicry on the authority of colonial discourse is profound and disturbing. For in 'normalizing' the colonial state or subject, the dream of post-Enlightenment civility alienates its own language of liberty and produces another knowledge of its norms" (1984: 126). Then, commenting on a passage by John Lock, Bhabha makes the following remarkable observation:

It is from this area between mimicry and mockery, where the reforming, civilizing mission is threatened by the displacing gaze of its disciplinary double, that my instances of colonial imitation come. What they all share is a discursive process by which the excess or slippage produced by the ambivalence of mimicry (almost the same, but not quite) does not merely "rupture" the discourse, but becomes transformed into an uncertainty which fixes the colonial subject as a "partial" presence. By "partial" I mean both "incomplete" and, "virtual." It is as if the very emergence of the "colonial" is dependent for its representation upon some strategic limitation or prohibition within the authoritative discourse itself. The success of colonial appropriation depends on a proliferation of inappropriate objects that ensure its strategic failure, so that mimicry is at once resemblance and menace. (1984: 127)

The mimicry Bhabha speaks of is not a simple objectification mirroring the mimicked; rather, it is a mock imitation that affirms the existential essence of the imitated precisely by emphasizing the colonially manufactured difference with which the Other identifies mistaking it for her own ontological, autonomous, identity. By virtue of being an imitation, the colonized self will always be referred back to the subjectivity of the colonizer whether the colonized situates herself in politics of resistance or in outright apologetic servitude for the colonial institution.

The "post-colonial" tragedy of Asia and Africa is that they reproduced European colonialism by adopting the European prescription for "sovereignty" in the form of nation-statism. Asia and Africa became mimics of Europe. Which Europe? The Europe that aborted the Enlightenment; the colonial Europe of nationalism and fascism; the Europe that had no space for its universalists, from Marx to Benjamin and from Louise Michel to Rosa Luxemburg; the Europe of the bourgeoisie that constructed the myth of race to dehumanize, enslave, and exterminate the Other. Essentially, in their very alleged act of national independence, the elites of the ruling groups replicated colonialism's model for institutionalizing biopower, in the nation-state, and by doing so they practically actualized the colonialist vision of the world. In the name of emancipation, these Asian and African new states have only reproduced excessive forms of unfreedom maintained by brutal violence whether against those who are internally colonized within each nation-state or within the racial majorities. Thus, within the peripheries new centers and peripheries were created, and within those peripheries of the peripheries new margins were created. Today, those who are marginalized in any nation-state in Asia and Africa are the invisible, nameless, and faceless oppressed who are subjected to every imaginable form of colonialism. Above everything else, they are denied an identity even within the language of colonial mimicry. For instance, Balochis are denied a name (they are referred to as Pakistanis or Iranians, which is the worst possible form of denial because they are colonized by Pakistan and Iran). Kurds in Turkey have been subjected to systemic discrimination, displacement, and, often, mass murder precisely because they are not Turks, yet even linguistically they are subjected to elimination because they are labeled "Turkish."

From the viewpoint of the institution of colonialism, the colonized becomes manageable, reproducible, recyclable, reformable, and even disposable especially when she falls into the trap of the colonial mimicry. It is no wonder that, from Mesopotamia to West Africa, the (supposedly postcolonial) nations invited their former colonizers to directly handle their national crises. For instance, today the French Republic is invited back to some of the former colonies to enhance, as it were, accountability and security where the mimic nation-states have been struggling, and failing, to become like their European creators. What a literal embodiment of Marx's statement, "the first time as tragedy, the second as farce" (2010d: 103). The original is brutally false, so the imitation could only be catastrophic. The original is both pathological and fatal, so the copied versions could only fatally pathologize life and pathologically mock death.

In tragedy, the trace of the loss is present. The distance with the bygone is made tangible at least in terms of subjective experience. The absence of the absent subject is present. Therefore, in tragedy, our experience remains to be auratic. However, when the trace of what is lost is eradicated, whether through museumization or other forms of commodification of the Other such as culturalization, we are being deprived of even the ability to be melancholic or nostalgic. The tragic could be a source for great art and the deepening of our life experiences, but when we lack even the sense of tragedy, we fail to perceive the tragic, and, instead, we will only become more detached from life as auratic experiences.

By virtue of being colonized within, the colonized cannot decide on what constitutes the tragic. Even her own suffering cannot be perceived as tragic enough to become the subject of art unless her suffering is re-perceived from the point of view of the colonizer. That is to say, only when the colonizer determines the tragic essence of an event can the event in question be experienced and re-presented as tragedy. A case in point is that of the death of Alan Kurdi, the three-year-old Kurdish child from Kobanê, Syria, whose body was found on a shore in Turkey on September 2, 2015, after he had been drowned in the Mediterranean with a group of other refugees. The photo of the face-down dead little boy was of course tragic, and it was perceived as such. What is strange is that multiple Kurdish artists, who are well aware of the unjustifiable deaths of children across Kurdistan on a daily basis were caught up in the Western perception of the tragedy of Alan Kurdi as they painted and repainted the image. Similarly, the vast majority of the Yezidi survivors of genocide live in Iraqi Kurdistan, suffering from all kinds of discrimination and neglect in refugee camps, but somehow the only survivor who was received by Kurdish politicians in Iraq has been Nadia Murad, after her tragic story received attention and recognition in the West. These same politicians could have invited Nadia Murad anytime or simply treated her and her fellow Yezidi survivors with the dignity they deserve. But alas, the person they suddenly decided to invite is not Nadia Murad, the Yezidi survivor, the triply marginalized whose main concern is the silenced victims of genocide, but a celebrity who received the Nobel Peace Prize. This of course only makes Nadia Murad's cause more deserving of our genuine support because if anything, it speaks of loss of the sense of tragedy in Iraq where most Yezidi survivors live. To give a final example of the phenomenon from the same place, in January 2015, as a UN Refugee Envoy, Angelina Jolie visited Iraqi Kurdistan where a major camp for Syrian refugees has been located since 2012. Something happened that is just as disturbing in terms of the utter insensitivity of the Kurdistan Regional Government's officials. According to several eyewitnesses, the politicians were more concerned with taking pictures with the famous Hollywood actress than discussing refugee affairs.

Experiences such as melancholy or nostalgia require subjects. The experiences may be painful, but if anything, they add more texture to the worldness of the subject. The content is sorrow, but it is a sorrow contained within the boundaries of an autonomous being, rendering her being in spatiality and history distinct. Auratic existence and experience are rendered impossible in the colonial universe where the colonized suffers. Her suffering is neither narratable in prose nor relivable in poetry. For the colonized is deprived of subjectivity. That is why, more often than not, it takes a white subject to author or co-author the biography of the colonized Other for the biography to be published and marketed globally. Even when a member of the colonized produces her autobiography, it is the marketability of the style and the language that determine the story's fate. The autobiographer must strive to produce a cultural commodity out of her life and world. The product must fit the demands and stereotypes of Western consumers, whose own aesthetic criteria are anything but autonomous thanks to the totalitarian effect of the culture industry.

Also, it is because of this loss of traces of subjectivity that the colonized, even when in a state of virtual enmity against the European, appeals to the European conscience as if it were by definition humanity's conscience. One of the ironic contradictions that attests to this is the repeated calls by the Syrian opposition forces on Europe and the United States to forcefully intervene in Syria against the Baathist regime. In fact, the dominant mood in Arabic media became one of frustration due to the purported European and American indifference toward the suffering of Syrians. Often, the European and American perceived subject is simply referred to as "the world" in these typical expressions of frustration (that the world is indifferent, etc.).

Following the American invasion of Iraq and the removal of the Baathist regime in 2003, these same platforms in the Arabic public sphere did everything they could, including providing free propaganda for Islamist forces affiliated with Al-Qaida, to mobilize against the American troops in Iraq and the post-Saddam Iraqi government. Similarly, the liberal Arab intelligentsia typically accused Arab regimes across North Africa of relying on the (imperialist) Western powers to remain in power; as soon as the Arab Spring uprisings began, the same intelligentsia, without any sense of irony, established a popular discourse around blaming the West (morally) for not supporting the uprisings. Ultimately, these opinion making elites proved over and over again to be both desperately against and for Western intervention, which is exemplary of the state of being deeply colonized.

More broadly, regimes that are openly non-democratic go through the motion of arranging (sham) elections, as if by some degree of imitation, they could secure some degree of legitimation. Most such regimes would not lose any more legitimacy among their ruled people if they plainly and publicly dismiss the whole scheme of elections. In fact, they might gain a stronger grip of power without those sham elections that function more like regular reminders of those regimes' utter hypocrisy. The assumed target of the performative act, and therefore the object of the cheating, is not the already disempowered people within the country, but rather it is the West qua "the world." Contrary to what they usually claim, these leaders have fully internalized the white man's notion of legitimacy as legitimacy per se. In other words, while a despotic leader from, say, Central Asia or West Africa, may commit whatever crosses his mind against his "nation," it never occurs to him to simply disregard the election show altogether. That is so precisely because the targeted audience of the performance is not the allegedly sovereign nation but the white man, whose assumed standard for political legitimacy the dictator from Central Asia or West Africa has internalized as unignorable.

The colonized is turned into something inherently inauthentic qua a mechanically reproducible copy, an auraless persona, whose sole significance is essentially to glorify the imitated authenticity that is the colonial subject, the white European. Through engineering and implementing the colonial subjugation, the European colonizer supernaturalized the colonial subjectivity. That is to say, European colonialism aimed at both the thingification of the colonized and the divinification of the colonizer at the same time. In her very auralessness, which is produced through, not despite, the postcolonial, the so-called independent nation-state, the former victim of colonialism constantly functions as a reference to the aura of the colonizer. In her mimic presence, even her absence is demolished. Her presence eradicates every trace of her own being in the world qua a subject. In addition, in the presence of this (mentally) colonized subject, the absence of the European colonizer's self is made present. As a result, all spaces become the European colonizer's space. The European colonizer is no longer defined by her spatial presence, but spatiality is defined in reference to her. It should go without saying, the universalized European subject certainly does not represent the European universalists/communists, from Karl Marx to Walter Benjamin. To the contrary, these universalists were themselves marginalized, and ultimately denied every citizenship, employment, and space in Europe.

Even when the (mentally) colonized expresses her anger and dissatisfaction with her state of unfreedom, she reaffirms the omnipresence of the colonizer by virtue of operating within the colonial frame of reference. The (mentally) colonized operates within a discourse that is fundamentally structured around colonial modes of perception and signification. Once the internal colonialism is accomplished, every move by the colonized only further dissolves her own being as a subject, which is at the same time the fuel for the light that illuminates the statues of the deified self of the dominant. In this sense, most African and Asian nation-states, from India to Ethiopia, have only eternalized, internalized, and universalized the colonial project that was invented by the racist, not the universalist/communist, European. However, within these peripheries, there have always been other centers of imperialism and colonialism producing margins within the margins of the peripheries. The center–margin dynamics within the global peripheries are no less brutal than the global ones. Therefore, a lot of the same relations of subjugation, including the role of religion, are produced and reproduced within the global peripheries as well, and this is something many on the left have failed to take into account or even notice.

While my claims regarding the deification of the colonized subject may be read as a metaphor, the theological conversion of the colonized renders the transformation literally true. When the mentally colonized person reflects and wants to do something about her state of enslavement, she appeals to the colonial God. The more agony she experiences, the more desperate and devoted she becomes in her total submission to what she perceives as the ultimate source of truth, justice, and beauty. The agony of the colonized is obviously caused by colonialism, yet, thanks to colonial theology, that agony constantly results in further glorification of the colonial self and that self's system of values. To the racist colonizer, on the other hand, the Other's very existence is a problem, so practically no amount of conversion, submission, and peacefulness will satisfy her. We should also keep in mind that while the othered Other's difference is a source of fear, her similarity is even more feared by the dominant. The story of the Cherokee people in the nineteenth century under colonialism is among the clearest embodiments of this. First, they were forced into assimilation in the name of "civilizing" them, in which conversion to Christianity was among the most central measures. When the Cherokees succeeded in being assimilated, the white ruling groups wasted no time to subject them to mass violence and displacement, once more. They, as it were, became too similar to the whites. In Mexico, more often than not, the missionaries wanted to convert the colonized peoples, but they insisted on not teaching them Spanish in order to keep them in the position of subjugation even within the institution of religion.

Today, the anti-immigration policies in Europe may be legitimized in the name of (European) protectionism, but it is not hard to detect the real fear beneath the surface, which is a fear of the Other actually becoming European. This fear is the same that motivated decision-makers to forbid the so-called race mixing, especially between African Americans and white Americans, in the era of slavery. Colonizers want the Other to become similar as a copy of the colonial subject, not as a subject per se. The point is to make the Other a reflection, a mechanically reproducible image, of the colonizer's subject. When we are told that God had created humans in his own image, the point is the glorification of the creator, and the creature is deserving of respect only insofar as she is a reflection of the creator. The merit of such a copied existence, whether in theology or colonialism, is entirely dependent on its reproducibility as an inauthentic image of the sole entity that is entitled to subjecthood, the divine or the colonizer, respectively.

In Fanon's works, there is arguably nothing more central than his concern about the anti-colonial struggle on the existential and ontological levels. He was well aware of the fact that the African cause will be lost if Africans fail to liberate themselves from the frame of reference that had been drawn by the European colonizers. Of course, Fanon was not so naive as to call for a return to "authentic" cultures because that would be another form of internalizing the colonial project. In fact, he explicitly expressed his concern about the culture talk that has been produced by the colonialist Europeans (for instance, see Fanon 2004: 154–5, 172). To him, African liberation could only mean victory over the tribalist world imposed by the European colonizers on Africa and the rest of the world. He refused to fall into the trap of playing the Other of Europe. A Fanonian Africa is indeed the Africa that would disappoint the European colonialist precisely because it would be an Africa that owns a true universality, instead of letting the racist European to claim universality. The political revolution, in Fanon's thought, is inseparable from the existentialist philosophy of breaking through the limits of the possible by focusing on what is most definitive of the human ontology, namely, the will to be what one is not. Indeed, Fanon writes, "Thus human reality in-itself-for-itself can be achieved only through conflict and through the risk that conflict implies. This risk means that I go beyond life toward a supreme good that is the transformation of subjective certainty of my own worth into a universally valid objective truth" (1986: 70). Later he adds, "I am a part of Being to the degree that I go beyond it" (1986: 179). This is exactly the universalist project that is essentially negative, and among its immediate targets of negation are national, cultural, and religious categories. This is the philosophical locus of universalist revolutionaries who emerged from the margins and set out to negate the savagery of the totalitarian global regime of hierarchical discrimination. From Marx to Fanon, Rosa Luxemburg to Mao, Lenin to Ho Chi Minh, Trotsky to Che, and Biko to Ocalan, the project is that of reclaiming humanity not as it is determined by or in relation to the colonialist subject but rather as the universal truth that has not been actualized yet.

Moving from Negating Acts to a Revolution of Negation

The hegemony of the ruling groups is so totalitarian, only during regional or global crises will the loopholes become relatively visible for potential revolutionary perception and action. Even during those crises, the best revolutionary candidates, as both subjects and movements, are those who are situated in the margins of the margins. Because their normal circumstances are crises-ridden, in times of national, regional, or global crises, the marginalized are less traumatized than the privileged. Of course, this is not to say they suffer less fatality; to the contrary, like the poor everywhere, whether during pandemics or natural disasters, they are at risk of higher fatalities than other populations.

To disrupt a system of domination, its regime of value production must become a direct target of the revolutionary movements of dissent. "Value production" must be understood as capital, truth, and morality simultaneously. As long as one sector of the dominant mode of value production remains operating, the dominant regime will endure. It may adjust its policies of wealth distribution, racial relations, gender inequality, internal colonialism, or imperialism, but it does so precisely in order to deepen its hegemony and, thus, eternalize its domination.

The dialectics of hope and hopelessness is not a thought formula, but a theory that is both descriptive and transformative of the human world.

The postnihilist revolutionary becomes capable of perceiving the chains of her reality. Then, she gradually starts to become aware of the reality of the illusions that sustain the material reality. The journey to become a revolutionary is by no means purely intellectual. To the contrary, it is holistic both individually and socially, just as the revolutionary hope is both personal and universal at the same time. The holistic nature of the revolutionary transformation is rooted in the fact that systems of domination are totalitarian, that is, they have actualized unfreedom in all aspects of life. The negation of unfreedom, therefore, necessitates a project that is both holistic and universalist. Nonetheless, the spark of negativity and the ensuing awareness is worth visiting and revisiting. Therefore, a further clarification of the artistic personality of the postnihilist revolutionary is in order.

The postnihilist is spontaneous in her spatial activities, which is precisely how her body becomes a historical space for the revolution. Also in this sense, she becomes the revolution, leaving no chance for failure both as the body of the revolutionary subject and the revolution of the body of the oppressed. Her freedom is not dependent on the realization of a utopian world in the future; rather, it is realized in the spontaneity of her being in the world as a historical agent who undoes the conditions of unfreedom, starting with her own unfreedom. Through negating the reality of unfreedom, the revolutionary has already realized and been living her freedom. In essence, the postnihilist revolutionary subject and the postnihilist revolution are inseparable. What remains is the freedom of the rest of humanity, which is the postnihilist revolutionary project in the broader historical and societal sense. However, the rule does not change even in that universal sense insofar as the revolution is ultimately the historical and spatial outcome of the multiplicity of subjects becoming postnihilist, becoming the *subject* and the act of *revolution* at the same time.

The postnihilist revolutionary of course contemplates on her actions, but the contemplation for the most part takes place after she conducts her acts in everyday life. This spontaneous characteristic is exemplary of the contrast between the postnihilist personality and the personality of the dull empiricist. Like an artist, the postnihilist revolutionary does not plan but lives life in the only way that is meaningful, that is, spontaneously. The performative aspect is an inherent aspect of being spontaneous and, thus, it is the diametrical opposite of performing spontaneity, which dominates all bourgeois public spaces. Performativity is a political action's democratic measure. If the action's performative character is a secondary trait relative to any other trait, then the action might be exploiting democratic means for undemocratic ends.

Revolution is negative through and through. What appears to be revolutionary hope is nothing but the extraordinary motion initiated by the extraordinary comprehension of the naked truth of the hopelessness that pours out from every inch of reality. That motion may or may not accumulate enough force to create an extraordinary shift in the direction, speed, or the velocity of what is presently shaping what will be called the course of history during the next chapter of history. No one is more aware of the hopelessness of the existing order and the way history will be advancing moment by moment and day by day. In fact, what distinguishes a revolutionary is precisely her courage to look at the abyss of the present moment. It is the truth of the hopelessness that transcends her to a revolutionary subject, and in a few cases, like Rosa Luxemburg or Franz Fanon, to revolution itself. Rosa Luxemburg's declaration that "one must take history as it comes, whatever course it takes" is, therefore, the ultimate revolutionary way of being, of living, of thinking and acting. The revolutionary's tangible, historical, concrete freedom is not something that could be threatened precisely because she is fully aware how hopelessly she is unfree.

Postnihilism has already been crystalizing through some of the margins (in the margins of the global peripheries) that have the misfortune of being subjugated to multiple forms of exploitation and oppression not only at the hand of Western imperialism but also at the hand of regional imperial forces and fascist regimes. This geographic misfortune, however, has at the same time placed them in a unique epistemic situation where the maximum number of the factors of domination both in their singular brutality and compound hegemony can be perceived. Precisely because of this epistemic situationality, an emancipatory movement (armed with a revolutionary philosophy that is also crystallized by the same subject) entails the largest scope of freedom and inclusivity. Such an awareness has the ability to perceive the scope of the crises with which we are faced and has the potential power to negate the multilayered conditions of exploitation and unfreedom. In other words, the complexity of capitalist, nationalist, and patriarchal exploitation paired with the multiplicity of everyday forms of oppression to which the margins of the margins in the peripheries are subjected can be experienced only by those at the very bottom of the pyramid of domination.

Of course, such conditions naturally produce only the most hopeless prospects of embitterment, if for nothing else, because the capitalist system of accumulation is such that the more a group is underrepresented, the greater the surplus value allocated on them becomes, which often translates to being forced to selling not only their present labor but their entire future labor as well merely to secure food and shelter. While this proposition is true in the case of marginalized Americans as well, in the case of the marginalized in the global peripheries, the conditions of hopelessness reach their absolute limits. Unlike life in works of fiction and sentimental cinema produced for moral consumerism, in reality such miserable conditions of life do not, and cannot, produce saints, heroes, and stories of romance. On the contrary, the true tragedy of these oppressed groups is that they are forced to intensify their own subjugation by even further exploiting the most silenced among themselves. For understanding the brutality of limitless domination and exploitation, the Nazi concentration camps remain to be historical cases we all need to examine and reexamine. By putting in place a machine of bureaucracy that operated on the basis of instrumental rationality (like most bureaucracies everywhere) and technological apparatuses that operated on isolated features of efficiency of the sciences (like some state technological apparatuses of control today) the Nazis had their victims stripped of their human dignity before stripping them of their lives. When people are stripped of their human dignity, they could be transformed to mere tools of reproducing unlimited violence, as Zygmunt Bauman reminds us (2004: 86–7). All that to say we would be committing a terrible fallacy if we romanticize conditions of unfreedom, as it has often been done and offered as a lesson of morality. If anything, such cheap attempts to romanticize the subject of oppression play an organic role in naturalizing systems of oppression. An analogous case is the numerous literary attempts to romanticize the imagined character of the prostitute. Such writers, albeit unknowingly, attribute a sense of noble purposefulness to the conditions that give rise to prostitution at the expense of the commodified humanity of the prostitute and the irreducible suffering to which the prostitute is subjected in the reality of her everydayness.[5]

Conclusion: The Postnihilist as a Revolutionary

The spiritualist argument regarding the limits of reason, as the Enlightenment's central doctrine, already assumes the existence of an alternative, higher, reason. Therefore, the spiritualist doctrine immediately undermines its own reasoning. The moment an idea is formulated, a statement is articulated (whether that statement is an assertion of a myth or the law of gravity), human reason is at work. Denying that can only amount to attributing a transcendental feature to human reason. That means the spiritualist doctrine would entail the very opposite of its own main premise. Namely, it would affirm that human reason is limited, and that human reason is unlimited, at the same time.

The appeal to theism can only be based on reason's incapacity, but reason's incapacity must also mean that its realization of theism is a false one. By the same token, if the realization of theism is not false then reason's unlimited capacity is implied. To put it differently, if reason recognizes some form of rationality beyond its own reach, such as God, then God is not beyond its reach. If God is not beyond its reach, then reason is not limited, which can only mean God is reason itself only mystified. Feuerbach asked, "Have the Christians really done away with the eternity; that is, the reality of being? All they have done is to place it into a particular being, into the being of God which they thought of as its own ground and as being without beginning." Then he adds, and this is the crucial point, "Thought can never go beyond being, because it cannot go beyond itself; because reason consists only in positing being; because only this or that being, but not the genesis of being itself, can be thought" (1972). To correct the error, then, theology must be demystified, and that is precisely what Feuerbach meant when he argued that theology is part of anthropology, that we created God. Therefore, while spiritualists too realize that the bridge is on fire, they believe if they manage to stay asleep, they can survive in their dream space.

Our inability to see patterns of contradictions indicates that the ideological hegemony has reached a totalitarian point. When the norm is irrational, it is not natural. We must be suffering from something extraordinary when we act irrationally, against even our own interests. The bleakness of an age can be gauged by the commonality of its absurdities and the absurdity of its social practices. This book constantly points out undetected absurdities and uses them to problematize the normalized and internalized. The process as a whole aims to negate the ideological hegemony and, at the same time, construct a postnihilist philosophy that enables its reader to negate the limits of what is possible now, to realize that the alternative to the existing order cannot be conceived prior to negating the existing order. This postnihilist philosophy is revolutionary insofar as its ultimate goal is the creation of a space for imagining a world in which imagining alternative worlds is neither impossible nor necessary. The existing state of the world necessitates an alternative world, the realization of which is both intellectually and materially impossible unless we break free from its chains and start the journey of negations. The contradictions are sufficient to make us infer the rational conclusion that the existing order must be negated in its totality. Only after the first negation can we start to realize what kind of world can be created. All we can know now is that the world we will realize must replace inequality with equality, unfreedom with freedom. We may not know what equality and freedom are like, but we know too well what inequality and unfreedom are like.

Those of us who dare to reason that ultimately this socio-ecological catastrophe along with the endless forms of exploitation of people and environment can and must be stopped, those of us who dare to announce that capitalism is replaceable with an ecologically sustainable and historically more advanced order are habitually accused of being utopian. From internationally recognized social scientists to average university professors, from citizens who are not particularly interested in theories of history, society, or politics to first-year college students, most seem prepared to swiftly and confidently refute Marxism for its alleged utopian vision. It is particularly discourses based on reasoning denounced for being unrealistic.

In fact, faith-based mythological systems could claim anything, anything at all, no matter how absurd in its irrationality, without being denounced for making utopian and unrealistic claims. This brings us to the second phenomenon: that mass belief in utterly irrational and exclusionary dystopia is something that is proudly expressed in the public sphere. There are millions of preachers of expansionist religions who speak of worlds that are completely faith-based precisely because each one of them is utterly irrational on all accounts. Among the most obvious and central buildings of an

American, European, North African, or Middle Eastern town is the place where such public discourses about some universal justice and afterlife world are reproduced.

To make things worse, more often than not those who accuse the communist of being utopian are themselves among the masses who believe that the world is only a few thousand years old and that human beings rise up after death to enter a fully just kingdom. Of course, that is called spirituality, so it is not subjected to the same standards and assessments by our guardians of reality. What is spirituality if not a disguised psychological method to justify one's irrational submission to an order that is otherwise impossible to justify both rationally and ethically? What is spirituality if not placing all of existence as such on grounds that are exempted from rational judgment? Given that the perpetuation of relations of domination is dependent on the material and intellectual captivity of the majority, what is spirituality but an internalized management system that de-politicizes all that is political and politicizes all that is not political, and rationalizes all that is in the interest of the dominant and ridicules all that would otherwise be most obvious with minimal capacity of reason?

The fact that this irony of rationalization of mythology and mystification of rationality is overlooked speaks to both the destructiveness and the totalitarian nature of normalized regime of production and perception. There is something catastrophically wrong with public awareness when the majority of people do not perceive believing in a Disney-like second world as problematic but are quick to describe a world not based on misery and inequality as unrealistic, utopian, idealistic, and so on. Therefore, it is crucial to comprehend the scope of the current crisis with its various dimensions and manifestations before we can reasonably address the question of alternative possibilities to the existing order. Today the gloom on the horizon is so bleak that comprehending it takes a revolutionary courage to *know*, which in turn will lead to a revolutionary negation of reality.

Postnihilism replaces denial with negation. Denial is based on intentional ignorance, the conscious refusal to *know*, whereas negation entails rebellious actions and comes as a result of dialectical awareness of truth and truth making. The courage required here has to do with the fact that true knowing renders change inevitable. Once we know how bad things are, we will have no choice but to change them. By the same token, those who choose not to know do so to avoid having to act (or act precisely in order to not know).[6] Often the primary psychological function of a belief system is to make the state of not having to know a permanent state of being in the world. The belief in a supreme, metaphysical, being shields one from the curse of knowledge and all that knowledge leads to. Of course, the believer will still pursue knowledge, but only within a predetermined frame of production and consumption, within utilitarian and pragmatic boundaries. This reductionist and partial knowledge is therefore at the heart of what Marx calls the "ideological superstructure," which is not only determined by the existing social relations but also protective of those relations. Also, this form of knowledge is helpful in the sense that it shields the subject from the feeling of having to change the world; it sustains the conditions of ignorance. Contrary to that, negative knowledge is unsettling, troublesome, agitating, and transforming. It is the knowledge that inevitably leads to a shift in the modes of perception. The reality would no longer be seen as paradise or a path to return to (the lost) paradise. Conveniently, it is this knowledge that is associated with the "fall" into the world. The world, however, is simply another term for reality. It is not that there are multiple worlds; there are only multiple ways of perceiving the same world. Negative knowledge amounts to ceasing to view the world as paradise. Those of us who have fallen and those of us who are still in some sort of protective heaven live side by side, here and now.

Postnihilist revolutionaries are those who accept the reality in terms of perceiving it, that is, they do not deny it nor are they afraid to look at its abyss. They do not try to take refuge in spirituality, entertainment, actual narcotics, or deliberate ignorance. However, they reject the existing reality's legitimacy. They know reality and truth do not always mean the same thing. When he was only twenty-one, defending the youth's courage to dream against conservatism, Walter Benjamin wrote, "We, however, know something different, which experience can neither give to us nor take away: that truth exists, even if all previous thought has been an error" (2004b: 4).

Operating under the comforting conditions of metaphysics of universal justice is inherently anti-revolutionary. Those who are not prepared to go all the way in terms of negativity are revolutionaries' worst allies. They are the ones who start establishing the pillars of fascism even before the euphoria of riots disappears, and thanks to them revolutions have become associated with those short-lived moments that are followed by the return of despotism, terror, and oppression. That is the story of post-revolutionary Latin America, the 1979 revolution in Iran, and, more recently, the Arab Spring. For the next revolution, it is crucial for revolutionaries to realize that liberation theology is an oxymoron just as "egalitarian slavery," "emancipatory colonialism," or "feminist patriarchy" would be an oxymoron. A moralist complaint about greed, showing some humanitarian sentiment, or a few instances of anti-imperialist speech do not make postnihilists. A postnihilist is the one whose rebellion is inseparable from her intellectual fearlessness, a negator of the established truths and established knowledge production at the same time.

It is in the nature of domination to take place gradually and prepare for eternal endurance, whereas revolt is sudden as an event, unexpected as an action, and smashing as a force. A postnihilist revolutionary act is a Dionysian act. The calculating and compromising figure is a potential Stalin and the nice liberal believer in theology is a potential Khomeini. They may cite poetry and live as a bohemian now, but some other time, when the opportunity presents itself, they will leave no room for error in totalizing a system of counterrevolutionary terror. The only situation that is worse than fascism is a revolution in which fascists take part.

CHAPTER EIGHT

Postnihilist Theses on Revolution Summarized

The Priority of the Negation

As Adorno asserts, "wrong life cannot be lived rightly" (2005: 39). It should be straightforward for any historical materialist to realize that we cannot conceive a possible (right) alternative so long as we live under these (wrong) conditions. For precisely this reason, in order to know what is wrong and reject it, we do not necessarily need to know what is right. The alternative that is intrinsic to the idea of revolution is the negation of what is wrong, as opposed to the assertion of what is right. A postnihilist realizes that the world is not fixable, but that it is improvable through the conscious negation of structures of domination. We see this in the struggles of those who fought slavery. For they were not inspired by the promise of an ideal world in the future, but rather forced to act against conditions that were neither tolerable nor justifiable.

Freedom and equality are not ideals, as they are regularly portrayed. On the contrary, they are negated by force, so unfreedom and exploitation are the unnatural social modes. Moreover, because the social inequality that results from exploitation is founded and maintained by force, defeating it is an act of the negation of negation that amounts to rejecting what has been normalized without having to create anything unnatural. It is inequality that is maintained through systematic violence, which in turn dehumanizes the social modes of coexistence; therefore, insofar as it is a guiding principle, equality is not a utopian ideal but a state of being that needs to be gained within the historical moment.

Because the social unfreedom that results from exploitation is founded and maintained by force, defeating it necessitates a forceful, multidimensional act of negation. This amounts to rejecting what has been normalized, which does not require the creation of anything unnatural. In other words, the realization of freedom is violent only insofar as it requires undoing coercive power relations that sustain the violent state of inequality. Of course, none of that is to say that the negation of negation should simply take the form of a return to the state of nature. Rather, it must sublimate the existing modes of being, transcending both social modes of consciousness and the horizon of possibilities. What we call the state of nature is, after all, only a presumed state imagined within and by a specific historical consciousness.

Because the state of nature is a state that is not conscious of itself as such, merely being aware of that consciousness renders the (re)emergence of the state of nature impossible. Those who are conscious of the reactionary nature of inequality and the contradictions inherent in social hierarchy need to equip themselves with the essential dialectical knowledge to guard against relapses. Indeed, historically progressive consciousness struggles to negate the very conditions that necessitate its existence. Critical philosophy is, accordingly, a philosophy that is aware of its temporality and strives to actualize a world without itself. By the same token, a social movement can be called progressive if it is aware of its own negative existence, situated between newly emerging horizons of possibilities and the existing conditions that render creative imagination abnormal.

Negation I: Despair

The necessary pre-revolutionary moment is despair. The subject realizes that even existentially, the human condition is hopeless, which is precisely why she sees in the submission to social norms a reaffirmation of her own unfreedom. On this level, the struggle is relatively individualistic: there is only one way to live a life meaningfully. To discover one's way of life, despair is a prerequisite, for it transforms the person from a socially dictated self to a subject with subjectivity. Regaining the ability to experience the essential emptiness of the self amounts to the emancipation of the consciousness as the most defining space for subjectivity. It is the awareness of the inner emptiness and the general absurdity of existence that puts one in the position of being lost, being free. Before reaching the point of being lost, we do not dare to know, and, therefore, whatever we do will inevitably only further perpetuate our unfreedom.

Politically, Marx and Engel's doctrine of not having anything to lose is the grounds on which the first revolutionary step should be taken. For that reason, it is essential to negate one's own conditions of privilege that are built into collective identities, whether based on nationality, religion, or whatever else. Such collective identities, insofar as individuals are concerned, serve a primarily psychological function, namely, to make a meaningless life bearable through their accompanying mythologies. Erich Fromm explains the authoritarian personality's desperate urge to join a group in terms of mechanisms of escaping freedom. According to Fromm's analysis, the authoritarian personality's sense of insignificance is at the root of her readiness to submit to an oppressive power in return for a sense of belonging (Fromm 1965: 157–230). What the potential revolutionary must do is negate such illusionary meanings, hopes, and senses of belonging. Faced with the existential despair that follows this act of negation, the subject will then begin to gain the strength needed for the perpetual march toward a different world, regardless of whether the cause is popular or not at that specific historical moment.

In that very lonely first move, the revolutionary fully experiences her freedom for the first time. Because there is only one way to live a life meaningfully, that post-despair sense of freedom is essential. Prior to that, one can only live a predetermined life that contributes to the general unfreedom and misery of the human condition as such. Once one decolonizes one's own consciousness and starts the path of her only way of living, one is already a revolutionary. With that comes indestructible freedom, the potential power of which oppressors seem to sense instinctively. There is nothing that scares oppressors more than the body of a person who has become aware of her only way to live, her freedom. It is for that reason that fascists often subject the revolutionary's body to all kinds of torture, and, even after death, mutilation.

When despair is transcended to become the consciousness of freedom, the subject embraces resistance against the unfree world as the third moment of becoming. Because living as a free person in an unfree world is a contradiction, resistance, the third moment of the dialectical becoming, becomes the only way of life. The focus, then, shifts from whether a revolution is possible to the impossibility of living under the existing conditions of unfreedom. Most essential to emancipation is this consciousness. Without being aware of one's freedom, no power can make one free. It is only once one becomes aware of one's freedom, as the dialectical moment that negates and at the same time contains despair, that the unconditional and uncompromising rejection of domination becomes imperative. Therefore, true resistance is not premised on the question of the availability, feasibility, or plausibility of a potential alternative. Rather, it is the only possible way of being in the world as an autonomous subject.

For the hopeless ones, who are aware of their freedom and the imposed social unfreedom, negating domination is both existential and political at the same time. Let us take as an example the case of a Yezidi Kurdish woman who is rejected both as a right holder and as a living being. As a revolutionary, however, she actively rejects the world in which fascism is the norm. To secure a space for her being in the world, she must reject the existing order, that is, she must create a different truth beyond the current limits imposed by the oppressive reality and the reality of oppression. The very impossibility of a dignifying life yields creative possibilities that would otherwise be impossible. In other words, the path to despair and the path to revolution are one and the same. To live, she must be a revolutionary. What about those who joined the revolution when they had other options to live relatively comfortably? It is the ability to identify with the oppressed, that makes such revolutionaries realize both their life in an unfree world and their way of life as a path to freedom. It is a bourgeois illusion to think one could be free in a world where many others are enslaved. A world in which enslavement is still taking place is something that all of us should reject outright for the sake of the realization of our own universal potentiality, our own freedom.

This is where the true revolutionary lesson lies for the rest of us as well. We strive toward a level of awareness that will allow us to sincerely identify with the oppressed. In order for that to happen, again, we must negate our bourgeoisified conditions. Political awareness should be measured by the degree to which one can identify with those who are rejected by the existing system. With such an awareness, despair is inevitable, and the act of negating despair becomes essential for the realization of freedom. Therefore, the ability to live in the historical moment is inherently heroic and revolutionary. Once we gain the courage to live in the historical moment, the question will no longer be about the possibility of a rational and just world, but the impossibility of living in an irrational and unjust world, the impossibility of rationalizing and justifying a passive life in the existing world.

The revolutionaries who come from the margins and are not mentally colonized are too hopeless not to start a progressive revolution, and they will inevitably assume a negative orientation unimaginable to those self-proclaimed revolutionaries who oscillate between comfort and boredom. This is not to romanticize oppression. On the contrary, the effects of oppression are no less disturbing than oppression itself. However, with the courage to face hopelessness and embrace one's free will to choose to live in the historical moment, the circumstances of enslavement can be entirely transformed within a perpetual revolutionary way of being. Eventually, those revolutionaries who emerge from the margins of the margins of the margins may discover a path to universal emancipation, and their struggle becomes our only hope. Walter Benjamin wrote, "Only for the sake of the hopeless ones have we been given hope" (2004a). The statement can be turned around: the only hope we can have is the struggle of the hopeless ones.

Negation II: Oppression

The twentieth-century revolutions had predefined heroes and villains, friends and foes. As a result, the revolutionary movements themselves were always vulnerable to becoming counterrevolutionary as their social statuses changed. More often than not, as soon as they gained sovereignty, nationalist and national liberation movements assumed the position of oppressive, colonial, and imperialist forces against smaller and/or marginalized populations. The swiftness with which people can transition from being oppressed to being oppressors is such that former victims often use their past suffering as a justification to inflict more suffering on others. This is applicable to not only groups, but also individuals, and in terms of not only time, but also space. In fact, most of us alternate between positions of privilege and underprivilege as we move between spaces. An individual's identity can change from being an oppressor to being oppressed and vice versa simply by moving between different social spaces. For example, the worker who is oppressed in the workplace could be an oppressor in private space, toward her children or spouse.

To be more precise, in addition to social positioning, what determines whether an individual or a group is an oppressor or oppressed in any given space and time is their politics. Merely being in a position of privilege or dis-privilege does not necessarily dictate one's role in terms of relations of domination. While one's position could be one of privilege, one could choose to be on the side of the oppressed, or vice versa. A white man in a white majority society is in a position of privilege, but whether he is an oppressor or not depends on his political stance, broadly construed. Similarly, a non-white woman in a white majority society is clearly in a disadvantaged position, but she could at the same time be an oppressor depending on her politics and the specific space in which she operates. The same applies to social groups; in all cases, oppression is relative to circumstances and political practice.

A movement that is not aware of the multiplicity of oppression will most likely reproduce conditions of oppression. Therefore, revolutionary negation must be unconditional in its rejection of oppression and all-encompassing in scope regarding what constitutes domination. A subject's overall political identity is dependent on the extent to which she universally negates oppression. Class, race, and gender do not in and of themselves necessarily determine where a person or a group stands in relation to the oppressive existing order. Rather, it is the person or group's active negativity that determines their degree of progressiveness. A revolutionary subject is not defined by her perceived social identity, but rather by what she makes of that identity. One could argue that identity and the uniqueness of experience are politically significant only insofar as they lead to egalitarianism, which requires a universally conscious politics of negation. For there is nothing intrinsic in any minority identity to guard it against various forms of prejudices. Once again, without a negating consciousness, identitarianism could very well lapse back into essentialism and sectarianism.

Negation III: Thoushaltnotism

In the era of neoliberalism, critique has been reduced to mild complaints built into consumerism and expressed through the culture industry. The consumer has come to believe the lie that she can make impactful political choices through consumerism, for example, choosing to boycott specific companies or brands on the basis of certain causes. Popular music, stand-up comedy, and late-night talk shows similarly exempt the consumer–citizen from all possible guilt. The bourgeoisie at large can afford to live a purportedly moral life and speak "critically" about the problems we face, but how many have chosen to actively negate their own bourgeois conditions? Instead, the vast majority simply practice what can be termed *Thoushaltnotism*. By this I mean the morality that compels followers to refrain from committing certain acts, as opposed to actively engaging in undoing injustice.

In this post-political age, *thoushaltnotism* is the dominant moral doctrine of the many self-proclaimed anti-capitalists for whom resistance is just another cool word to throw around. The assumption that an honest application of prehistoric morality could actually fix the contemporary world is a prime example of the anti-revolutionary tendency that religious institutions have eternalized. Avoiding what are considered morally wrong individual acts and embracing a "peaceful and green" lifestyle leaves capitalism firmly intact, despite the fact that it is grounded in social, geographical, and ecological violence. *Thoushaltnotism* is the belief of doing one's part while being compliant with the system of domination. Animals, at the moment of their death, look into the eyes of the perpetrator, but the latter avoids that gaze. This has been the case for thousands of years. As entire societies of *thoushaltnotists*, we dismiss the gaze of the victim in order to be able to continue committing the normalized crimes that sustain our day-to-day lives. It takes only basic literacy to realize that our reality, both historically and geographically, is founded on unjustifiable acts of violence and exploitation against the most vulnerable in the human community and the natural world at large. Most of us simply choose not to understand.

Just as the guardians of reality are in fact far from being realistic, those who derive their moral code from *thoushaltnotism* fail even by ethical standards. A moralist is taught that she is responsible for what she herself does, so if she refrains from immoral acts, she is a good person as a matter of course. This would be a sound ethical principle if the human community at large were living in the ideal conditions of life. Failing that, any ethics worthy of consideration would also mandate subjects to do everything possible to stop injustice. Choosing not to do what one could do to decrease the suffering of others would then be unethical, rendering the *thoushalnotist* immoral. Indeed, we see this everyday as *thoushalnotists* choose to ignore the many millions of victims of fascism in today's world. In fact, societies grounded in *thoushaltnotism* contribute to the systemic violence against these victims.

In the same way that oppression is socially situated and politically shaped, morality is dependent on the dominant modes of production and perception. Portraying the crisis of capitalism as moral in nature only gives the bourgeoisie more leverage. For capitalism is more than capable of addressing its moral deficiencies, whether through fostering religious sentimentalism, humanitarianism, and semi-political activism or directly through the power of capital. The same people who systematically benefit from labor exploitation and ecological destruction can appear to be the most moralistic, from leading environmentally friendly lives to making considerable humanitarian donations. To give another example, the very institutions that are responsible for societal stratification and disparities on racial bases fanatically adopt the fashionable discourse of diversity and inclusion. Including a couple of "diverse" faces in promotional images has become a well-established strategy used by corporations and non-profit organizations alike. Even openly conservative political movements feel the need to recruit supporters and even candidates from the racialized groups they demonize. In all such instances, the motivation is the same: maintaining such appearances is good for business. The same regime that systematically marginalizes entire populations literally purchases a humanitarian façade to present itself as a morally sound system.

When ethics is abstracted from social relations of power and production, as is commonly done in analytic philosophy, critique becomes as ineffective as religious piety with regard to changing the world. If there is one thing we have learned from Marx, it is that morality itself is both a product of the dominant modes of production and an ideological means of normalizing the existing relations of domination. Take the moral discourse surrounding abortion, for instance. Is it not a clear example of a form of morality that sustains the existing modes of production whereby women are used as "means of production" owned by men? Of course, God too would support men's interests by prohibiting abortion. Having women submit to such a god represents the culmination of men's domination, whereby patriarchal modes of production are safeguarded by the oppressed themselves.

Throughout history, dominant forces have created numerous deities, and the dominated have faithfully eternalized them. In the process, the dominant has gained more hegemony, and the dominated have obtained just enough psychological comfort to divert their focus away from the miserable lives they lead, to deny the truth of their reality. Religion, as an ideological apparatus, has its evolutionary history. Prior to the Greek classical age, religion was part of everyday life but not necessarily as an institution aligned with the state. It was only at the historical moment when philosophical consciousness began questioning the Olympian gods' compliance with state politics that Athens invented institutionalized religion by criminalizing blasphemy. This institutional birth of religion officially concretized the inseparability of power and morality, official politics and official religion. The state gained the legal power to prosecute citizens in the name of religion.

Thus, the execution of Socrates at the sunset of the Greek classical age signifies a landmark in the evolution of religion in the West. Seven centuries later, the Roman empire adopted a more effective religious order: monotheism, which had been successfully incorporated into the ruling ideology in Persia in the form of Zoroastrianism. Ultimately, the Olympians had been too pluralistic to establish a perpetual system of domination,[1] so Christianity became necessary for founding a tyrannical moral regime. Of course, with the official birth of religiously sanctioned morality and politically sanctioned religion, domination entered a new era, the dark ages, which persists to this day in more than one sense and more than a few parts of the world.

Through changing moral norms, the dominant deprives its moral critics of their means of critique. As the unfreedom of the dominated deepens, their moral language becomes ever more useless as a means of critique. They may sense that something is fundamentally wrong, but in addition to normalizing its domination, the bourgeoisie has paralyzed modes of critique and homogenized perception. The bourgeoisie's ultimate victory did not come when it declared the end of history, at the end of the nineteenth century, but when the proletariat internalized liberal capitalism's declaration of the end of history at the end of the twentieth century. In short, the only imaginable way out of the dominant system became the end of the world, as Jameson noted (2003: 76). In Europe, even many Marxists turned to *thoushaltnotism*, especially in the form of environmentalism, to water down their former revolutionary ideology in the era of neoliberalism. In the meantime, in the United States, popular anti-capitalist discourse has started to center around a moral condemnation of the "greedy capitalist" and the 1 percent, as if the 99 percent stands outside the capitalist order and does not maintain it on a daily basis. When the historic moment of the Occupy Movement came, occupation was officially transformed into a metaphor on the margins of the metaphysics of morality. The Occupy Movement may have set out to occupy Wall Street, but the movement itself quickly became another space occupied by anti-capitalist moral sentiments. Obviously, any liberal solution to the crisis of liberalism further confirms the eternalization of capitalism, but in the absence of negative consciousness, contradictions cease to even create a sense of irony. Two premises need to be emphasized: (i) Liberalism is the ideological façade of capitalism and as such it is absurd to seek a liberal solution for the capitalist crisis. (ii) Liberalism as an ideology is grounded on bourgeois freedom and does not have any doctrine for social justice.

In conclusion, postnihilism as a revolutionary philosophy of negation has the following characteristics:

- Against positive alternativism: in order to know what is wrong and reject it, we do not necessarily need to know what is right. Furthermore, this should be pushed to its epistemological limit to argue that in order to be able to grasp an alternative, it is imperative to first negate the existing conditions that paralyze imagination.

- Against psychological positivity: despair, not optimism, is an essential moment that could dialectically shape revolutionary will.

- Against the ahistorization of identities: oppression is both situational and political, so postnihilism is universalist in its negativism, and that is precisely why it is capable of both recognizing and transforming local progressive struggles.

- Against *thoushaltnotism*: critical theory becomes devoid of its revolutionary potential when it is reduced to moral criticism as opposed to the critique of the totality of unfreedom inherent in bourgeois society and its reactionary poles.

NOTES

1 The Philosophy and the Plan of the Present Work

1 Enzo Traverso comes close to making a similar point, but he prefers the term "post-fascism" to refer to today's fascist ideologies (2019). For instance, he states, "fascism has not only been transnational or transatlantic, but also transhistorical" (2019: 20). Umberto Eco too realizes that there is a problem in attempting to grasp fascism as an ideology (1995). He writes,

> On the contrary, fascism had no quintessence. Fascism was a fuzzy totalitarianism, a collage of different philosophical and political ideas, a beehive of contradictions. Can one conceive of a truly totalitarian movement that was able to combine monarchy with revolution, the Royal Army with Mussolini's personal milizia, the grant of privileges to the Church with state education extolling violence, absolute state control with a free market? (1995)

What is truly ironic is that even the philosophizer of Mussolini's Fascism admits in the clearest expressions that there is no such thing as the Fascist ideology. For instance, he asserts,

> the doctrine of Fascism is not a philosophy, in the ordinary sense of the term, and still less is it a religion. It is also not an explicated and definitive political doctrine, articulated in a series of formulae. The truth is that the significance of Fascism is not to be measured in the special theoretical or practical theses that it takes up at one or another time. As has been said at its very commencement, it did not arise with a precise and determinate program. (Gentile 2002: 21)

2 The Indispensability of Universal Anti-fascist Solidarity: A Return to Normal Is Neither Possible nor Desirable

1 Adorno offers a powerful psychoanalytical account of the inner unity of a fascist group whose members share the same object of projection, the "great little man." The "great little man" is a reference to the father figure who functions as both the fetishized locus of authority and someone who

   (supposedly) understands and speaks the language of the common people (see Adorno 2001a, 2004).

2 In cinematic work, this psychological dynamic is depicted very well in the character Remy (Michael Rapaport) in *Higher Learning* (Singleton 1995).

3 For instance, in *Totem and Taboo*, first published in 1913, Freud writes, "The psycho-analysis of individual human beings, however, teaches us with quite special insistence that the god of each of them is formed in the likeness of his father, that his personal relation to God depends on his relation to his father in the flesh and oscillates and changes along with that relation, and that at bottom God is nothing other than an exalted father" (2001: 171). In *The Future of an Illusion*, originally published in 1927, he strongly argues that "the primal father was the original image of God, the model on which later generations have shaped the figure of God" (1961: 42).

4 Perhaps this confusion is reflective of the camouflage tactics used by most fascist movements today. In Enzo Traverso's words,

> Today, the rise of the radical right displays a semantic ambiguity: on the one hand, almost no one openly speaks of fascism—with the notable exceptions of the Golden Dawn in Greece, Jobbik in Hungary, or the National Party in Slovakia—and most observers recognize the differences between these new movements and their 1930s ancestors. On the other hand, any attempt to define this new phenomenon does imply a comparison with the interwar years. (2019: 18)

5 For instance, see Griffin (2006, 2018); Laqueur (1997); Paxton (1998, 2004). That said, there is still a sense of scholastic obligation to return to the first historical models of fascism, at least in terms of deriving the definition. Jason Stanley's 2018 book, *How Fascism Works*, is among the orthodox approaches to fascism within the liberal tradition, and it warns the American public about the resemblances between Trumpism and fascism. Nonetheless, Stanley also makes his case by relying on the two historical cases of Fascism and Nazism. While his arguments for the comparison are strong, the book does not break free from the reductionist limits of the liberal tradition.

6 While this does not mean Marxist accounts of fascism were not guilty of their own form of reductionism, among the useful analyses of fascism are those of the German Critical Theorists, such as Theodor Adorno (2001a, 2004), Max Horkheimer (2005), Walter Benjamin (1979), and Herbert Marcuse (1998, 2002), and psychoanalyst Marxists such as Wilhelm Reich (1946) and Eric Fromm (1965).

7 Karl Polanyi's *The Great Transformation* provides a detailed account of the capitalist root and stem of fascism (2001; originally published in 1944). He goes as far as denying any essential correlation between nationalism and fascism, arguing that "It was a case of symbiosis between movements of independent origin" (2001: 250). "In reality," Polanyi asserts, "the part played by fascism was determined by one factor: the condition of the market system" (2001: 250). Fascism was far from becoming a serious international threat in its first phase, 1917–23, and in the second phase, 1924–9. "After 1930," however, "when

market economy was in a general crisis," fascism became "a world power" (2001: 251).

3 The Two-Headed Beast of Capitalism and Nation-Statism

1 Of course, one has to cite Benedict Anderson (2006) for his definition of nation as an "imagined community," but one also needs to keep in mind that while the imagined could create a certain reality, that reality still lacks the durable truth to maintain it for a prolonged period of time. What is missing, therefore, in Anderson's account is precisely a philosophy of history beyond the immediate reality of the age of nation-states.

2 Sheldon Wolin wrote an important book on what he calls, "inverted totalitarianism" to designate "a system that represents the political coming-of-age of corporate power" (2010: xiii).

3 Being an example of the dysfunctional totalitarian model, the Iranian regime has failed miserably in the struggle against the coronavirus outbreak (Deutsche Welle 2020). The first confirmed cases of infection were reported on February 19 (Fassihi 2020), yet it was only on March 17 that the regime finally decided to shut down some shrines (Marizad 2020). The Iranian regime is in the unenviable situation whereby it is left with two shattering options: (1) closing religious public spaces, which would negate the ideological premise of the regime or (2) keeping religious public spaces accessible, which would exacerbate the pandemic and eventually undermine the regime's control over society. The regime draws its legitimacy from religious sanctity, but that same sanctity limits its scientific authority, which is the most essential authority during such an outbreak. Normally, it is opponents of the theocracy who represent a threat to the regime's control of public space. This time around, for the most part, it has been conservative segments of the population who seem to have played the main role in rendering the outbreak catastrophic. This conservative base continued visiting religious sites while the regime remained reluctant to prevent them from doing so. In Turkey, the situation has not been much better. Erdogan's populist regime has been trying its best to put up the appearance of the only state that has been successful in both preventing the outbreak and also helping the rest of the world, including the United States, to do so as well (Kocyildirim 2020). While the virus continues to hunt lives in Turkey, Erdogan's regime is busy maneuvering with Russia, Greece, the EU, and Libya to maintain the position of an imperial power in the region. For Erdogan, as for a typical fascist leader, the loss of human lives does not necessarily constitute a crisis—only loss of power and influence does.

4 This is exactly what Arendt notices in her *The Origins of Totalitarianism* when she writes,

> The transformation of the state from an instrument of the law into an instrument of the nation had been completed; the nation had conquered the state, national interest had priority over law long before Hitler could

pronounce "right is what is good for the German people." Here again the
language of the mob was only the language of public opinion cleansed of
hypocrisy and restraint. (1979: 275)

5 Karl Polanyi argued that only in the 1930s, when the market economy faced a
major crisis, did fascism become a world power (2001: 251).

6 Unsurprisingly, any obsession with a return to nature as the path to ultimate
salvation runs the risk of slipping into the fascistic formula of communities,
even if it is contextualized within a seemingly anti-fascist discourse.

7 Even before the coronavirus, in reference to the ecological crisis, the UN
repeatedly warned its nation-state parents about the impending catastrophe
(IPCC 2018).

4 Capitalism and the Ecological Deadlock

1 It was not until NASA scientist James E. Hansen's testimony before the US
Senate in 1988, at the start of an exceptionally warm summer, that the human
toll on the environment started to gain mainstream currency.

2 Even scientific research sponsored by the US government explicitly points to
imminent catastrophes resulting directly from human-driven climate change
(Ludden and Joyce 2018). Also in 2018, the Global Change Research Program
published its fourth National Climate Assessment, documenting the anticipated
repercussions of climate change on a variety of levels, from marginalized
communities to the ecosystem and the economy (USGCRP 2018). A more recent
Australian report asserts that by 2050 the disaster will be so severe that it could
mean "the end of human global civilisation as we know it" (Spratt and Dunlop
2019: 7). In short, the effects of climate change are only growing clearer, and
our window of opportunity to prevent changes of catastrophic proportions is
extremely limited.

3 This anti-socialist tendency has been especially strong in the United States.
Thanks to the increased awareness of and concern for social justice among
Millennials and Generation Z, as well as the rising popularity of Bernie Sanders
as an influential self-proclaimed socialist, the public aversion to the term has
decreased considerably. Still, according to a recent poll, most Americans would
still refuse to vote for a qualified presidential candidate who identifies as a
socialist (McCarthy 2019).

4 For more on the concept of ecological imperialism, see Foster and Clark (2004).

5 "Americans make up only 4.5% of the world's population and yet consume
nearly 20% of its energy" (World Population Balance 2019).

6 Bernie Sanders, a self-proclaimed socialist, avoided calling upon "workers" in
his campaign for the 2016 Democratic presidential nomination, perhaps because
it would have estranged the many workers who do not wish to see themselves
as such. Thus, more or less like Hillary Clinton, his rhetoric was focused on the
plight of "middle class" voters.

7 Ironically, the belief that the English, French, and German proletariat would rise up to put an end to capitalism in Europe opening the door for the socialist age was embraced rather dogmatically even by the Bolshevik thinkers, including Lenin and Trotsky themselves. This resulted in a tragic underestimation of the actual power and potential historical significance of the proletarian revolutions in Asia and Latin America by many orthodox Marxists, including Trotsky, despite his legendary struggle for internationalism to the last day of his life.

8 For more on this, see Zink and Geyer (2016); Hickel (2018).

5 Culturalism as an Ideological Crisis

1 It is worth noting that Hegel makes a direct connection between freedom and truth while simultaneously associating "culture" with the form of the universal. In Hegel's own words, "Thus subjective Spirit gains emancipation in the Truth, abnegates its particularity and comes to itself in realizing the truth of its being." Adding,

> Culture is essentially concerned with Form; the work of Culture is the production of the Form of Universality, which is none other than Thought. Morality, Government, Constitutions, etc., must be conformed to general principles, in order that they may accord with the idea of Free Will and be Rational. Thus only can the Spirit of Truth manifest itself in Subjective Will—in the particular shapes which the activity of the Will assumes. (2001: 435–6)

2 Benedict Anderson (2006) makes a valid point about the historical correlation between the fall of the Christian universality and the rise of nationalism, which retained most of the mythical elements of Christianity.

3 This observation is based on my visits to two large Zarathustrian sites in Amédi and Duhok, respectively, in Iraqi Kurdistan.

4 Also see the introduction by Gisela Catanzaro to the English edition of Grüner's book.

5 Hobsbawm draws a similar connection between the reactionary nature of nationalism, even in its progressive phase, and romanticism (1996: 120).

6 Stefan Ihring (2014) makes a definitive case, based on historiographical evidence, for the link between Kemalism and Nazism especially in terms of the former's influence on the latter.

7 For a very interesting use of "culture" as cross-generational passed how-to knowledge in nonhuman animals, which reinforces my point, see Heidt (2020).

6 Refuting the No-Alternative Rhetoric

1 Domenico Losurdo raised this excellent question, which like most great ideas becomes obvious only after a thinker points it out. Losurdo unreservedly

condemns the crimes committed by Stalinist regimes and invites us to ask crucial questions about racist genocides committed by liberal capitalism. Then he raises a profoundly critical question in regard to the economic and political policies of liberal democracies: how is the United States's "food diplomacy," which has been used to starve entire populations, such as those of Iraq and Cuba, different from "man-made famine," of which Stalin and Mao are rightly accused? If anything, the politics of preventing millions of people from access to food and medicine in the name of "food diplomacy" is an intentional man-made famine, the consequences of which are no mystery even before it is implemented (Losurdo 2015: 309–12). Losurdo points to historical revisionism's strategies that have led to widespread misconceptions regarding the revolutionary tradition from 1789 to 1917 (2015: 165–83). Even the so-called American "civil war" has been the main target of revisionism to delegitimize it, as Losurdo explains in the first two chapters of his book. To add to Losurdo's argument, it should be noted that there was no consent about 1860–5 period, as various labels were deployed to designate it depending on the respective ideological affiliations. Only after 1907 did it become somewhat customary to refer to the events as "civil war" due to a declaration by the congress in that year. However, if we compare it to the reign of terror that followed the French Revolution of 1789, it turns out that the rate of violence and casualties both numerically and proportionally (relative to the total population of either country respectively) was higher in the United States, reaching 750,000 casualties according to more recent estimations (US Census, 2019; US Department of Defense and American Battlefield Trust, 2021). The rate of dead would come to 1/41 compared to 1/50 in the French case. Add to that the brutality to which Blacks and Natives were subjected to, which is usually not counted. In 1860, there were 4.4 million Blacks and 27 million whites in the United States; 4 million of the total Black population were enslaved, with nearly 47 percent of them in the south.

2 Karol Modzelewski, the Russian-born Polish humanist Marxist who opposed the dictatorship regime in Poland, famously told the new ruling elite of Poland that he "didn't sit eight and a half years in jail to build capitalism" (quoted in Ost 2019). Modzelewski's proclamation exquisitely captures the false neoliberal claim of victory.

3 David Harvey addresses various dimensions of the neoliberal hegemony in his classic book *A Brief History of Neoliberalism* (2007). For instance, he writes, "Neoliberalization required both politically and economically the construction of a neoliberal market-based populist culture of differentiated consumerism and individual libertarianism. As such it proved more than a little compatible with that cultural impulse called 'post-modernism' which had long been lurking in the wings but could now emerge full-blown as both a cultural and an intellectual dominant" (Harvey 2007: 42).

4 Also see Marx (2010b: 142).

5 In a comment on the Paris Commune, Marx writes, "the working class … have no ideals to realize, but to set free elements of the new society with which old collapsing bourgeois society itself is pregnant" (2010c: 335). In a more direct passage on the negative character of communism, in the *1844 Manuscripts*,

Marx argues that "if we characterise *communism* itself because of its character as negation of the negation, as the appropriation of the human essence through the intermediary of the negation of private property—as being not yet the *true,* self-originating position but rather a position originating from private property" (2010a: 313; italics in original).

6 Marx in the *1844 Manuscripts* describes the communist movement as "a self-transcending movement" (2010a: 313).

7 Making the negative core of Marxist communism clear, Lenin wrote,

> There is no trace of an attempt on Marx's part to make up a utopia, to indulge in idle guesswork about what cannot be known. Marx treated the question of communism in the same way as a naturalist would treat the question of the development of, say, a new biological variety, once he knew that it had originated in such and such a way and was changing in such and such a definite direction. (2014: 122; italics added)

Indeed, this is confirmed by a major scientific authority of all times. Namely, Einstein in 1949 stated, "since the real purpose of socialism is precisely to overcome and advance beyond the predatory phase of human development, economic science in its present state can throw little light on the socialist society of the future" (2009).

8 Even in the few contexts in *Capital* where "communism" is mentioned, we cannot find anything remotely resembling a positive description of a communist society. For example, in *Capital I*, in a footnote, Marx states, "Hence in a communistic society there would be a very different scope for the employment of machinery than there can be in a bourgeois society" (2010e: 396). In *Capital II*, we find what might be read as a description of communism when he writes, "if we conceive society as being not capitalist but communist, there will be no money capital at all in the first place, nor the disguises cloaking the transactions arising on account of it" (2010f: 314). However, even this is merely a negatively described aspect of a communist society.

9 I make this argument in more detail in "Negativity as the Compass of Revolution: A Marxist Rejection of the No-Alternative Ethos." *Science & Society*, Vol. 86, No. 3, July 2022, 409–38.

10 For more on this, see Ahmed 2008b. The main idea in this article, which is the Nietzschean contradiction between awareness and the ability to act, originated in a lecture by Bela Egyed at Carleton University in 2006.

11 It is also worth mentioning that for Trotsky (Anglo-Saxon) pragmatism was stubbornly against dialectical thinking and as such deeply anti-revolutionary (2012: 158–60). Interestingly, he made a similar link between dull empiricism and the lack of imagination when he described Stalin's mind as "stubbornly empirical, and devoid of creative imagination" (1970: 506).

12 Engels used the expression "inductive asses" (qtd. in Bloch 2018: 97) to refer to positivists whose thought is fanatically limited by the empirical.

13 Constructivists and critical theorists have dwelled on this point (see Cox 1981; Wallerstein 2006; Linklater 2007).

14 Personally, I have been told this multiple times in various ways and at least
    once in these exact or very similar words by a refugee scholar, who assumed,
    albeit falsely, that I had been a refugee in the United States (not that my status
    would make a difference in the problematic expectation about refugees).

15 On more than one occasion, during a series of invited talks on the Black Lives
    Matter hosted by an academic platform in New York in 2020, a scholar from
    an Ivy League university actually made such an argument. I should also add
    that the platform's passive acceptance of the racist act was no less problematic.
    Perhaps, the fallacy of the racist argument was not apparent to those present,
    which is indicative of their own racist mentality, but one would think that at
    least as proud liberal authors and educators they would have reacted to the
    moral objectionability of the racist speech.

16 In his *Philosophy of History*, Hegel (2001) recognized this substantial
    difference between the ability to think in terms of general concepts versus
    immediacy of belief, but instead of recognizing the difference as individual
    differences of concrete persons and their material conditions of life, he offers
    an essentializing account that carries clear symptoms of racism, culturalism,
    and orientalism.

17 See, for example, Bishop and Green (2008).

18 Simon Jarvis captures this aspect of Adorno's thought: "Adorno's utopian
    negativity, instead, works through immanent critique. It cannot provide a
    blueprint for what the good life would be like, but only examines what our
    'damaged' life is like. It hopes to interpret this damaged life with sufficient
    attention and imagination to allow intimations of a possible, undamaged life to
    show through" (1998: 9).

7 The Marginalized and Their Cosmopolitan Episteme of Emancipation

1   It seems the statement is Žižek's own wording of an idea induced from what
    Benjamin expressed loosely with regard to the rise of fascism following the
    Second World War. In other words, Žižek himself deserves equal, if not more,
    credit for the insightful statement.

2   Foucault, in his groundbreaking *The Order of Things* (1994), unearths what
    knowledge meant in the sixteenth century.

3   Basically, that is the reasoning behind the doctrine of "just war." Somehow,
    every war is believed to be a just war by some and a criminal war by others.

4   Étienne Balibar has done impressive work arguing that there is no such thing
    as no violence (2002: see Chapter 7).

5   Benjamin made a somewhat similar point in a letter in 1913:

        To you, a prostitute is some kind of beautiful object. You respect her as
        you do the Mona Lisa. … But in so doing, you think nothing of depriving

thousands of women of their souls and relegating them to an existence in an art gallery. As if we consort with them so artistically! Are we being honest when we call prostitution "poetic"? I protest in the name of poetry. (Quoted in Eiland and Jennings 2014: 56)

6 Rebecca Solnit's book *Hope in the Dark* (2016) is an example of false knowledge in order not to act, and her type of activism is exemplary of acting not to know.

8 Postnihilist Theses on Revolution Summarized

1 On the Greek gods, Nietzsche writes, "A religion of life speaks out of them, not one of duty or of asceticism, or of spirituality. All of these forms breathe the triumph of being, an abundant feeling for life accompanies their cult. They do not demand: in them the present, whether good or evil, is deified" (1997: 85).

BIBLIOGRAPHY

1st Infantry Division (n.d.), *Soldier's Handbook to Iraq*. Available online: https://fas.org/irp/world/iraq/1IDguide.pdf (accessed June 13, 2021).

Adorno, T. (1973), *Negative Dialectics*, London: Routledge and Keegan Paul.

Adorno, T. (2000), *Problems of Moral Philosophy*, ed. Thomas Scröder, trans. R. Livingstone, London: Polity.

Adorno, T. (2001a), "Freudian Theory and the Pattern of Fascist Propaganda," in J. M. Bernstein (ed.), *The Culture Industry: Selected Essays on Mass Culture*, 132–57, London: Routledge.

Adorno, T. (2001b), "Culture Industry Reconsidered," in J. M. Bernstein (ed.), *The Culture Industry: Selected Essays on Mass Culture*, 98–106, London: Routledge.

Adorno, T. (2004), "Antisemitism and Fascist Propaganda," in S. Crook (ed.), *Stars Down to Earth and Other Essays on the Irrational in Culture*, 218–32, London: Routledge.

Adorno, T. (2005), *Minima Moralia: Reflections on a Damaged Life*, London: Verso.

Adorno, T. (2006a), *The Culture Industry: Selected Essays on Mass Culture*, ed. J. M. Bernstein, London: Routledge.

Adorno, T. (2006b), *History and Freedom: Lectures 1964–1965*, ed. R. Tiedemann, trans. R. Livingstone, Cambridge: Polity Press.

Agamben, G. (1998), *Homo Sacer: Sovereign Power and Bare Life*, trans. Daniel Heller-Roazen, Stanford, CA: Stanford University Press.

Ahmed, S. (2008a), "Mass Mentality, Culture Industry, Fascism," *Kritike: An Online Journal of Philosophy*, 2 (1): 79–94.

Ahmed, S. (2008b), "Wisdom Poisons Life," *Philosophical Frontiers*, 3 (2): 1–11.

Ahmed, S. (2011), "Return of Revolutions?" *Critical Legal Thinking*, last modified April 12, 2011. Available online: https://criticallegalthinking.com/2011/04/12/return-of-revolutions/ (accessed June 14, 2021).

Ahmed, S. (2016), "Being a Kurdish-Turkish Mistake" [Interview by Robert Leonard Rope], *OpenDemocracy*, September 18. Available online: https://www.opendemocracy.net/en/being-kurdish-turkish-mistake/ (accessed June 14, 2021).

Ahmed, S. (2019a), "One Hundred Years After World War I, Are We Heading Back to the Abyss." *OpenDemocracy*, June 30. Available online: https://www.opendemocracy.net/en/transformation/one-hundred-years-after-world-war-i-are-we-heading-back-abyss/ (accessed June 14, 2021).

Ahmed, S. (2019b), *Totalitarian State and the Destruction of Aura*, Albany, NY: SUNY Press.

Ahmed, S. (2019c), "The 21st-Century Crossroad of Islamism and Enlightenment," *TelosScope*, last modified December 10. Available online: https://www.telospress.com/the-21st-century-crossroad-of-islamism-and-enlightenment-part-1-the-historical-crossroad-of-an-ideological-crisis/ (accessed June 14, 2021).

Ahmed, S. (2020), "When We Lose the Ability to be Shocked, Fascism has Already Arrived," Institute for Social Ecology. Available online: http://social-ecology.org/wp/2020/05/when-we-lose-the-ability-to-be-shocked-fascism-has-already-arrived/ (accessed May 2, 2020).

Ahmed, S. (2021), "Universal Discrimination and the Democratic Camouflaging of Culturalism," *LINKS: International Journal of Socialist Renewal*, March 27. Available online: http://links.org.au/universal-discrimination-democratic-camouflaging-culturalism (accessed June 14, 2021).

Aleem, Z. (2020), "Why Brazil's President Jair Bolsonaro Joined a Protest Calling for a Military Coup," *Vox*, April 19. Available online: https://www.vox.com/covid-19-coronavirus-world-international-response/2020/4/19/21227218/bolsonaro-brazil-coronavirus-protests-coup (accessed June 14, 2021).

Allen, R. (1833), *The Life, Experience, and Gospel Labors of the Rt. Rev. Richard Allen: To which Is Annexed, the Rise and Progress of the African Methodist Episcopal Church in the United States of America: Containing a Narrative of the Yellow Fever in the Year of Our Lord 1793: With an Address to the People of Color in the United States*, Philadelphia: F. Ford and M.A. Riply.

Amnesty International (2017), *Blood-Soaked Secrets*, London: Amnesty International. Available online: https://www.amnesty.org/download/Documents/MDE1394212018ENGLISH.PDF (accessed June 14, 2021). Also available online in Persian: https://www.amnesty.org/download/Documents/MDE1394212018PERSIAN.PDF (accessed June 14, 2021).

Amnesty International (2020), "Turkey: Imprisoned Journalists, Human Rights Defenders and Others, Now at Risk of Covid-19, Must Be Urgently Released," Amnesty International, March 30. Available online: https://www.amnesty.org/en/latest/news/2020/03/turkey-imprisoned-journalists-human-rights-defenders-and-others-now-at-risk-of-covid-19-must-be-urgently-released/ (accessed June 14, 2021).

Anderson, B. (2006), *Imagined Communities: Reflections on the Origins and Spread of Nationalism*, London: Verso.

Anthropocene Working Group (AWG) (2019), "Results of Binding Vote by AWG," Subcommission on Quaternary Stratigraphy. Available online: http://quaternary.stratigraphy.org/working-groups/anthropocene/ (accessed June 14, 2021).

Arendt, H. (1979), *The Origins of Totalitarianism*, San Diego, CA: Harcourt Brace and Company.

Arendt, H. (1998), *The Human Condition*, Chicago: University of Chicago Press.

Augustine, A. (1871), *The City of God*, trans. Rev. Marcus Dodss, Edinburgh: T&T Clark.

Augustine. A. (2003), *Confessions*, trans. R. S. Pine-Coffin, London: Penguin Books, 2003.

Azzam, A. Y. (1980), *Al-Saratan Alahmar* [The Red Cancer], Amman: Maktabat al-Aqsa.

Badiou, A. (2010), *The Communist Hypothesis*, trans. D. Macey and S. Corcoran, London: Verso.

Balibar, É. (1991), "Racism and Nationalism," in E. Balibar and I. Wallerstein (eds.), *Race, Nation, Class: Ambiguous Identities*, 37–67, London: Verso.

Balibar, É. (2002), *Politics and the Other Scene*, trans. C. Jones, J. Swenson, and C. Turner, London: Verso.

Balibar, É. (2007), *The Philosophy of Marx*, trans. C. Turner, London: Verso.

Barry, J. (1999), "Marxism and Ecology," in A. Gamble, D. Marsh and T. Tant (eds.), *Marxism and Social Science*, 259–79, Urbana: University of Illinois Press.

Bauman, Z. (2004), *Identity: Conversations with Benedetto Vecchi*, Cambridge: Polity Press.

BBC News (2020), "Coronavirus: Bolsonaro Fires Health Minister over Pandemic Response," *BBC News*, April 16. Available online: https://www.bbc.com/news/world-latin-america-52316150 (accessed June 14, 2021).

Benjamin, W. (1979), "Theories of German Fascism: On the Collection of Essays War and Warrior," *New German Critique*, 17 (Spring): 120–8.

Benjamin, W. (2004a), "Goethe's Elective Affinities," in M. Bullock and M. W. Jennings (eds.), trans. S. Corngold, *Selected Writings, Volume 1, 1913–1926*, 297–360 Cambridge, MA: Harvard University Press.

Benjamin, W. (2004b), "Experience," in M. Bullock and M. W. Jennings (eds.), trans. S. Corngold, *Selected Writings, Volume 1, 1913–1926*, 297–360, Cambridge, MA: Harvard University Press.

Benjamin, W. (2006), "On the Concept of History," in H. Eiland and M. W. Jennings (eds.), trans. H. Zohn, *Walter Benjamin: Selected Writings, Volume 4, 1938–1940*, 389–400, Cambridge: Belknap Press of Harvard University Press.

Berardi, B. (2015), *Heroes: Mass Murder and Suicide*, London: Verso.

Berlin, I. (2013), *Karl Marx: Thoroughly Revised Fifth Edition*, Princeton: Princeton University Press.

Bernstein, E. (1893), *Ferdinand Lassalle as a Social Reformer*, trans. E. Marx Aveling, London: Swan Sonnenschein.

Bernstein, E. (1897), "Karl Marx and Social Reform," *Progressive Review*, 7 (April). Available online: https://www.marxists.org/reference/archive/bernstein/works/1897/04/marx-reform.htm (accessed June 15, 2021).

Bernstein, E. (1909), *Evolutionary Socialism*, trans. E. C. Harvey, Independent Labour Party.

Bhabha, H. (1984), "Of Mimicry and Man: The Ambivalence of Colonial Discourse," *October*, 28: 125–33.

Biehl, J. (2015), *Ecology of Catastrophe: The Life of Murray Bookchin*, Oxford: Oxford University Press.

Biko, S. (1987), I *Write What I Like: Steve Biko; A Selection of His Writings*, ed. A. Stubbs, C. R. Johannesburg: Heinemann.

Bishop, M., and M. Green (2008), *Philanthrocapitalism: How the Rich Can Save the World*, New York: Bloomsbury Press.

Bloch, E. (2018), *On Karl Marx*, trans. J. Maxwell, London: Verso.

Blomberg, T. G. (2003), *Punishment and Social Control*, New York: Aldine de Gruyter.

Bonilla-Silva, E. (2003), *Racism without Racists: Color-Blind Racism and the Persistence of Racial Inequality in the United States*, Lanham: Rowman & Littlefield.

Britton, F. L. (2012), *Behind Communism*, London: Ostara.

Brum, E. (2018), "How a Homophobic, Misogynist, Racist 'Thing' Could Be Brazil's Next President," *The Guardian*, October 6. Available online: https://www.theguardian.com/commentisfree/2018/oct/06/homophobic-mismogynist-racist-brazil-jair-bolsonaro (accessed June 15, 2021).

Burç, R. (2016), "Erdogan's Plan for the Kurds: Destroy, Rebuild, Pacify," Telesur. Available online: http://www.telesurtv.net/english/opinion/Erdog

ans-Plan-for-the-Kurds-Destroy-Rebuild-Pacify-20160303-0031.html (accessed June 15, 2021).

Burley, S. (2017), *Fascism Today What It Is and How to End It*, Chicago, CA: AK Press.

Buruma, I. (2021), "Racism and Enlightenment," Persuasion, February 22. Available online: https://www.persuasion.community/p/ian-buruma-racism-and-enlightenment (accessed June 15, 2021).

Castillo, M. (2011), "Electronic Waste: Where Does It Go and What Happens to It?" Time, January 14. Available online: http://techland.time.com/2011/01/14/electronic-waste-where-does-it-go-and-what-happens-to-it/ (accessed June 15, 2021).

CBC News (2016), "Ontario Looks at 2-Year Hold on Bottled Water Business," CBC/Radio Canada, October 16. Available online: http://www.cbc.ca/news/canada/kitchener-waterloo/aberfoyle-wellington-ontario-2-year-hold-bottled-water-1.3807950 (accessed June 15, 2021).

Charles, L. (2006), *Borat: Cultural Learnings of America for Make Benefit Glorious Nation of Kazakhstan*, Beverly Hills, CA: 20th Century Fox Home Entertainment.

Chisholm, Dan, Kim Sweeny, Peter Sheehan, Bruce Rasmussen, Filip Smit, Pim Cuijpers, and Shekhar Saxena (2016), "Scaling-Up Treatment of Depression and Anxiety: A Global Return on Investment Analysis," *Lancet Psychiatry*, 3 (5): 415–24.

Cohen, P. (2020), "'Still Catching Up': Jobless Numbers May Not Tell Full Story," *New York Times*, last modified May 28. Available online: https://www.nytimes.com/2020/05/28/business/economy/coronavirus-unemployment-claims.html?searchResultPosition=1.

Conquest, R. (2000), *Reflections on a Ravaged Century*, New York: W. W. Norton.

Cox, R. W. (1981), "Social Forces, States and World Orders: Beyond International Relations Theory," *Millennium*, 10 (2): 126–55.

Curtis, M. (1979), *Totalitarianism*, New Brunswick, NJ: Transaction Books.

Deutscher, I. (2015), *The Prophet: The Life of Leon Trotsky*, London: Verso.

Deutsche Welle (2020), "Iran Faces Catastrophic Death Toll from Coronavirus," *DW*, March 17. Available online: https://www.dw.com/en/iran-faces-catastrophic-death-toll-from-coronavirus/a-52811895 (accessed June 13, 2021).

Durie, R. (2009), "Gilles Deleuze," in J. Edkins and N. Vaughan-Williams, *Critical Theory and International Theory*, 125–36, London: Routledge.

Eiland, H., and M. W. Jennings (2014), *Walter Benjamin: A Critical Life*, Cambridge, MA: Harvard University Press.

Einstein, A. (2009), "Why Socialism?" *Monthly Review*, 61 (1). Available online: https://monthlyreview.org/2009/05/01/why-socialism/ (accessed June 15, 2021).Eco, U. (1995) "Ur-Fascism (Book Review)," *New York Review of Books*, June 22, 12. https://search.proquest.com/docview/1311529717?accountid=14637.

Essed, P. (1991), *Understanding Everyday Racism: An Interdisciplinary Theory*, Newbury Park, CA: SAGE.

Fanon, F. (1986), *Black Skin, White Masks*, trans. C. L. Markmann, London: Pluto.

Fanon, F. (2004), *The Wretched of the Earth*, trans. Richard Philcox, New York: Grove Press.

Fassihi, F. (2020), "Power Struggle Hampers Iran's Coronavirus Response," *New York Times*, March 17. Available online: https://www.nytimes. com/2020/03/17/world/middleeast/coronavirus-iran-rouhani.html (accessed June 15, 2021).

Feuerbach, L. (1972), "Toward a Critique of Hegel's Philosophy," trans. Z. Hanfi, Marxist Archive. Available online: https://www.marxists.org/reference/archive/ feuerbach/works/critique/ (accessed June 15, 2021).

Feuerbach, L. (2008), *The Essence of Christianity*, trans. G. Eliot, MSAC Philosophy Group.

Filmer, R. (1949), *Patriarcha and Other Political Works*, ed. P. Laslett, Oxford: Basil Blackwell.

Foster, J. B., and B. Clark (2004), "Ecological Imperialism: The Curse of Capitalism," *The Socialist Register*, 40: 186–201.

Foster, J. B., and B. Clark (2018), "The Robbery of Nature: Capitalism and the Metabolic Rift," *Monthly Review*, July 1. Available online: https://monthlyrev iew.org/2018/07/01/the-robbery-of-nature/ (accessed June 15, 2021).

Foster, J. B. (1999), "Marx's Theory of Metabolic Rift: Classical Foundations for Environmental Sociology," *American Journal of Sociology*, 105 (2): 366–405.

Foucault, M. (1984), "Nietzsche, Genealogy, History," in P. Rabinow (ed.), *The Foucault Reader*, 76–100, New York: Pantheon Books.

Foucault, M. (1994), *The Order of Things: An Archeology of the Human Sciences*, trans. Les Mots et les choses, New York: Vintage Books.

Foucault, M. (1995), *Discipline and Punish: The Birth of Prison*, trans. A. Sheridan, New York: Vintage Books. Originally published as (1975), *Surveiller et punir: Naissance de la prison*, Paris: Gallimard.

Freire, P. (1968), *Pedagogy of the Oppressed*, New York: Seabury Press.

Frej, W. (2016), "Not Treating Depression and Anxiety Costs the World $1 Trillion a Year," *Huffington Post*, 13 April.

Freud, S. (1949), *Group Psychology and the Analysis of the Ego*, Toronto: The Hogarth Press.

Freud, S. (1961), *The Future of an Illusion*, trans. and ed. J. Strachey, New York: W. W. Norton.

Freud, S. (1962), *Civilization and Its Discontents*, trans. and ed. J. Strachey, New York: W. W. Norton.

Freud, S. (2001), *Totem and Taboo*, trans. J. Strachey, London: Routledge.

Freyenhagen, F. (2013), *Adorno's Practical Philosophy: Living Less Wrongly*, Cambridge: Cambridge University Press.

Fromm, E. (1965), *Escape from Freedom*, New York: Avon Books.

Fromm, E. (2004), *Marx's Concept of Man*, trans. T. B. Bottomore, London: Continuum.

Fukuyama, F. (1989), "The End of History?" *The National Interest*, 16 (Summer): 3–18.

Fukuyama, F. (1992), *The End of History and The Last Man*, New York: Free Press.

Gallup (2017), "*U.S. Lower- and Middle-Income Consumer Spending from July 2016 to July 2017, by Month (in U.S. Dollars)*," Statista. Available online: https://www.statista.com/statistics/205250/us-self-reported-lower-inc ome-consumer-spending-by-month/ (accessed June 15, 2021).

Genocide Watch (n.d.), "Genocide Alerts: Current Alerts." Available online: https://www.genocidewatch.com/copy-of-current-genocide-watch-aler (accessed August 27, 2020).

Gentile, G. (1995), "Fascism as a Total Conception of Life," in *Fascism*, ed. Roger Griffin. Oxford: Oxford University Press.

GMF (2017), "Global Distribution of CO_2 Emissions from Fuel Consumption by Region in 2007," Statista. Available online: https://www.statista.com/statistics/267796/global-distribution-of-co2-emissions-from-fuel-consumption/ (accessed June 15, 2021).

Goebbels, J. (1935), "Communism with the Masks Off," Calvin University's German Propaganda Archive. Available online: https://research.calvin.edu/german-propaganda-archive/goeb58.htm (accessed June 15, 2021).

Gorz, A. (2012), *Capitalism, Socialism, Ecology*, trans. M. Chalmers, London: Verso.

Graham, L. (2016), "Rule of Law at Risk in Turkey," *CNBC*, July 20. Available online: https://www.cnbc.com/2016/07/20/rule-of-law-at-risk-in-turkey.html (accessed June 15, 2021).

Gramsci, A. (1971), *Selections from the Prison Notebooks*, New York: International.

Griffin, R. (2006), *The Nature of Fascism*, London: Routledge.

Griffin, R. (2018), *Fascism*, Cambridge: Polity Press.

Grüner, F. (2020), *The Haitian Revolution: Capitalism, Slavery, and Counter-Modernity*, trans. R. McGlazer, London: Polity.

Gutiérrez, G. (1988), *A Theology of Liberation: History, Politics, and Salvation*, trans. C. Inda and J. Eagleson, Maryknoll, NY: Orbis Books.

Haraway, D. (2013), "The Biopolitics of Postmodern Bodies: Constitutions of Self in Immune System Discourse," in T. Campbell and A. Sitze (eds.), *Biopolitics: A Reader*, 273–309, Durham, NC: Duke University Press.

Harding, S. (1986), *The Science Question in Feminism*, Ithaca, NY: Cornell University Press.

Harper's Magazine, (2020), "A Letter on Justice and Open Debate," July 7, *Harper's*: https://harpers.org/a-letter-on-justice-and-open-debate/.

Harvey, D. (2007), *A Brief History of Neoliberalism*, New York: Oxford University Press.

Hegel, G. W. F. (2001), *The Philosophy of History*, trans. J. Sibree, Kitchener, ON: Batoche Books.

Heidt, Amanda (2020), "Watch an Example of Chimpanzee 'Culture,' as One Fishes for Termites," sciencemag.org, May 28. Available online: https://www.sciencemag.org/news/2020/05/watch-example-chimpanzee-culture-one-fishes-termites?utm_campaign=news_daily_2020-06-23&et_rid=582645261&et_cid=3376596 (accessed June 13, 2021).

Hickel, J. (2018), "Why Growth Can't be Green: New Data Proves You Can Support Capitalism or the Environment – But It's Hard to Do Both," Foreign Policy, September 12. Available online: https://foreignpolicy.com/2018/09/12/why-growth-cant-be-green/ (accessed June 15, 2021).

Higher Learning (1995), [Film] Dir. J. Singleton, USA: Columbia Pictures. DVD.

Hobsbawm, E. J. (2012), *Nations and Nationalism Since 1780: Programme, Myth, Reality*, Cambridge: Cambridge University Press.

Hobsbawm, E. J. (1994), *The Age of Extremes: The Short Twentieth Century 1914–1991*, New York: Vintage Books.

Hobsbawm, E. (1996), *The Age of Revolution 1789–1848*, New York: Vintage Books.

Horkheimer, M., and T. W. Adorno (2002), *Dialectic of Enlightenment: Philosophical Fragments*, trans. E. Jephcott, ed. G. S. Noerr, Stanford, CA: Stanford University Press.

Horkheimer, M. (2005), "The Jews and Europe," in E. Mendieta (ed.), *The Frankfurt School on Religion: Key Writings by the Major Thinkers*, 225–42, London: Routledge.

Horkheimer, M. (2019), [video]. https://www.youtube.com/watch?v=n V5EBHePKRc

Hosfeld, R. (2013), *Karl Marx: An Intellectual Biography*, trans. B. Heise, New York: Berghahn Books.

Human Rights Watch (2016), "Make It Safe: Canada's Obligation to End the First Nations Water Crisis," Human Rights Watch, June 7. Available online: https:// www.hrw.org/report/2016/06/07/make-it-safe/canadas-obligation-end-first-nati ons-water-crisis (accessed June 15, 2021).

Human Rights Watch (2019), "Brazil: Bolsonaro Celebrates Brutal Dictatorship," Human Rights Watch, March 27. Available online: https://www.hrw.org/ news/2019/03/27/brazil-bolsonaro-celebrates-brutal-dictatorship

Ihring, S. (2014), *Attatürk in the Nazi Imagination*, Cambridge: The Belknap Press of Harvard University.

International Council of Nurses (2021), "The Global Nursing shortage and Nurse Retention," ICN: https://www.icn.ch/sites/default/files/inline-files/ICN%20 Policy%20Brief_Nurse%20Shortage%20and%20Retention.pdf.

IMF (2019), "The 20 Countries with the Lowest Gross Domestic Product (GDP) Per Capita in 2016 (in U.S. Dollars)," Statista. Available online: https://www. statista.com/statistics/256547/the-20-countries-with-the-lowest-gdp-per-capita/ (accessed June 15, 2021).

IPCC (2018), "Global Warming of 1.5°C," The Intergovernmental Panel for Climate Change. Available online: https://www.ipcc.ch/sr15/chapter/chapter-2/ (accessed June 15, 2021).

Jameson, F. (2003), "Future City," *New Left Review*, 21 (May–June): 65–79. Available online: https://newleftreview.org/issues/ii21/articles/fredric-jameson-fut ure-city (accessed June 15, 2021).

Jarvis, S. (1998), *Adorno: A Critical Introduction*, Cambridge: Polity Press.

Kaneda, T., and G. Dupuis (2017), "2017 World Population Data Sheet with Focus on Youth," PRB, August 14. Available online: https://www.prb.org/2017-world-population-data-sheet/ (accessed June 15, 2021).

Kautsky, K. (1946), *Social Democracy Versus Communism*, trans. D. Shub and J. Shaplen, New York: Rand School Press.

Khalidi, A. (2018), "Turkey Arrests Over 150 Kurdish Politicians, Journalists, and Activists," *Kurdistan24*, October 9. Available online: https://www.kurd istan24.net/en/news/939789af-29fd-43d8-9a33-297ae922d1a6 (accessed June 15, 2021).

Klein, N. (2007), *The Shock Doctrine: The Rise of Disaster Capitalism*, New York: Metropolitan Books.

Kocyildirim, E. (2020), "Only 1 Case? Turkey's Coronavirus Coverup Is a Disaster Waiting to Happen," *The National Interest*, March 11. Available online: https://nationalinterest.org/blog/middle-east-watch/only-1-case-turkeys-coronavirus-coverup-disaster-waiting-happen-131817 (accessed June 15, 2021).

Kotkin, S. (2017), *Stalin: Waiting for Hitler, 1929–1941*, New York: Penguin Press.

Krieg, G. (2017), "The 14 Most Shocking Comments from Trump's Charlottesville News Conference," CNN, last modified August 16. Available online: https://www.cnn.com/2017/08/15/politics/donald-trump-charlottesville-lines/index.html (accessed June 15, 2021).

Laqueur, W. (1997), *Fascism: Past, Present, Future*, Oxford: Oxford University Press.

Lebowitz, M. (2008), "An Alternative Worth Struggling For," *Monthly Review*, 60 (5). Available online: https://monthlyreview.org/2008/10/01/an-alternative-worth-struggling-for/ (accessed June 15, 2021).

Lefebvre, H. (2014), *Critique of Everyday Life*, trans. J. Moore, London: Verso.

Lenin, V. I. (1978), *State and Revolution: Marxist Teaching about the Theory of the State and the Tasks of the Proletariat in the Revolution*, Westport, CT: Greenwood Press.

Lentin, A. (2014), "Post-Race, Post Politics: The Paradoxical Rise of Culture after Multiculturalism," *Ethnic and Racial Studies*, 37 (8): 1268–85. https://doi.org/10.1080/01419870.2012.664278.

Linklater, A. (2007), "Critical Theory," in Martin Griffiths (ed.), *International Relations Theory for the Twenty-First Century: An Introduction*, 47–59, London: Routledge.

Losurdo, D. (2015), *War and Revolution: Rethinking the 20th Century*, trans. G. Elliott, London: Verso.

Löwenthal, L., and N. Guterman (2021), *Prophets of Deceit*, London: Verso.

Ludden, J., and C. Joyce. (2018), "What You Need to Know about the New U.S. Climate Assessment," *GBH News*, November 26. Available online: https://www.wgbh.org/news/national-news/2018/11/26/what-you-need-to-know-about-the-new-us-climate-assessment.

Luke, T. W. (2020), *Screens of Power: Ideology, Domination, and Resistance in Informational Society*, Candor, NY: Telos Press.

Luxemburg, R. (2004), *The Rosa Luxemburg Reader*, ed. P. Hudis and K. B. Anderson, New York: Monthly Review Press.

Luxemburg, R. (2013), *The Letters of Rosa Luxemburg*, London: Verso.

Luxemburg, R. (2020), *Reform or Revolution?*, Paris: Foreign Languages Press.

Makiya, K. (1993), *Cruelty and Silence: War, Tyranny, Uprising, and the Arab World*, New York: W. W. Norton.

Makiya, K . (1998), *Republic of Fear: The Politics of Modern Iraq*, updated edn., Berkeley: University of California Press.

Makiya, K. (2006). "Putting Cruelty First: An Interview with Kanan Makiya (Part 2)," *Dissent Magazine*, Spring. Available online: https://www.dissentmagazine.org/wp-content/files_mf/1389810881d4Interview.pdf.

Marcuse, H. (1998), "State and Individual Under National Socialism," in D. Kellner (ed.), *Technology, War, and Fascism: Collected Papers of Herbert Marcuse*, vol. 1: 67–92, London: Routledge.

Marcuse, H. (2002), *One-Dimensional Man: Studies in the Ideology of Advanced Industrial Society*, London: Routledge.

Marizad, M. (2020), "Hard-Line Shiites Storm Iran Shrines Closed over Coronavirus," *NBC News*, March 17. Available online: https://www.nbcnews.com/news/world/hard-line-shiites-storm-iran-shrines-closed-over-coronavirus-n1161366 (accessed June 15, 2021).

Marx, K., and F. Engels (1978), "Manifesto of the Communist Party," in R. C. Tucker (ed.), *The Marx-Engels Reader*, 2nd edn., 469–500, New York: W. W. Norton.

Marx, K., and F. Engels (2010), "The German Ideology," in *Marx and Engels, Collected Works*, vol. 5, trans. C. Dutt and W. Lough, 19–452, London: Lawrence & Wishart.

Marx, K. and F. Engels (1852–61), "Articles by Marx in New-York Daily Tribune," Marx Engels Archive. Available online: https://www.marxists.org/archive/marx/works/subject/newspapers/new-york-tribune.htm (accessed May 10, 2020).

Marx, K. (1967), *Writings of the Young Marx on Philosophy and Society*, trans. and ed. L. D. Easton and K. H. Guddat, Garden City, NY: Doubleday.

Marx, K. (1970), *Critique of Hegel's Philosophy of Right*, trans. A. Jolin and J. O'Malley, Cambridge: Cambridge University Press. Available online: https://www.marxists.org/archive/marx/works/1843/critique-hpr/ (accessed June 15, 2021).

Marx, Karl (1976), "Preface," in *A Contribution to the Critique of Political Economy*, 2–7, Peking: Foreign Languages Press.

Marx, K. (1994), *Karl Marx: Selected Writings*, ed. L. H. Simon, Indianapolis, IN: Hackett.

Marx, K. (2010a), "Economic and Philosophic Manuscripts 1844," trans. C. Dutt, *Marx and Engels, Collected Works*, vol. 3: 229–346, London: Lawrence & Wishart.

Marx, K. (2010b), "Letters from the Deutsch-Französische Jahrbücher," in trans. C. Dutt, *Marx and Engels, Collected Works*, vol. 3: 133–45, London: Lawrence & Wishart.

Marx, K. (2010c), "The Civil War in France," in trans. Barrie Selman, *Marx and Engels, Collected Works*, vol. 22: 307–69, London: Lawrence & Wishart.

Marx, K. (2010d), "The Eighteenth Brumaire of Louis Bonaparte," in *Marx and Engels, Collected Works*, vol. 11, 99–197, London: Lawrence & Wishart.

Marx, K. (2010e), *Capital I*, vol. 35 of *Marx and Engels, Collected Works*, 7–852, London: Lawrence & Wishart.

Marx, K. (2010f), *Capital II*, vol. 36 of *Marx and Engels, Collected Works*, London: Lawrence & Wishart.

Material Flow Analysis Portal (2018), "Global Trends of Material Use," MaterialFlows.net. Available online: http://www.materialflows.net/global-trends-of-material-use/ (accessed June 15, 2021).

McCarthy, J. (2019), "Less than Half in U.S. Would Vote for a Socialist for President," Gallup, May 9. Available online: https://news.gallup.com/poll/254120/less-half-vote-socialist-president.aspx (accessed June 15, 2021).

Mekonnen, M. M., and A. Y. Hoekstra (2016), "Four Billion People Facing Severe Water Scarcity," *Science Advances*, 2 (2): 1–6. Available online: https://advances.sciencemag.org/content/advances/2/2/e1500323.full.pdf (accessed June 15, 2021).

Midsommar (2019), [Film] Dir. A. Aster, Santa Monica: Lions Gate Entertainment Inc. DVD.

Miranda, D. (2019), "Bolsonaro Wants to End Democracy in Brazil. Here's One Way He Could Do It," *The Guardian*, November 21. Available online: https://www.theguardian.com/commentisfree/2019/nov/21/bolsonaro-brazil-military-dictatorship-violence (accessed June 15, 2021).

Nietzsche, F. (1997), "The Dionysian Worldview," trans. C. Crawford, *Journal of Nietzsche Studies*, 13: 81–97.

Ost, D. (2019), "I Didn't Sit Eight and a Half Years in Jail to Build Capitalism," *Jacobin*. May 19. Available online: https://jacobinmag.com/2019/05/karol-modz elewski-poland-solidarity-democratic-socialism (accessed June 15, 2021).

Patnaik, U., and P. Patnaik (2019), "Neoliberal Capitalism at a Dead End," *Monthly Review*, 3: 20–31.

Paxton, R. O. (1998), "The Five Stages of Fascism," *Journal of Modern History*, 70 (1): 1–23.

Paxton, R. O. (2004), *The Anatomy of Fascism*, New York: Alfred Knopf.

Perrigo, B. (2019a), "The Indian Government Is Revoking Kashmir's Special Status. Here's What That Means," *Time*, August 5. Available online: https://time.com/5644356/india-kashmir-article-370/ (accessed June 15, 2021).

Perrigo, B. (2019b), "India's Government Wants to Block Some Muslims From Citizenship. Here's What to Know About a Controversial New Bill," *Time*, December 10. Available online: https://time.com/5746688/india-citizenship-amendment-bill/ (accessed June 15, 2021).

Polanyi, K. (2001), *The Great Transformation: The Political and Economic Origins of Our Time*, Boston, MA: Beacon Press.

Raymond, W. J. (1978), *Dictionary of Politics: Selected American and Foreign Political and Legal Terms*, Lawrenceville, VA: Brunswick.

Razack, S. H. (2001), *Looking White People in the Eye: Gender, Race, and Culture in Courtrooms and Classrooms*, reprint edn, Toronto: University of Toronto Press.

Rees, J. (1998), *The Algebra of Revolution: The Dialectic and the Classical Marxist Tradition*, London: Routledge.

Reich, W. (1946), *The Mass Psychology of Fascism*, trans. T. P. Wolff, New York: Orgone Institute Press.

Rodat, S. (2017), "Cultural Racism: A Conceptual Framework," *Revista de Stiinte Politice* (54): 129–40.

Rubicon Project (2016), "Average Spending on Holiday Shopping in the United Kingdom (UK) in 2015 and 2016 (in GBP per capita)." Statista. Available online: https://www.statista.com/statistics/633617/christmas-shopping-average-spending-capita-uk/ (accessed June 15, 2021).

Rupert, M. (1994), "Alienation, Capitalism and the Inter-State System: Towards a Marxian/Gramscian Critique," in S. Gill (ed.), *Gramsci, Historical Materialism and International Relations*, 67–92, Cambridge: Cambridge University Press.

SIPRI (2000), "SIPRI Yearbook 2000: Armaments, Disarmament and International Security," Stockholm International Peace Research Institute. Available online: https://www.sipri.org/sites/default/files/2016-03/SIPRIYB00mini.pdf (accessed June 15, 2021).

SIPRI (2016), "SIPRI Yearbook 2016: Armaments, Disarmament and International Security," Stockholm International Peace Research Institute. Available online: https://www.sipri.org/sites/default/files/YB16-Summary-ENG.pdf (accessed June 15, 2021).

Smith, D. (1979), "A Sociology for Women," in J. Sherman and E. T. Beck (eds.), *The Prism of Sex: Essays in the Sociology of Knowledge*, 135–87, Madison: University of Wisconsin Press.

Sollenberger, R. (2020), "Trump Declares Support for Armed Protestors Storming Michigan Capitol," *Salon*, May 1. Available online: https://www.salon.com/2020/05/01/trump-declares-support-for-armed-protestors-storming-michigan-capitol-these-are-very-good-people/ (accessed June 15, 2021).

Solnit, R. (2016), *Hope in the Dark: Untold Histories, Wild Possibilities*, Chicago: Haymarket Books.

Spratt, D., and I. Dunlop (2019), *Existential Climate-Related Security Risk: A Scenario Approach*, Melbourne: Breakthrough—National Centre for Climate Restoration. Available online: https://docs.wixstatic.com/ugd/148cb0_a1406e0143ac4c469196d3003bc1e687.pdf (accessed June 15, 2021).

Special Rapporteur on Extreme Poverty and Human Rights (2019), "Climate Change and Poverty." Available online: https://www.ohchr.org/Documents/Issues/Poverty/A_HRC_41_39.pdf.

Spurgeon, C. H. (2020), *Cheque Book of the Bank of Faith*, Abbotsford, WI: Aneko Press.

SRC (2019), "Planetary Boundaries Research," The Stockholm Resilience Centre. Available online: https://www.stockholmresilience.org/research/planetary-boundaries.html (accessed June 15, 2021).

Stanley, J. (2018), *How Fascism Works: The Politics of Us and Them*, New York: Random House.

The Ford International Weekly (1920), "The International Jew: The World's Problem," May 22. Available online: https://upload.wikimedia.org/wikipedia/commons/3/34/19200522_Dearborn_Independent-Intl_Jew.jpg (accessed June 15, 2021).

Traverso, E. (2016a), *Fire and Blood: The European Civil War, 1914–1945*, trans. D. Fernbach, London: Verso.

Traverso, E. (2016b), *Left-Wing Melancholia: Marxism, History, and Memory*, New York: Columbia University Press.

Traverso, E. (2019), *The New Faces of Fascism: Populism and the Far Right*, trans. D. Broder, London: Verso.

Trotsky, L. (1970), *My Life: An Attempt at an Autobiography*, New York: Pathfinder.

Trotsky, L. (2012), *Writings in Exile*, ed. K. Chattopadhyay and P. Le Blanc, London: Pluto Press.

US Census Bureau (2019), "Population of the United States from the Final Census Conducted before the Civil War in 1860, by Race and Gender," Statista, July 8. Available online: https://www-statista-com.libproxy.union.edu/statistics/1010196/population-us-1860-race-and-gender/ (accessed February 10, 2021).

US Department of Defense and American Battlefield Trust (2021), "Number of Military Fatalities in All Major Wars Involving the United States from 1775 to 2021," Statista, January 10. Available online: https://www-statista-com.libproxy.union.edu/statistics/1009819/total-us-military-fatalities-in-american-wars-1775-present/ (accessed February 10, 2021).

US Environmental Protection Agency (2011), "Electronics Waste Management in the United States Through 2009," EPA. Available online: https://bit.ly/3wEiNVD.

USGCRP (2018), *Impacts, Risks, and Adaptation in the United States: Fourth National Climate Assessment*, vol. 2, ed. D. R. Reidmiller, C. W. Avery, D. R. Easterling, K. E. Kunkel, K. L. M. Lewis, T. K. Maycock and B. C. Stewart, Washington: U.S. Global Change Research Program.

Van Dijk, T. A. (2011), "Discourse Analysis of Racism," in J. H. Stanfield II (ed.), *Rethinking Race and Ethnicity in Research Methods*, 43–66, Walnut Creek, CA: Left Coast Press.

Virno, P. (2013), "Labor, Action, Intellect," in T. Campbell and A. Sitze (eds.), *Biopolitics: A Reader*, 245–68, Durham, NC: Duke University Press.

Wallerstein, I. (2006), *World Systems Analysis: An Introduction*, Durham, NC: Duke University Press.

Ward, L., and J. Strashin (2019), "Sex Offences Against Minors: Investigation Reveals More Than 200 Canadian Coaches Convicted in Last 20 years," *CBC*, February 10. Available online: https://www.cbc.ca/sports/amateur-sports-coac hes-sexual-offences-minors-1.5006609?cmp=newsletter-The+Buzzer+-+Mon day+Feb+11+2019 (accessed June 15, 2021).

Weaver, M. (2016), "Turkey Rounds Up Academics Who Signed Petition Denouncing Attacks on Kurds," *The Guardian*, January 15. Available online: https://www.theguardian.com/world/2016/jan/15/turkey-rounds-up-academics-who-signed-petition-denouncing-attacks-on-kurds (accessed June 15, 2021).

WGBH Educational Foundation (2009), "China: Digital Dumping Ground," [Video] PBS. Available online: http://www.pbs.org/frontlineworld/stories/ghana 804/video/video_index.html (accessed June 15, 2021).

Wheen, F. (2000), *Karl Marx: A Life*, New York: W. W. Norton.

Williams, R. (1983), *Keywords: A Vocabulary of Culture and Society*, New York: Oxford University Press.

Witte, G. (2020), "As Protesters Swarm State Capitols, Much of the Coronavirus Backlash Is Coming from Within," *Washington Post*, April 3. Available online: https://www.washingtonpost.com/national/as-protesters-swarm-state-capitols-much-of-the-coronavirus-backlash-is-coming-from-within/2020/04/22/e4d7b1ee-84c8-11ea-a3eb-e9fc93160703_story.html (accessed June 15, 2021).

Wodak, R. and M. Reisigl (2015), "Discourse and Racism," in D. Tannen, H. E. Hamilton and D. Schiffrin (eds.), *The Handbook of Discourse Analysis*, 2nd ed., vol. 1: 576–96, West Sussex, UK: Willey Blackwell.

Wolin, S. S. (2010), *Democracy Incorporated: Managed Democracy and the Specter of Inverted Totalitarianism*, Princeton, NJ: Princeton University Press.

World Bank (2018), "*GNI Per Capita, Atlas Method (Current US$)*," The World Bank. Available online: https://data.worldbank.org/indicator/NY.GNP.PCAP. CD?locations=CD (accessed June 15, 2021).

WPB (2019), "Population and Energy Consumption," *World Population Balance*. Available online: https://www.worldpopulationbalance.org/population_energy (accessed June 15, 2021).

Wright, S. (1998), "The Politicization of 'Culture,'" *Anthropology Today*, 14 (1): 7–15.

Xu, Y., and V. Ramanathan (2017), "Well Below 2°C: Mitigation Strategies for Avoiding Dangerous to Catastrophic Climate Changes," *Proceedings of the National Academy of Sciences of the United States of America*,

114 (39): 10315–23. Available online: https://www.pnas.org/content/pnas/early/2017/09/13/1618481114.full.pdf (accessed June 15, 2021).

Zenith International (2012), "Sales Volume Growth of Bottled Water in Leading Countries Worldwide in 2011, by Country (Change to Prior Year)," Statista. Available online: https://www.statista.com/statistics/252214/bottled-water-volume-growth-by-leading-country/ (accessed June 15, 2021).

Zenith International (2014), "Bottled Water Consumption Worldwide from 2007 to 2017," Statista. Available online: https://www.statista.com/statistics/387255/global-bottled-water-consumption/ (accessed June 15, 2021).

Zink, T., and R. Geyer (2016), "There Is No Such Thing as a Green Product," Stanford Social Innovative Review. Available online: https://ssir.org/articles/entry/there_is_no_such_thing_as_a_green_product# (accessed June 15, 2021).

Žižek, S., and B. Gunjević (2012), *God in Pain: Inversions of Apocalypse*, New York: Seven Stories Press.

Žižek, S. (1994), "Introduction: The Specter of Ideology," in S. Žižek (ed.), *Mapping Ideology*, 1–33, London: Verso.

Žižek, S. (2008a), *In Defence of Lost Causes*, London: Verso.

Žižek, S. (2008b), *Violence: Six Sideways Reflections*, New York: Picador.

Žižek, S. (2012), *Less than Nothing: Hegel and the Shadow of Dialectical Materialism*, London: Verso.

Žižek, S. (2014), *Event: Philosophy in Transit*, Brooklyn, NY: Melville House.

INDEX

www.ingramcontent.com/pod-product-compliance
Ingram Content Group UK Ltd.
Pitfield, Milton Keynes, MK11 3LW, UK
UKHW022250060726
473012UK00003B/134